STUDENT-TO-STUDENT COUNSELING

Student-to-Student Counseling

An Approach to Motivating Academic Achievement

By WILLIAM F. BROWN

PUBLISHED FOR THE HOGG FOUNDATION FOR MENTAL HEALTH
BY THE UNIVERSITY OF TEXAS PRESS, AUSTIN AND LONDON

Library of Congress Cataloging in Publication Data

Brown, William Frank, 1920–
  Student to student counseling.

  (The Hogg Foundation research series)
  Bibliography: p.
  1. Student counselors. 2. Personnel service in
higher education. I. Title. II. Series.
  LB2343.B73   378.1'94'22   76-38536
ISBN 0-292-77500-8

Composition by G&S Typesetters, Austin
Printing by Capital Printing Company, Austin
Binding by Universal Bookbindery, Inc., San Antonio

*To my wife, Mary, whose loving devotion and
loyal understanding have given my life
real significance*

CONTENTS

PLATES

FIGURES

FOREWORD

The rapid increase in the number of individuals seeking education beyond high school is reaching the point where some form of higher education may soon become as universal as secondary schooling was only a generation ago. Doubling the number of college students in the past decade has placed a severe strain on traditional modes of higher education, making it necessary to devise innovative ways of reaching and helping the individual student. One of the most promising new methods for offering guidance to the beginning college student involves the employment of upper-division students as counselors of freshmen. Growing out of twenty years of research on motivating academic achievement, *Student-to-Student Counseling* contains a fresh approach to this important problem.

Relying heavily upon resources existing in any college for advising and motivating students, William F. Brown has developed a system that has proven its effectiveness in a wide variety of situations. Upperclassmen are given special training in the academic counseling of beginning students, using highly structured materials designed especially for this purpose. The counseling takes place at the beginning of the first year when the student is most receptive to help. A program for an entire freshman class in a small college can be organized and conducted by a single professionally trained counselor on a very modest budget. In addition to the improved study habits, attitudes, and motivation of beginning students, a side benefit is the experience gained by the upperclassmen serving as counselors.

The American Personnel and Guidance Association judged Dr. Brown's work on student-to-student counseling so highly that he

was given the 1967 Nancy C. Wimmer Award for the most out-
standing contribution to improved counseling and guidance practices in America. The Hogg Foundation for Mental Health has
supported his research and development on a small scale since
1956. It is our firm belief that the failure of many thousands of
students to cope effectively with the personal, social, and academic
demands of college life represents a tragic waste where even a
small improvement would be a major contribution to society.

WAYNE H. HOLTZMAN

PREFACE

The intent of this book is to show, by example, how needed expansion of counseling services for beginning college freshmen may be achieved, effectively and economically, through the use of carefully selected, trained, and supervised student counselors, backed up by interested and informed faculty advisors. The book primarily reports the operation of such a counseling program on the campus of Southwest Texas State College in San Marcos, Texas. Sufficient research evidence has been collected, however, to confirm that the student-counseling-student approach may be employed effectively in a variety of other situations.

This book is directed primarily at personnel workers concerned with solving the counseling squeeze currently faced by so many colleges and universities. Counselor educators should also find much here that will be useful in stimulating their students to think about the potentialities inherent in assigning counseling responsibilities to support personnel receiving only limited training. With the focus placed upon the student counselor himself, it is reasonable to assume that he, too, will use the book for reference and discussion, especially during his training period. Finally, this study should attract readers from among administrative personnel in higher education—presidents, deans, and chairmen—who are attempting to adjust to the realities of increasing student involvement and relaxed admissions policies.

The student-counseling-student approach, as described in this report, is a concept that has evolved out of an eighteen-year program of testing and counseling research initiated in 1952. The thirty major investigations comprising this research effort have focused on three objectives: (1) to examine and evaluate the importance of learning motivation and learning behavior as determinants of scholastic success in high school and college, (2) to construct and validate appropriate testing and counseling materials based upon the motivational orientation approach to predicting scholastic success and analyzing scholastic failure, and (3) to develop and evaluate effective approaches for counseling students on their past, present, and future academic adjustment problems. The ultimate goal for this research activity was to produce a practical, economical, and effective counseling program for helping students adjust to the academic and social demands of college.

The initial focus of research activity was on the construction and validation of appropriate testing materials for assessing academic attitudes and study skills. Once this effort was well under way, additional investigations were initiated in an attempt to define critical motivational elements through factor analysis and item analysis procedures. The development and field-testing of appropriate counseling materials and procedures was the third phase of the continuing research effort. Finally, a number of projects were undertaken to ascertain the effectiveness and adaptability of the student-to-student approach to providing academic adjustment counseling.

During the initial four years of the program, 1952–1955, financing was obtained through institutional research support provided by the Testing and Counseling Center at The University of Texas and the Human Resources Research Office at George Washington University. Between 1956 and 1965, the research activity was entirely supported by a series of grants from the Hogg Foundation for Mental Health at The University of Texas. The ESSO Education Foundation funded most of the research effort from 1966 through 1970, although modest funding was also received through institutional research support provided by Southwest Texas State College.

The test development projects reported in Chapter 2 span seventeen years and involve students attending twenty colleges and twenty-six high schools; the student-to-student counseling projects reported in Chapter 5 span eleven years and involve students attending ten colleges and twelve high schools. Altogether, various aspects of the total research program have involved approximately 42,500 students enrolled at sixty high schools and colleges located in fifteen different states. The final investigation entailed cross-cultural research to determine the effectiveness of student-to-student counseling for Spanish-speaking students.

The research findings from the thirty investigations have supported the following conclusions: (1) academic attitudes and study skills are important determinants of scholastic success in high school and college, (2) motivational orientations must be considered when counseling high school and college students on their scholastic difficulties, and (3) student counselors can utilize the motivational orientation approach to provide effective academic adjustment counseling for high school and college students.

Taken together, these three conclusions offer an approach for partially solving the counseling squeeze of higher education. The primary purpose of this book is to describe the investigations and to report the findings that support these conclusions. A second objective is to delineate the essential operational characteristics of a successful peer counseling program and to examine the adaptability of the approach to other campuses.

Like most authors, I am indebted to far more people than I can mention here. First, I want to acknowledge the research support provided by the Hogg Foundation for Mental Health and the ESSO Education Foundation. My sincerest thanks also go to the administration of Southwest Texas State College, both past and present members, particularly President John G. Flowers and Deans Alfred H. Nolle and Martin O. Juel, for their faith in my judgment and confidence in my belief that the student-counseling-student approach could provide an effective answer to our counseling needs. I am especially grateful to my long-time friend and colleague, Dr. Wayne H. Holtzman, for his encouragement and advice, without which the investigation would have surely faltered. Finally, I wish to affirm the debt owed to my initial group of student counselors—Veleda Deschner, Jan Eudy, Betty Ludwig, Dorene Weferling, Glenn Campbell, Gilbert Moehnke, Wilburn Peese, and Nathan Wehe. The success of our unique counseling program was due, in large measure, to their interest and effort in making student-to-student counseling a meaningful activity for all concerned.

WILLIAM F. BROWN
San Marcos, Texas

STUDENT-TO-STUDENT COUNSELING

1. The Case for
Student-to-Student Counseling

According to the U.S. Office of Education (116), the total college enrollment has skyrocketed from 1.5 million students in 1940 to 2.3 million in 1950, 3.6 million in 1960, and 7.4 million in 1970. There are more than five times as many college students now as there were thirty years ago, with nearly two-thirds of this unprecedented growth occurring during the 1960's. It is further anticipated that this increase in college enrollment will continue, with an estimated 9.3 million students attending college in 1975 and 11.4 million in 1980. Thus the number of young people entering college has more than doubled during the past decade and is expected to increase at least another 50 percent during the next decade.

Constantly increasing enrollments are forcing a rapid expansion of college facilities and services. Restrictions imposed by financial and personnel limitations, however, have compelled administrators to reexamine practically every phase of college operation. The urgent requirement is to enlarge, revise, or reduce college activities, as appropriate, to obtain the greatest return on investment.

THE COUNSELING SQUEEZE OF HIGHER EDUCATION

One consequence of the student "population explosion" has been to focus attention upon the need for effective counseling services. During the past ten years, many of the nation's senior colleges and universities have been forced to adopt a selective admission program based upon standardized test scores and high school grades. At other senior colleges and universities, the push by the disadvantaged for educational opportunity has resulted in a trend toward relaxed admission requirements, which is bringing in many students who lack the necessary basic skills for effective scholarship. The rapidly expanding community-college movement, with its open admission policy, has recruited large numbers of students who need considerable help in improving their academic skills. Consequently, programs to provide academic adjustment counseling for new students have received increasing emphasis at most colleges and universities. The objective for these programs is to maximize the likelihood of academic success for those who are admitted. The importance of this goal is underscored by the fact that, at present, only four out of ten entering college freshmen eventually receive the bachelor's degree.

At most colleges, however, the freshmen arriving on campus each fall are so numerous that it is virtually impossible for each to receive individual attention from college personnel workers and faculty members. In fact, the student population explosion, combined with limited personnel and financial resources, has actually restricted or reduced freshman counseling services on some college campuses. Thus, freshman orientation sometimes consists of little more than a welcoming assembly followed by a brief conference with an overworked or indifferent faculty advisor. After that, the freshman is often left to his own resources in adjusting to the college community.

On most college and university campuses, however, considerable effort is made to provide a meaningful orientation program for new students. While varying in approach, content, and duration, many of these programs are elaborate and expensive, with much time and effort being expended in planning and providing a series of orientation experiences designed to assist the personal-social-academic adjustment of the incoming freshman. Unfortunately, however, published reports (53, 65, 72, 87, 88, 97) on the effectiveness of these freshman-week activities indicate that there is little or no evidence to support the contention that such orientation programs help new students to relate themselves more meaningfully to the academic community. The available evidence (1, 2, 63, 105) also indicates a lack of results for the typical six- to eighteen-week college orientation course that freshmen are required to attend on many campuses. Such courses appear to be of limited effectiveness except where student participation is entirely voluntary and where study skills instruction is primarily emphasized. Even then, the research findings are inconsistent in terms of demonstrating long-term improvement in effective study behavior.

One possible reason for the failure of such college orientation programs may be the credibility factor. These programs are almost always planned, directed, and staffed by professional personnel, with limited involvement of students except in such assisting roles as campus guide or dormitory proctor. Today's generation gap tends to decrease the believability of statements made by adults and to increase the acceptability of information received from peers. Students listen to students more readily than they do to adults. Thus, adult-dominated orientation programs are unlikely to be effective in helping incoming students, because their credibility will likely be questioned by these students.

Needing information, advice, help, and reassurance during this period of adjustment, however, the freshman naturally turns to his more experienced peers for assistance. Sometimes he is given excellent help, but frequently he is provided erroneous or biased information or receives superficial or ill-informed assistance. Although so haphazard a process obviously leaves too much to fortuity, it is not likely to be replaced by a systematic program of individual counseling by professional guidance workers. The limitations imposed by available supply (amount of time and size of staff) and probable demand (number of students and variety of problems) make such a solution untenable on all but a very few campuses.

The problems described above underscore the fact that many colleges simply do not have the financial and personnel resources to maintain an adequate counseling program utilizing conventional procedures. The high academic mortality rate for freshmen, however, indicates an urgent requirement for more and better freshman counseling. Available statistics (55, 94, 117) suggest that the freshman-year attrition rate typically approaches 40 percent, with this figure remaining fairly constant throughout the 1960's. Unless effective steps are taken, however, this already alarming retention rate can be expected to drop sharply with the increasing input of disadvantaged students lacking the necessary preparation for effective scholarship. Colleges and universities are thus caught between an increasing requirement for improved counseling services and the rising cost and dubious effectiveness of their existing orientation programs. What is the answer to this counseling squeeze faced by so many institutions of higher education? Obviously, the philosophy and methodology of conventional counseling programs must be reviewed, and more effective and economical counseling approaches must be found.

One promising solution to the problem is the increased utilization of those largely untapped counseling resources available on all campuses—the faculty and the students. Unfortunately, the faculty member's traditional role as friend and confidant of the student has become increasingly difficult to maintain as a consequence of the trend toward larger classes, busier schedules, and more formalized instruction. As colleges and universities have grown in size, the problems of communication have further tended to impersonalize student-faculty relationships. Consequently, the students themselves are the only readily available and largely unused human resource to be found on the typical college campus.

During the past two decades, there has been a significant change in the traditional stereotype of the student's role in the counseling process. The developing trend has been to give the student an increasingly greater role in his own counseling. In many college counseling programs, this role has been expanded to the end that student counselors, acting in close cooperation with faculty advisors and personnel workers, are actively participating in the early counseling of freshmen. Because freshmen need immediate information and reassurance during their initial period of adjustment, college counseling programs are increasingly turning to upperclassmen to assist in the initial orientation of new students to the college community and to help freshmen in adapting to life in college residence halls.

REPORTED USE OF STUDENT-COUNSELING-STUDENT PROCEDURES

Two surveys have been made to determine the extent to which upperclassmen are being utilized to provide counseling for beginning freshmen. A survey of counseling services in institutions of higher learning made by Hardee and Powell (102) in May, 1956, included a half dozen questions concerning the use of student counselors during the 1955–56 academic year. A comprehensive survey of the use of student counselors in senior colleges and universities during the 1963–64 academic year was undertaken by Brown and Zunker (49, 131) in November, 1963. Since the two surveys were made eight years apart, a comparison of the reported findings should point up trends in the use of student-to-student counseling and identify new developments in this area of collegiate counseling activities.

Results for the 1955–56 National Survey

The 1955–56 survey revealed that 147 out of 218 colleges, or 67.4 percent, employed student-counseling-student procedures. Hardee and Powell found that almost all the student counselors worked either in the orientation program for new students or in the residence halls where new students are housed. Personal-social adjustment was the major area in which students were reportedly used as counselors. Academic problems and religious concerns were other areas in which upperclassmen were reported to be counseling freshmen.

As reported to Hardee and Powell, the selection and training of student counselors usually left much to be desired. Students entrusted with counseling responsibilities were typically selected with considerable care. However, the selection process apparently placed greatest emphasis on social behavior and attitudes, to the possible neglect of academic values. Students selected to serve as counselors were normally upperclassmen chosen for their personal qualifications and for their social accomplishments as reflected by their records. Leadership experience appeared to play a weighty role in the selection process, with most of the counseling aides being drawn from student government bodies, service and religious organizations, and recognized leaders in residence halls and honorary groups. In short, selection appeared to be based on the hope that the counselors might "counsel by example" of their own attitudes and behavior.

The training of student counselors was too often haphazard in planning and short in duration. Almost all programs utilizing student counselors were reported to provide training for selectees. Workshops, conferences, lectures, and informal discussion sessions were the procedures usually employed, with personnel deans normally providing leadership for the training enterprises. Some programs reportedly attempted to teach trainees something about the philosophy and objectives of the personnel program, and to supply information regarding effective procedures and techniques for conducting interviews and group discussions. However, analysis of the training received by student counselors indicated that most training programs were short and superficial. Hardee and Powell (102, p. 229) summarized the situation as follows: "The content of training procedures varies considerably according to the function which students are expected to fulfill. From a scrutiny of manuals, memoranda, and other printed materials prepared to aid in this training, it seems that much of the training is intended to facilitate mechanical procedures. Student counselors are provided with schedules, lists of required activities, or similar materials and are instructed in the proper guiding of new students or checking on their early activity to see that schedules are adhered to and that requirements are met."

Results for the 1963–64 National Survey

The 1963–64 survey by Brown and Zunker provides a much more detailed examination of the use of student-counseling-student procedures. A special questionnaire was designed to obtain the following information about the selection, training, and use of undergraduate student counselors: (*a*) places where student counselors were systematically used on the college campus, (*b*) types of counseling activities routinely performed by student counselors, (*c*) types of guidance materials routinely used by student counselors, (*d*) criteria employed in the selection of student counselors, (*e*) amount of formal training given to student counselors, (*f*) personnel directly involved in giving training to student counselors, (*g*) instructional procedures used in training student counselors, and (*h*) payment received by student counselors for their services. A copy of their Student Counselor Utilization Survey is included as Appendix A.

The questionnaire was mailed to a 20 percent stratified random sampling of four-year colleges and universities in the forty-eight contiguous states. A detailed description of the mail-out procedure employed in this survey is available elsewhere (130). Response to the questionnaire was exceptionally good in that it was returned by 95.2 percent of the sampled institutions. This unusually high questionnaire return rate suggests that there is much interest in the potentialities inherent in student-to-student counseling.

Of the responding institutions with a total enrollment over two thousand, 41 out of 65, or 63.1 percent, reported using undergraduate student counselors to assist in the counseling of freshmen. Student counselors were used in 77 out of 115, or 67.0 percent, of the responding institutions with a total enrollment under two thousand. Tables 1 through 9 report the data obtained from the returned questionnaires for the 118 colleges and universities using student-to-student counseling.

WORK PERFORMED BY STUDENT COUNSELORS

It is apparent from the results reported in Table 1 that most student counselors are assigned to duties in the residence halls. Although comparatively few colleges report their use elsewhere, the limited assignment of student counselors to instructional departments, study habits clinics, and testing and counseling centers does suggest a trend toward their regular use to provide routine counseling on academic adjustment problems, especially at the smaller institutions.

As reported in Table 2, institutions using student-to-student counseling indicate that such counseling is most often accomplished on an individual basis. Whereas individualized counseling is more often the case at the larger institutions, small-group counseling is used more often at the smaller colleges.

Table 3 shows that new-student orientation and residence hall supervision are the two functions most often performed by student counselors. Personal-social problems counseling, study habits counseling, and subject matter tutoring were also reported to be provided by student counselors at over one-third of the colleges sampled. Subject matter tutoring and vocational guidance were reportedly given more often by student counselors at the larger institutions.

Table 4 clearly indicates that freshman handbooks and college

TABLE 1

Places Where Student Counselors Are Systematically Used

Location	Enrollment under 2,000 No.	Enrollment under 2,000 %[a]	Enrollment over 2,000 No.	Enrollment over 2,000 %[b]	Total No.	Total %[c]
Residence halls	69	89.6	36	87.8	105	89.0
Student social center	17	22.1	7	17.1	24	20.3
Student religious center	7	9.1	4	9.8	11	9.3
Instructional departments	8	10.4	3	7.3	11	9.3
Study habits clinic	6	7.8	0	0.0	6	5.1
Testing and counseling center	5	6.5	0	0.0	5	4.2

[a] Percentage is based on 77 responding institutions.
[b] Percentage is based on 41 responding institutions.
[c] Percentage is based on 118 responding institutions.

TABLE 2
Size of Counselee Group Routinely Counseled
by Student Counselors

How Counseling Is Accomplished	Enrollment under 2,000		Enrollment over 2,000		Total	
	No.	%ª	No.	%ᵇ	No.	%ᶜ
Individual students	56	72.7	36	87.8	92	78.1
Small groups of 2–6 students	26	33.8	9	22.0	35	30.1
Intermediate groups of 7–20 students	18	23.4	8	19.5	26	22.0
Large groups of 21 or more students	9	11.7	8	19.5	17	14.4

ª Percentage is based on 77 responding institutions.
ᵇ Percentage is based on 41 responding institutions.
ᶜ Percentage is based on 118 responding institutions.

TABLE 3
Types of Counseling Activities Routinely Performed
by Student Counselors

Counseling Activity	Enrollment under 2,000		Enrollment over 2,000		Total	
	No.	%ª	No.	%ᵇ	No.	%ᶜ
New student orientation	71	92.2	35	85.4	106	89.8
Residence hall supervision	67	87.0	36	87.8	103	87.3
Personal-social problems counseling	34	44.2	18	43.9	52	44.1
Study habits counseling	33	42.9	17	41.5	50	42.4
Subject matter tutoring	24	31.2	18	43.9	42	35.6
Religious counseling	9	11.7	1	2.4	10	8.5
Education program planning	5	6.5	5	12.2	10	8.5
Vocational guidance	0	0.0	5	12.2	5	4.2
Psychological test interpretation	2	2.6	0	0.0	2	1.7

ª Percentage is based on 77 responding institutions.
ᵇ Percentage is based on 41 responding institutions.
ᶜ Percentage is based on 118 responding institutions.

TABLE 4
Counseling Materials Routinely Used by Student Counselors

Counseling Materials	Enrollment under 2,000		Enrollment over 2,000		Total	
	No.	%[a]	No.	%[b]	No.	%[c]
Freshman handbook or guide	62	80.5	31	75.6	93	78.8
College catalog	53	68.8	33	80.5	86	72.9
Biographical or personal history forms	12	15.6	8	19.5	20	16.9
College academic records	12	15.6	8	19.5	20	16.9
Standardized test results	9	11.7	5	12.2	14	11.9
College personnel records	6	7.8	2	4.9	8	6.8
Occupational briefs	4	5.2	3	7.3	7	5.9
High school transcript	0	0.0	3	7.3	3	2.5

[a] Percentage is based on 77 responding institutions.
[b] Percentage is based on 41 responding institutions.
[c] Percentage is based on 118 responding institutions.

catalogs are the materials most frequently used by student counselors. College academic records, biographical data forms, and standardized test results were reportedly being used by student counselors at more than 10 percent of the institutions sampled, thereby confirming a trend toward using student counselors to provide systematic guidance on academic adjustment problems. It should be noted, however, that only the scores from scholastic ability tests and study habits questionnaires were routinely being used in such counseling, with the scores from other types of standardized tests rarely being made available to the student counselors.

SELECTION AND TRAINING OF STUDENT COUNSELORS

The criteria used for the selection of student counselors are reported in Table 5. The main criteria used to select student counselors are previous leadership experience, residence hall director's evaluation, college grade average, faculty member evaluation, and peer acceptance rating. The larger institutions place relatively greater emphasis upon the residence hall director's evaluation and college grade average, whereas the smaller institutions place relatively greater emphasis upon peer acceptance ratings.

The total training time provided for undergraduate student counselors is reported in Table 6. Almost half of the larger institutions

TABLE 5
Basis for the Selection of Student Counselors

Criteria Used in Selection	Enrollment under 2,000		Enrollment over 2,000		Total	
	No.	%[a]	No.	%[b]	No.	%[c]
Previous leadership experience	61	79.2	33	80.5	94	79.7
Residence hall director's evaluation	50	64.9	34	82.9	84	71.2
College grade average	45	58.4	33	80.5	78	66.1
Faculty member evaluations	43	55.8	23	56.1	66	55.9
Peer acceptance ratings	27	35.1	14	10.0	41	34.7
Scholastic ability test scores	7	9.1	6	14.6	13	11.0
Personality appraisal questionnaire scores	7	9.1	5	12.2	12	10.2
Study habits survey scores	2	2.6	0	0.0	2	1.7

[a] Percentage is based on 77 responding institutions.
[b] Percentage is based on 41 responding institutions.
[c] Percentage is based on 118 responding institutions.

TABLE 6
Total Training Time Provided for Student Counselors

Training Time	Enrollment under 2,000		Enrollment over 2,000		Total	
	No.	%[a]	No.	%[b]	No.	%[c]
No systematic training	33	42.9	7	17.1	40	33.9
1–3 hours of training	10	13.0	6	14.6	16	13.6
4–6 hours of training	16	20.8	5	12.2	21	17.8
7–10 hours of training	4	5.2	2	7.3	6	5.1
11–20 hours of training	6	7.8	8	19.5	14	11.9
More than 20 hours of training	8	10.4	12	29.3	20	16.9

[a] Percentage is based on 77 responding institutions.
[b] Percentage is based on 41 responding institutions.
[c] Percentage is based on 118 responding institutions.

reported giving more than ten hours of training, whereas only 18 percent of the smaller institutions provided more than ten hours of systematic training for their student counselors. These differences were both significant and unexpected. In fact, the training time provided at the larger institutions reflects much greater concern about the preparation of student counselors than had been reported by Hardee and Powell. Although total training time was not specifically reported, they had concluded that the training of student counselors was most often haphazard in planning and short in duration.

The personnel directly involved in training student counselors is reported in Table 7. Personnel deans and residence hall directors are those most often involved in the training of student counselors at both large and small institutions. The larger institutions,

TABLE 7
Personnel Directly Involved in Training Student Counselors

Personnel	Enrollment under 2,000		Enrollment over 2,000		Total	
	No.	%[a]	No.	%[b]	No.	%[c]
Residence hall directors	43	55.8	29	70.7	72	61.0
Dean of men and/or dean of women	47	61.0	23	56.1	70	59.3
Dean of students	43	55.8	22	53.7	65	55.1
Director of testing and counseling	18	23.4	16	39.0	34	28.8
Student counselors	14	18.2	17	41.5	31	26.3
Professional counselors	9	11.7	15	36.6	24	20.3
Academic dean	13	16.9	6	14.6	19	16.1
Psychology faculty members	12	15.6	4	9.8	16	13.6
Education faculty members	6	7.8	5	12.2	11	9.3
Director of student union	6	7.8	3	7.3	9	7.6
College chaplain	6	7.8	2	4.9	8	6.8
Other faculty members	2	2.6	4	9.8	6	5.1
Other administrative personnel	3	3.9	3	7.3	6	5.1

[a] Percentage is based on 77 responding institutions.
[b] Percentage is based on 41 responding institutions.
[c] Percentage is based on 118 responding institutions.

TABLE 8

Instructional Procedures Utilized in Training Student Counselors

Procedure	Enrollment under 2,000 No.	%[a]	Enrollment over 2,000 No.	%[b]	Total No.	%[c]
Group discussions	59	76.6	34	82.9	93	78.8
Lectures	32	41.6	31	75.6	63	53.4
Demonstrations	12	15.6	17	41.5	29	24.6
Reading assignments	13	16.9	11	26.8	24	20.3
Role playing	11	14.3	5	12.2	16	13.6
Practice exercise	7	9.1	8	19.5	15	12.7
Buddy-system training	7	9.1	2	4.9	9	7.6

[a] Percentage is based on 77 responding institutions.
[b] Percentage is based on 41 responding institutions.
[c] Percentage is based on 118 responding institutions.

TABLE 9

Payment Received by Student Counselors

Payment	Enrollment under 2,000 No.	%[a]	Enrollment over 2,000 No.	%[b]	Total No.	%[c]
Unpaid	28	36.4	13	31.7	41	34.7
Paid all or part of room and board	17	22.1	17	41.5	34	28.2
Paid a fixed total sum	20	26.0	5	12.2	25	21.2
Paid on hourly rate basis	7	9.1	2	4.9	9	7.6
Paid on monthly rate basis	2	2.6	5	12.2	7	5.9
Paid by tuition grant	4	5.2	2	4.9	6	5.1

[a] Percentage is based on 77 responding institutions.
[b] Percentage is based on 41 responding institutions.
[c] Percentage is based on 118 responding institutions.

however, make greater use of the residence hall director than do the smaller colleges. Likewise, larger institutions make greater use of professional counselors and the director of testing and counseling, probably because such professional personnel workers are more readily available there. Finally, experienced student counselors are more often involved in the training activity at the larger institutions than at the smaller colleges.

The instructional procedures utilized in training student counselors are reported in Table 8. Group discussion and lectures are the principal procedures employed at both the large and the small institutions, with lectures being used more extensively by the larger colleges and universities. Demonstrations, practice exercises, and reading assignments are likewise more often used by the larger institutions. The fact that demonstrations were routinely used by over 40 percent of the larger institutions would tend to confirm the earlier observation that there is increasing concern about the preparation of student counselors.

The pay given to student counselors is reported in Table 9. Approximately one-third of the sampled colleges did not pay their student counselors. Where payment was made, the most frequent methods were to pay all or part of the student's room and board or to pay the student a fixed sum for his services. The larger institutions reported a preference for paying room and board, while the smaller colleges preferred to pay a fixed sum. Several of the larger colleges also reported paying their student counselors a fixed monthly rate. The differences found are probably a reflection of the greater financial resources available to the larger colleges and universities.

Almost two-thirds of the questionnaires received from the 118 institutions using student counselors contained spontaneous comments in the space provided. The majority of these statements indicated a highly positive reaction to the value of including student counselors in college and university counseling programs. The respondents indicated that the major value to be realized from the use of student counselors was their effectiveness as "big brother" or "big sister" in helping new students adjust to the college campus. Recognition of the value of the proximity factor in student-to-student counseling was implicit throughout these spontaneous comments. Several statements made by the respondents also reflected a desire to expand the counseling activities of student counselors beyond their traditional role of dormitory monitor or orientation-week guide.

Comparison of Survey Findings

For the 1955–56 and 1963–64 surveys, respectively, 67.4 percent and 65.6 percent of the returned questionnaires reported the regular use of student-counseling-student procedures. Thus both surveys found organized student-to-student counseling to be in wide use on the nation's college campuses. The 1963–64 survey, when compared with the 1955–56 findings, also indicates an increasing concern about the selection and training of student counselors, especially at the larger institutions. Analysis of responses to the two surveys suggests a definite trend toward more systematic selection procedures, increased training time, and improved instructional methods and materials. Comparison of the two studies further suggests a developing trend toward using student counselors to provide systematic counseling on academic adjustment problems and to employ them on a continuing basis in settings other than the freshman residence halls. The problems involved in the effective utilization of student-to-student counseling need further careful study, however, for both surveys show that many institutions are employing haphazard procedures in the selection, training, and supervision of their student counselors.

RATIONALE FOR THE STUDENT-COUNSELING-STUDENT APPROACH

Administrators and faculty members are beginning to recognize that colleges need to do much more than they are to maximize the likelihood of graduation by those whom they admit. In view of the trend toward open admissions and recruitment of students from disadvantaged backgrounds, the time has certainly come for a reassessment of the "sink-or-swim" philosophy that so many colleges take toward their entering freshmen. No longer should the freshman year be considered a period when the academically unfit are screened out so that the survivors can then be educated. Instead, each entering freshman should be helped to make a satisfactory adjustment to the collegiate learning environment so that he can quickly begin to realize his academic potentialities.

One problem, of course, is that the financial and personnel costs are prohibitive for many institutions if the needed services are to be provided through conventional counseling procedures using professional personnel workers. Another problem is that the usual orientation approaches have typically not produced significant results, probably due, at least in part, to the fact that such programs are adult directed and lack credibility for many beginning freshmen. More economical and effective counseling approaches simply must be found, and the expanded use of student-to-student counseling appears to be one of the more promising solutions to the counseling squeeze of higher education.

Many reasons may be advanced to support the expanded use of student-to-student counseling procedures. First, it assures wider and earlier counseling contact with freshmen than is possible with the professional staff alone. Second, it counteracts the influence of the inevitable, extensive, and unstructured advising of beginning freshmen by randomly encountered upperclassmen. Third, it permits the systematic exploration of preventive measures for the common adjustment problems encountered by the typical beginning freshman. Fourth, it affords an opportunity for meaningful leadership experience to students selected as counselors. Fifth, it provides for improved communication channels between students and administrators. Finally, it supplies a practical approach that is economical from the standpoint of both financial and personnel costs.

Two additional reasons for the expanded use of student counselors require closer examination. First, analysis of a typical college counselor's duties reveals that much of the work is clerical in nature, with a great deal of the counselor's time being consumed in the performance of routine activities, such as the interpretation of requirements or the correction of misinformation. The use of supervised student counselors to perform these relatively routine operations would free the professional staff to handle more specialized counseling activities. Second, the student counselor has the advantage of "believability," and, hence, greater acceptance by freshmen. Because he "speaks the same language and shares the same problems," the student counselor is probably in a more favorable position than professional staff members for discussing deficient study skills and negative academic attitudes with freshmen. Educators and psychologists have long recognized that peer-delivered information and advice frequently receives readier acceptance by the typical eighteen-year-old than does the counsel given by teachers and parents. After all, it is a well-established characteristic of today's teen-age culture that advice received from one's peers is vastly superior to the counsel of authority figures representing the "establishment" position.

Some college administrators will, of course, be apathetic or opposed to the expanded use of student-counseling-student procedures. They will point out that the process is potentially dangerous because student counselors may not recognize the point at which a problem exceeds their capabilities. Needless to say, this same objection could also be voiced about the use of faculty advisors. Although such concern is not without justification, effective operational procedures can be developed to minimize the danger. Systematic selection and training procedures, continuous supervision by a qualified program director, comprehensive delineation of the student counselor's duties and limitations, and open channels for consultation and referral—all can be designed to protect both the counselor and the counselee from student counselor excesses.

Admittedly, these measures will still leave much to the judgment of the student counselor. Freshmen will naturally turn to upperclassmen to obtain information and advice, however, and the assistance thus obtained, while often biased in content and haphazard in delivery, still possesses the advantage of high credibility. Why not, therefore, make effective use of the ready acceptability of peer-delivered information? An organized program of student-to-student counseling should offer many advantages over leaving the student-counseling-student process to fortuity. Not the least of these might be a significant reduction in the credibility gap between students, faculty members, and administrators.

2. The Case for Study Habits and Attitudes Counseling

A problem of major concern to the nation's colleges and universities is the attrition of a sizable portion of each year's freshman class because of scholastic difficulties. The development and validation of instruments designed to predict the future academic achievement of entering college freshmen has long been one of the major subjects for educational and psychological research. A survey of the literature concerned with factors influencing student success and failure in college discloses that numerous tests have been created for the specific purpose of identifying students likely to encounter scholastic difficulties, while tests developed for use in other areas have been diverted to this purpose in large numbers. Achievement tests, aptitude measures, interest inventories, and personality questionnaires have been used with widely varying degrees of success. However, the best of our present test batteries are typically unable to account for more than half of the variance in the prediction of subsequent academic achievement.

Aptitude measures and achievement tests have both been developed to a high degree of perfection and the better instruments of either type often yield correlation coefficients approaching .60 with an external criterion, such as one-semester grade averages or grades in specific subject matter fields. When utilized together for the prediction of various scholastic attainment criteria, aptitude and achievement test combinations have sometimes yielded multiple correlation coefficients exceeding .70; however, this is the exception rather than the rule. While additional refinement of aptitude and achievement testing methodology will undoubtedly improve the quality of such instruments, this improvement is unlikely to yield materially greater correlation with the usual criterion of academic achievement.

Aptitude tests and achievement measures appear to have approached their maximum usefulness as predictive instruments, thereby suggesting the need for a comprehensive program of research leading to the construction and validation of nonintellectual predictors of scholastic success. Research reporting the predictive efficiency of interest inventories and personality questionnaires, although somewhat ambiguous and conflicting, fails to indicate any consistent significant relationship between such scores and the academic success of college freshmen. Analyses of responses to standardized personality and interest inventories have succeeded in identifying some of the distinctive characteristics and modes of adjustment differentiating high- and low-scholarship students. Nevertheless, the measurement of such traits has proven most elusive. Studies utilizing such instruments to predict academic success in college have produced very meager results.

By contrast, a variety of investigations comparing the behavior and attitudes of high-achieving and low-achieving college freshmen has confirmed the importance of motivational factors as a significant determinant of college scholarship. Studies utilizing observation, interview, and questionnaire techniques have revealed many behavioral and attitudinal differences between high-scholarship and low-scholarship students. For example, Tiebout (120), in a three-year clinical study, found a striking similarity in the clinical picture of students whose scholastic records were poorer than their intelligence test scores would predict. He found that attitudes of candidness and defensiveness in analyzing their weaknesses were characteristic of academic overachievers and underachievers, respectively. Specifically, low-scholarship students were found to exhibit three behavioral characteristics in common: (a) a tendency to gloss over failures and shortcomings and view them in an optimistic light, (b) a tendency to make much too high an appraisal of their net accomplishments, and (c) a tendency to rationalize their poor record of achievement by blaming poor study habits, poor teaching, and other outside factors. In short, Tiebout found that the low-scholarship student habitually rationalized or ignored his failures and exaggerated or distorted his successes in order to maintain a favorable impression of himself. He also found that academic underachievers tended to be governed by strong hedonistic principles.

Brown, Abeles, and Iscoe (31) likewise found significant behavioral differences in their comparison studies of high- and low-scholarship students. The data obtained from three separate studies suggested a common pattern for low-achieving students. This typical behavior pattern was labeled "activity delay" and appeared to be characterized by one or more of the following: (a) an unwillingness to conform to academic requirements, routines, and regulations, (b) a sense of irresponsibility toward commitments made, and (c) a lack of decisiveness of action and a tendency to procrastinate. From the results obtained, the researchers concluded that factors of negative interest and motivation were primary contributors toward low scholarship and that the student's attitude toward academic life may be as important as study habits, study aids, tutorial possibilities, or native intelligence.

In another study, Brown and Abeles (30) found that façade orientation scores were related significantly and negatively to subsequent academic achievement in college. Façade orientation was defined as a readiness, or willingness, to resort to façade in situations where self-interest dictates that one make a favorable impression. High- and low-academic achievers were found to differ significantly in their orientation toward the use of façade, with high- and low-scholarship students being characterized by conservatism and liberalism, respectively, in their façade orientation.

Questionnaires aimed at uncovering the study skills and academic attitudes that differentiate high-scholarship and low-scholarship students have mostly found significant differences in motivational orientations rather than significant variations in study mechanics. After making an intensive survey of the how-to-study literature, Brown and Holtzman (38, 39, 83) concluded that attitude, set, and motivational characteristics with regard to the academic situation were of greater importance than purely mechanical procedures of studying. While efficiency in study procedures was characteristic of high-scholarship students, efficient study skills could be considered as tools at the disposal of any student. The important consideration was what motivates the student to use or not to use these tools.

The conclusion about the importance of motivational factors was further reinforced by a series of discussion seminars conducted by Brown (13, 29). Over a period of four years, small groups of successful high school and college students met and compared the study behavior and scholastic motivation of high- and low-scholarship students. After these differences had been discussed at length, each group prepared a list of suggestions to be given to all students wishing to earn better grades. Analysis of the information thus obtained revealed that the study behavior of successful and unsuccessful students differed meaningfully in three important respects: (*a*) *organization for studying*, or their efficiency in organizing their study time, study materials, or study area; (*b*) *techniques for studying*, or their efficiency in reading textbooks, taking notes, writing reports, or preparing for tests; and (*c*) *motivation for studying*, or their realistic understanding of the need for studying and the importance of efficient study habits.

The findings from a variety of research investigations thus suggest the following conclusions about potentiality versus probability of academic success. Academic ability, as measured by standardized aptitude and achievement tests, yields information that represents the student's *potentiality* for future academic performance.

The *probability* of subsequent academic performance being at or near the student's measured potential depends upon the degree of steady, vigorous, motivated, effective effort put forth by the student. Overachieving and underachieving students are, respectively, found to be characterized by positive and negative academic beliefs, values, and expectations. Academic achievement is, then, directly related to both the student's level of academic ability and his level of scholastic motivation.

Investigating the Probability Factor in Scholastic Success

Research findings indicate that the counseling of students experiencing scholastic difficulties should take into account both potential for academic attainment and motivation for scholastic success. The counselor's problem, of course, is how to accomplish the latter in an effective, organized manner. Before meaningful counseling on motivational problems can be accomplished, appropriate psychometric strategics and materials must be developed and the critical motivational factors and interactions must be defined. Two research approaches were especially appropriate to achieve these objectives. First, systematic test construction and validation techniques could be employed to develop the necessary psychometric approaches. Once this effort has produced acceptable instruments, an attempt to define critical motivational elements through factor analysis procedures could then be undertaken.

Academic Attitudes and Scholastic Success

The Survey of Study Habits and Attitudes (37, 43), hereafter referred to as SSHA, was developed to meet the need for a self-inventory of study behavior and study motivation that would provide a valid prediction of subsequent academic achievement. The SSHA is a self-report questionnaire consisting of 100 statements distributed systematically across four 25-item subscales. In addition to a total Study Orientation score and area scores for Study Habits and Study Attitudes, the questionnaire also yields four subscale scores—Delay Avoidance, Work Method, Teacher Approval, and Education Acceptance. Separate forms are available for high school and college, with the item content of the two editions being identical except for minor changes in wording necessitated by differences in instructional procedures, academic requirements, and study conditions at the two levels.

The purposes of the SSHA are as follows: (*a*) to identify students whose study habits and attitudes are different from those of students who earn high grades, (*b*) to aid in understanding students having academic difficulties in their current study program, and (*c*) to provide a basis for helping such students improve their study habits and attitudes and thus more fully realize their best potentialities. The SSHA is not intended to be primarily a selection tool, since its usefulness for that purpose would be limited by its dependence on the frankness of student responses.

Development of the SSHA covered fifteen years and required eight revisions in item content. Construction of the SSHA began with an exhaustive review of the literature and a series of group discussions with college freshmen concerning the motivational differences between good and poor students. A total of 234 items was compiled from group interviews, existing inventories on study habits, studies using observational techniques to differentiate good and poor students, and reports on related experiments in the field of learning. These items were generally of two kinds—those dealing primarily with the mechanics of studying and those concerned mainly with motivation to do well in academic work. Subsequent development of the SSHA included six major phases involving a total of nearly 21,000 high school and college students.

Using grade-point averages as a criterion, a series of item analyses and questionnaire revisions produced a 75-item SSHA, which was published in 1953 (37). The 1953 SSHA provided a 36-item scoring key for men and a 29-item scoring key for women, with the two keys containing only 22 common items. Validity of the 1953 SSHA ranged from .27 to .66 for men and from .26 to .65 for women, with the average validity coefficient being .42 and .45 for men and women, respectively. Correlations between the SSHA and a typical scholastic aptitude test were .25 and .34, respectively, for men and women. The predictive power of the 1953 SSHA was thus shown to rest on its measurement of traits largely untouched by the usual scholastic aptitude test.

Soon after publication of the 1953 SSHA, further research was undertaken to improve the questionnaire's usefulness for counseling purposes by developing and validating meaningful subscales and separate high school and college editions. Developmental work on the revised SSHA included three stages. First, additional items were developed covering attitudinal areas not tapped by the original instrument. Second, subscales having both diagnostic and prognostic utility for the counseling process were constructed. Third, the usefulness of the derived subscales for academic counseling was systematically evaluated.

In the revised SSHA, published in 1964, 65 items remained unchanged, 5 items received minor changes in wording, and 30 new items were added to the 70 retained statements. All of the scored items in the 1953 SSHA were retained unchanged in the revised SSHA. Construction of subscales began with fifteen psychologists independently analyzing the 100 SSHA statements and subjectively categorizing them into areas. Consensus as to the placement of each item provided the basis for the initial construction of subscales. The a priori subscales thus derived were then assessed by correlational analyses to determine homogeneity of item content. Subscale purification by transfer of items to more appropriate subscales eventually produced four 25-item SSHA subscales. Each of the 100 SSHA items was then correlated with each of the four subscale scores to provide statistical justification for the item content of each subscale. SSHA scores, grade-point averages, and scholastic aptitude test scores were also intercorrelated for 12,660 students in grades seven through thirteen. From the data obtained it was concluded that each of the SSHA subscales measured traits that play a significant role in the academic achievement, that the traits being assessed were not appreciably related to measured scholastic aptitude, and that these traits were sufficiently independent for counseling purposes.

In addition to statistical evaluations, the operational use of the SSHA subscales in academic adjustment counseling was systematically investigated (20). Specifically, the revised SSHA was employed to counsel approximately 6,680 entering college freshmen on their potential academic adjustment problems. Analysis of follow-up data supported two conclusions. First, the revised SSHA was suitable for use in a program of academic adjustment counseling designed to facilitate counselee awareness of the importance of effective study habits and positive study attitudes. Second, freshmen counseled about deficiencies in their study habits and attitudes, when compared with matching uncounseled freshmen, generally earned better grades during their initial semester in college.

A unique feature of the revised SSHA is the Counseling Key, which was developed to help counselor and counselee identify academic behavior and scholastic motivation that are different from those characteristic of high-scholastic achievers. The Counseling Key identifies critical responses on the answer sheet by item number so that the counselor and counselee can look up these items in the SSHA booklet. Discussion of the student's reasons for answering as he did usually provides meaningful information about his study habits and the attitudes behind them. A detailed analysis of the student's specific study problems is thus made a practical element in trying to diagnose the nature of a student's academic difficulties. Utilization of the SSHA Counseling Key is described in detail elsewhere (37, 41, 43).

Research findings have thus shown the SSHA to be a useful predictor of academic achievement. Its correlation with various measures of scholastic aptitude is low enough to indicate that the predictive power of the SSHA rests on its measurement of traits largely untouched by aptitude tests. Its effectiveness as a predictor of future academic attainment reflects its systematic development and rigorous cross-validation, using empirical criteria of scholastic success. Construction and validation of the original and the revised SSHA are described in a series of reports published elsewhere (4, 7, 38, 39, 40, 43, 56, 64, 83, 84, 85).

There is positive evidence, however, that prediction is better when the students are interested in their results than when they are not. For example, one study (41, 64) using the 1953 SSHA revealed a sharp difference in the correlation between SSHA scores and one-semester freshman grades for students who expressed a strong interest in the meaning of their SSHA scores compared to the correlation for those students who did not express such interest. When the SSHA was administered at the beginning of the semester, a group of 411 freshmen at the University of Texas was told that anyone who was interested could obtain his score and have it interpreted if he would contact one of the authors. For the 90 women and 98 men who were sufficiently motivated to make inquiry, the correlations between SSHA total score and grades at the end of the semester were .65 and .71, respectively. For the remaining 223 freshmen, the correlations were .43 for women and .41 for men.

Other researchers have sought to evaluate the predictive efficiency and counseling usefulness of the SSHA. Popham and Moore (100) tested the hypothesis that college students' scores on the SSHA evidenced a significantly stronger relationship to earned grades than they did to measured intellectual aptitude. Research findings confirmed this hypothesis and it was concluded that the SSHA measures something other than academic aptitude, which is significantly associated with scholastic success. Lum (92) and Popham (99) compared the SSHA scores of scholastic overachievers and underachievers and found significant differences in their self-reported study orientation. Overachievers evidenced stronger motivation for studying, tended to be more self-confident, and appeared to have a greater capacity for working under pressure. Underachievers showed a marked tendency to procrastinate, tended to rely upon external pressures to complete assignments, and voiced more criticism of educational methodology and philosophy. The research findings by independent investigators thus confirmed the usefulness of the SSHA for counseling students having academic difficulties.

Study Skills and Scholastic Success

The Effective Study Test (13), hereafter referred to as EST, was developed to meet the need for an objective-type test that would measure a student's knowledge about efficient study procedures instead of inventorying his self-reported study habits and attitudes. The EST is a true-false test consisting of 125 statements distributed systematically across five 25-item subscales. In addition to the total Study Effectiveness score, the test yields five subscale scores— Reality Orientation, Study Organization, Writing Behavior, Reading Behavior, and Examination Behavior. Separate high school and college forms are available, with the item content for the two editions being identical except for minor changes in wording necessitated by differences in instructional procedures, academic requirements, and study conditions at the two levels.

The EST was specifically designed to serve the following three purposes: (*a*) to identify students likely to encounter future academic difficulties due to their limited knowledge of effective study procedures, (*b*) to aid in understanding students encountering academic difficulties in their current study program, and (*c*) to provide a basis for helping such students improve their study skills and thus more fully realize their academic potential. Although the EST is intended to be used primarily for counseling and teaching, its predictive validity is evidence of its relevance as a screening instrument to identify students having deficient study skills.

Development of the EST has covered five years and required six revisions in item content. Construction of the EST began with an exhaustive review of the how-to-study literature and a series of group discussions with college freshmen concerning differences in the study behavior of good and poor students. During the literature review and group discussion phase, a pool of 264 true-false questions was compiled from interview data, existing study habits questionnaires, and related research reports. Using grade-point averages and total test scores as criteria, a series of difficulty-discrimination item analyses were completed over a three-year period. The accompanying elimination or revision of test items eventually produced the final five-scale, 125-item, true-false test.

The EST has been validated at a variety of Texas high schools and colleges. The criterion used in all high school validation studies was the one-year grade-point average. The high-school-level EST was validated on 2,354 students enrolled in grades nine through twelve at six different Texas high schools. The obtained validity coefficients varied from .52 to .77, with the average correlation being .60 for the twenty-four groups tested. Other research findings showed that, when the intelligence factor was controlled, the resulting partial correlations were .39 and .54, respectively, with grade-point averages and achievement test scores. The criterion used in the college validation research was the first-semester grade-point average. The college-level EST was validated on 1,114 entering freshmen at two Texas colleges. The obtained validity coefficients were .54 and .57, and correlations between the EST and a typical scholastic aptitude test were only .28 and .29. Construction and validation of the EST are reported elsewhere in detail (13).

Research results obtained for high school and college versions of the EST show the test to be a valid predictor of academic achievement at both levels. Furthermore, the correlation between EST and typical tests of scholastic aptitude is modest enough to indicate that the former measures traits that play an important role in scholastic success but that are not assessed by the latter. From the available data it may be concluded that study skills knowledge, as measured by the EST, is meaningfully related to scholastic achievement even when the influence of intelligence has been cancelled out.

Factorial Analyses of Scholastic Success

The attempt to define critical motivational elements through factor analysis procedures involved two studies of freshmen enrolled at Southwest Texas State College. Selected standardized tests and experimental measures were administered to all first-semester freshmen during the fall semesters of 1954 and 1956. The scores thus obtained were intercorrelated and factor analyzed in order to examine significant variable interactions and to define critical motivational factors.

The initial factorial investigation was undertaken to demonstrate a number of specific hypotheses derived from the proposition that academic achievement in college is a function not only of scholastic ability but also of certain motivational orientations. The three areas of motivational orientation considered in the inquiry were academic attitude, peer-group affiliation, and life-style orientations.

A total of eleven tests, questionnaires, and rating forms were administered to 213 women and 199 men comprising the 1954–55 freshman class at Southwest Texas State College. The four standardized instruments used in the study yielded five scores; the seven experimental instruments developed for the investigation yielded twenty-one scores. The academic ability tests were administered to all entering freshmen at the beginning of the fall semester. Six weeks later, all beginning freshmen were given the academic attitude and life-style orientation questionnaires. The peer evaluation forms were completed at the end of the fall semester.

Two indices of high school scholarship and three criteria of college achievement were also employed in the investigation. A high school quarter rank obtained from high school transcripts and a high school percentile rank computed from data procured through direct correspondence with principals provided the indices of secondary school scholarship. Initial academic achievement in college was assessed by a first-semester grade-point average. Extracurricular participation ratings made by appropriate members of the college administration and evaluated participation scores derived from college newspaper and yearbook data afforded two estimates of early social achievement. Very brief descriptions of these thirty-one variables may be found in Appendix B. Detailed descriptions of the experimental instruments and the achievement criteria may be found elsewhere (5).

Analysis of the data was accomplished in three phases. First, separate intercorrelation matrices were computed for men and women. Second, separate factor analyses were made of the correlation matrices obtained for each sex. Finally, the variable having the highest loading was selected to represent each obtained factor, and multiple regression analyses were computed to determine the relative contribution of each factor to the prediction of academic achievement.

Using Thurstone's complete centroid technique, a factor analysis was performed for each sex, and five factors were extracted from each correlation matrix. Zemmerman's graphical procedure was used in rotating the axes defined by the centroid factor loadings. Satisfactory solutions were obtained after fifteen graphical rotations for men and thirteen graphical rotations for women. Four common factors and one unique factor were obtained for each sex. Two of the common factors, scholastic ability and acceptance *of* peer group, had almost identical loadings for both sexes, whereas there were significant discrepancies between loadings obtained for men and women on the factors for academic attitude and acceptance *by* peer group. The unique factor obtained for women was identified as life-style orientation, while the fifth factor found for men was defined by the indices of academic achievement in high school and college. Obtained intercorrelation matrices, factor loadings before and after graphical rotation, and defining variables for all extracted factors are reported elsewhere for both sexes (5, 45).

The variable having the highest loading for each factor was selected to represent that factor in a multiple regression analysis, with the criterion variable being the first-semester grade-point average. For both sexes, the most efficient regression equation for the prediction of academic achievement was the combination of a typical measure of scholastic ability and two measures of motivational orientation—academic attitude as measured by the SSHA and acceptance by the peer group as a study companion. For women, the regression of academic achievement upon these three defining variables yielded a multiple correlation coefficient of .76, which accounted for about 58 percent of the criterion variance. The same regression equation for men accounted for approximately 52 percent of the criterion variance with a multiple correlation of .72.

The intercorrelation, factor, and multiple regression analyses provided definitive evidence that indices of motivational orientation, especially measures of academic attitude and acceptance by peers, are significantly related to scholastic achievement but tend to operate independently of academic ability. When such motivational orientations were considered in addition to scholastic ability, the gains in predictive efficiency were found to be substantial for both sexes. Thus the research findings indicated that the probability of initial scholastic success in college is improved significantly when the student reports having positive academic attitudes and is accepted by the members of his peer group.

The initial factorial investigation was undertaken to test four hypotheses concerning the relationship between certain motivational orientations and academic achievement in college. The first postulation was stated as follows: Positive academic attitude, or a positive motivational orientation toward scholastic attainment, is characteristic of high-scholarship students, whereas the reverse is characteristic of low-scholarship students. For both men and women, correlations between the two measures of academic attitude and an index of initial academic achievement in college were significant beyond the .001 level of confidence. Furthermore, factor analyses yielded an academic attitude factor for each sex, thereby demonstrating that the measures represented an independent factorial dimension in the study.

The second hypothesis was stated as follows: Being accepted by, being peripheral to, or being rejected by one's classmates is related significantly to scholastic achievement; that is, high-scholarship students positively value and are positively valued by the members of their peer group, whereas the reverse is typical of low-scholarship students. All five measures reflecting acceptance by peers were correlated significantly with the academic achievement of women, whereas only one proved to be a significant correlate of male grade-point averages. The hypothesis that acceptance *by* one's peers is related significantly to academic success was thus strongly confirmed for women but received only minimal support for men. The hypothesized relationship between acceptance *of* one's peers and scholastic achievement was not significantly supported for either sex. In fact, the factor analyses for men and for women both yielded separate factors for acceptance *by* peer group and acceptance *of* peer group, thereby demonstrating that the two types of peer acceptance operated as relatively independent factorial dimensions. The research findings indicated that the probability of satisfactory scholastic success during the freshman year of college is further increased when the individual is accepted by the peer group. However, the results also suggested that such peer acceptance is more important for freshman females as a correlate of academic achievement.

The third hypothesis was stated as follows: High-scholarship students indicate a history of adherence to the role behaviors and value apprehensions of the upper-middle-class family life style, whereas low-scholarship students indicate a different orientation and background. For both men and women, three of the measures of life-style orientation developed for the inquiry were found to be significant predictors of subsequent academic achievement. The postulated life-style orientation factor was extracted for the female sample but failed to materialize for men. The existence of this motivational element as an independent factorial dimension was thus demonstrated only for women. The research findings, however, do support the hypothesis that life-style orientation and academic achievement in college are related significantly.

The final assumption was stated as follows: The three motivational elements—academic attitude, peer-group affiliation, and life-style orientation—operate independently of scholastic ability in the prediction of academic achievement. Correlation between scores obtained from the scholastic ability tests and scores derived from the motivational orientation measures ranged from low to moderate for both sexes, thereby supporting the hypothesis that the experimental variables, especially academic attitude and peer acceptance scores, are relatively independent of scholastic ability measures. Factor analysis results for both sexes showed the obtained academic attitude and peer acceptance factors to be relatively independent of the scholastic ability factor and of each other. The postulated life-style orientation factor was not found for men, however, and the measures developed to assess this motivational element had appreciable loadings on the scholastic ability factor extracted for both sexes. Although the evidence is less definitive for life-style orientation, the research results indicate that all three hypothesized elements of motivational orientation do tend to operate independently of academic ability.

The initial factorial investigation significantly supported the proposition that academic achievement in college is a function not only of scholastic ability but also of certain motivational orientations. A second factorial investigation was undertaken two years later in order to examine further the relationship between scholastic and social success in college and selected measures of ability, achievement, attitude, and adjustment. The focus of this follow-up inquiry was on the interaction of scholastic and social achievement and the identification of predictor indices for the latter.

From the student viewpoint, academic achievement is but one aspect of a successful college career. Many students assign equal (or perhaps even greater) importance to social achievement in college. Social achievement may be defined operationally in terms of the degree of social recognition gained for participation in campus extracurricular activities, including both activities that are organized and sponsored and those that are informal and unsponsored. Although educators generally have recognized that academic achievement and social achievement are both of importance to the student, little study has been made of the interaction between the two variables, and prediction research for the latter variable appears to be almost nonexistent.

A total of twelve tests, questionnaires, and sociometric devices, yielding fifty-seven predictor measures, was utilized in the follow-up study. The predictor measures included indices of scholastic ability, academic achievement, academic attitude, life-style orientation, personality need structure, peer-group affiliation, and personal and family adjustment. Criteria for initial scholastic and social achievement in college were, respectively, the first-semester point-hour grade average compiled from registrar's records and the extracurricular participation index derived from yearbook, newspaper, and other recorded data. An index of secondary school scholarship, the high school percentile rank, was computed from data procured through direct correspondence with school principals. Very brief descriptions of these sixty variables may be found in Appendix C. Detailed descriptions for the experimental instruments and the achievement criteria are available elsewhere (6).

The research population included all first-semester freshmen enrolled at Southwest Texas State College during the fall semester of the 1956–57 long session. The three tests measuring scholastic ability and academic achievement were administered to all entering freshmen at the beginning of the fall semester. Six weeks later, the beginning freshmen were given the seven questionnaires assessing academic attitudes, life-style orientation, personality need structure, and personal and family adjustment. Two sociometric devices for evaluating peer-group affiliation were completed by the freshmen at the end of the fall semester. Complete data were obtained for all 286 women and 242 men comprising the 1956–57 freshman class.

Computation and factor analysis of correlation matrices were accomplished independently for men and women. Computation of product-moment correlation coefficients between variables, extraction of factors by Thurstone's complete centroid technique, and rotation of extracted centroid loadings to a quartimax solution were accomplished on an IBM 650 electronic computer. Factoring was continued until seven factors were extracted for men and eight factors were extracted for women. The quartimax loadings obtained for each factor were then graphically plotted against those for all other factors.

Five of the factors extracted for each sex were considered to be common factors because of almost identical defining variables for men and women. These five common factors are defined chiefly by variables measuring scholastic ability, academic attitudes, personal problems, peer acceptance, and manifest personality needs. Measures of social adjustment, family adjustment, and social orientation define the unique factors obtained for women. Additional factors obtained for men were a factor reflecting hedonistic orientation and an instrument factor measuring personal and social adjustment.

Examination of the male and female intercorrelation matrices indicated that the best predictors of the scholastic success criterion, one-semester grade-point averages, were the indices of scholastic ability, scholastic achievement, and academic attitude. The best predictors of the social success criterion, extracurricular participation index, were current peer-group acceptance and social orientation as reflected by biographical data. The correlations obtained between objective criteria of scholastic and social success in college were .26 and .19 for men and women, respectively. The two aspects of a successful college career were thus found to be operating as largely independent variables during the first semester of the freshman year.

The two factorial investigations at Southwest Texas State College confirm the importance of motivational orientations in making scholastic success predictions and in providing academic adjustment guidance. In both studies, academic attitude emerged as a well-defined factor operating independently of an equally well-defined scholastic ability factor. A third well-defined factor, peer-group affiliation, also appeared to be a significant determinant of college success—both scholastic and social. The importance of the peer-group affiliation factor is confirmed by investigations reported by Posey (101) and by Brown and McGuire (6, 46). Both studies found a substantial relationship between low peer-group acceptance and low scholastic achievement and between high peer-group acceptance and high scholastic achievement. Each investigation concluded that peer-group affiliation is significantly related to initial social and scholastic success in college.

Sex Roles and Academic Expectations

Findings from research on the probability factor in academic success suggested that sex-based differences in beliefs, values, and expectations were important variables requiring further investigation. Research leading to publication of the 1953 SSHA (4, 37, 40, 64, 85) had resulted in separate scoring keys for men and women. Furthermore, the 36-item male scoring key and 29-item female scoring key contained only 22 common items. The authors concluded that differences in the responses of men and women to SSHA items indicated the possibility of strong sex differences in such attributes as attitude, set, and motivation in the academic situation.

Two factorial investigations into the relationship between motivational orientations and scholastic success (5, 9, 45) had likewise revealed characteristic differences in the role behavior of male and female freshmen. In the 1954–55 investigation, the life-style orientation factor was extracted for the female sample but failed to materialize for the male sample. Acceptance by the peer group was also found to be a more important correlate of scholastic success for the female freshmen. In the 1956–57 study, factor analysis yielded two unique factors for men and three unique factors for women in addition to the five factors common to both sexes. Measures of social adjustment, family adjustment, and social orientation defined the unique factors obtained for women. The unique factors extracted for men reflected hedonistic orientation and personal-family adjustment problems. The results for both factor analyses thus suggested that motivational orientations should be interpreted in keeping with the disparity of experiences and expectations acquired in male and female sex roles. Other researchers (118, 122, 127) had also confirmed the need for further examination and utilization of sex differences in the educative process. However, there was very little evidence in the literature to support the existence of positive action in this direction.

These research findings clearly suggested the need for systematic investigation of significant sex differences in motivational orientations toward scholastic success. Consequently, two studies were made of male and female responses to the 100 items comprising the revised SSHA (8, 47, 107). The 1956–57 and 1963–64 freshman classes at Southwest Texas State College provided the male and female research samples for these analyses. The same 1963–64 research samples were also utilized in making an analysis of male and female responses to the 125 statements comprising the EST.

In the initial investigation (8), the revised college-level SSHA was administered to all first-semester freshmen approximately six weeks after the fall semester began. Response distributions for each SSHA statement were tabulated separately for the 243 males and 286 females comprising the 1956–57 freshman class. The chi-square significance test was then employed to identify those items having significantly different response distributions for the male and female samples. The analysis of male and female responses to the 100 SSHA statements revealed 28, 14, 8, and 11 items, respectively, which were significant at the .001, .01, .02, and .05 levels of confidence. On 59 of the 61 significant items, women scored significantly better than men; on the remaining two items, male responses averaged significantly higher.

The self-reported academic attitudes of the female freshmen were thus found to be decisively more favorable toward, and accepting of, the academic environment and its demands than were those of the male freshmen. Two conclusions were drawn from the initial investigation into differences in male and female academic attitudes. First, the self-reported study habits and attitudes of first-semester college freshmen showed highly significant sex-related differences. Second, where significant sex-related differences were found, the female sample almost always averaged higher scores than did the male sample.

Although the initial investigation revealed significant sex-related response differences for 61 of the 100 SSHA items, no effort had been made to match or control the male and female research samples on such important variables as scholastic ability, living conditions, or high school background. The research findings could have been influenced significantly by such uncontrolled variables. Consequently, it was decided to replicate the study with proper controls before accepting the findings as a basis for action. The follow-up study (47, 107) also sought to identify significant sex-based differences in the study knowledge of first-semester freshmen and to compare these with identified differences in male and female academic attitudes.

The college-level SSHA and EST were administered to all entering freshmen at the beginning of the fall semester of the 1963–64 academic year. From the original population of 897 freshmen, 327 men were individually matched with 327 women so as to provide matching samples of male and female first-semester freshmen. The matching operation was designed to control such variables as age, measured scholastic ability, high school grade average, high school size, and current place of residence. The distribution of responses to all items on the 100-item SSHA and the 125-item EST were then tabulated separately for the male and female samples. Finally, the chi-square significance test was employed to identify those items having significantly different response distributions for males and females. Analysis of answers to the 100 SSHA statements identified 65 items having significant sex-based response differences; analysis of answers to the 125 EST questions revealed 26 items having significant response differences for male and female freshmen. Furthermore, female freshmen scored higher than male freshmen on all significant items for both instruments. The research results thus clearly demonstrated that male and female freshmen enrolled at Southwest Texas State College do tend to approach academic assignments differently, with female freshmen tending to have more positive academic attitudes and more effective study skills than do their male counterparts.

Table 10 presents the number and percent of items significant at the .001, .01, .02, and .05 levels of confidence for both the SSHA and the EST. Whereas 65 percent of the SSHA items showed significant sex-related response differences, only 21 percent of the EST questions did so. Inspection of Table 11 further suggests that the male freshmen do not use what they know about effective study methods as much as do the female freshmen. This fact becomes

TABLE 10
Comparison of SSHA and EST Questions Found to Have
Significant Sex-Related Response Differences
(N = 327 male-female pairs)

Significance Level	SSHA		EST	
	No. of Items	% of Items	No. of Items	% of Items
.05	7	7.0	6	4.8
.02	6	6.0	9	7.2
.01	20	20.0	9	7.2
.001	32	32.0	2	1.6
Total	65	65.0	26	20.8

TABLE 11
SSHA Items Having Sex-Related Response Differences
Significant beyond the <.001 Level of Confidence
(N=327 male-female pairs)

No.	Item	Scale*	X^2
73.	I complete my homework assignments on time.	DA	51.32
14.	I give special attention to neatness on themes, reports, and other work to be turned in.	WM	46.43
32.	Unless I really like a course, I believe in doing only enough to get a passing grade.	EA	45.01
10.	My teachers criticize my written reports as being hastily written or poorly organized.	WM	33.19
82.	I am careless of spelling and the mechanics of English composition when answering examination questions.	WM	33.19
5.	When I get behind in my schoolwork for some unavoidable reason, I make up my back assignments without prompting from the teacher.	DA	32.65
25.	I lay aside returned examinations, reports, and homework assignments, without bothering to correct errors noted by the instructor.	DA	30.34
85.	I study three or more hours per day outside of class.	DA	29.82
12.	Even though I don't like a subject, I still work hard to make a good grade.	EA	28.47
13.	Even though an assignment is dull and boring, I stick to it until it is completed.	DA	26.79
89.	I keep my assignments up to date by doing my work regularly from day to day.	DA	25.67
54.	When in doubt about the proper form for a written report I refer to an approved model to provide a guide to follow.	WM	25.05
81.	With me, studying is a hit-or-miss proposition depending on the mood I'm in.	DA	24.50
2.	In preparing reports, themes, term papers, etc., I make certain that I clearly understand what is wanted before I begin work.	WM	24.13
1.	When my assigned homework is extra long or unusually difficult, I either quit in disgust or study only the earlier parts of the lesson.	DA	23.91
52.	I feel that my grades are a fairly accurate reflection of my ability.	EA	22.83

* The SSHA provides four subscales as follows: DA=Delay Avoidance; WM =Work Methods; TA=Teacher Approval; and EA=Education Acceptance.

Table 11 (continued)

No.	Item	Scale*	X^2
90.	If time is available, I take a few minutes to check over my answers before turning in my examination paper.	WM	22.68
95.	I feel that students cannot be expected to like most teachers.	TA	21.32
78.	When preparing for an examination I arrange facts to be learned in some logical order—order of importance, order of presentation in class or textbook, order of time in history, etc.	WM	19.32
72.	I strive to develop a sincere interest in every course I take.	EA	17.92
24.	I feel that students are not given enough freedom in selecting their own topics for themes and reports.	EA	17.37
39.	I feel that teachers are overbearing and conceited in their relations with students.	TA	17.13
70.	I copy the diagrams, drawings, tables, and other illustrations that the instructor puts on the blackboard.	WM	16.90
55.	The illustrations, examples, and explanations given by my teachers are too dry and technical.	TA	16.76
94.	When tests are returned, I find that my grade has been lowered by careless mistakes.	WM	16.68
31.	When explaining a lesson or answering questions, my teachers use words that I do not understand.	TA	16.63
30.	I have trouble with the mechanics of English composition.	WM	16.50
100.	I believe that grades are based upon a student's ability to memorize facts rather than upon the ability to "think" things through.	EA	16.32
67.	I think that football coaches contribute more to school life than do the teachers.	TA	16.02
23.	I feel that teachers are too rigid and narrow-minded.	TA	15.89
19.	I think that teachers like to exercise their authority too much.	TA	14.05
36.	I feel confused and undecided as to what my educational and vocational goals should be.	EA	13.85

* The SSHA provides four subscales as follows: DA=Delay Avoidance; WM =Work Methods; TA=Teacher Approval; and EA=Education Acceptance.

readily apparent when attention is given to the significance levels. At the .001 level of confidence, there were twenty times as many significant items on the SSHA as on the EST. The number of significant items at the .01 level of confidence was three times as many for the SSHA as for the EST. The ratio of items significant at the .02 and .05 levels were about the same for the two instruments.

Table 11 lists, in rank order by obtained chi-squares, the thirty-two SSHA statements showing a sex-based response difference significant at or beyond the .001 level of confidence. Examination of these items suggests that the female freshmen were conscientious about completing academic assignments, whereas the male freshmen often exhibited a negative or indifferent attitude toward their study requirements. Female freshmen also seemed to realize the advantages of neatness, organization, and attention to details, while male freshmen tended toward carelessness, disorganization, and minimal effort in the completion of academic tasks. Furthermore, women reported a higher degree of acceptance of academic requirements and routines, whereas men more often reported restlessness, inability to concentrate, and a lack of motivation to work on academic assignments. While the men more often reported procrastination in completing academic assignments, the women more often reported a systematic punctuality in meeting academic requirements. Confusion or indecision about future vocational goals and criticism or rejection of current educational activities were more often reported by the male freshmen. The men were also more inclined to rationalize their shortcomings by placing the blame for their poor academic performance upon their teachers. In fact, the male freshmen tended to label their teachers as rigid, narrow-minded, overbearing, conceited, dry, boring, sarcastic, and unfair. Female freshmen tended to take the opposite viewpoint when evaluating their instructors.

The research findings from both studies confirmed that men and women enrolled as freshmen at Southwest Texas State College do exhibit significantly different beliefs, values, and expectations about academic activities. Furthermore, female freshmen were found to have more positive academic attitudes and to use more efficient study procedures than did their male counterparts. The identified differences in male and female academic attitudes suggest that the counseling process should take greater cognizance of the motivational orientations of the two sexes. It would further appear that specific counseling procedures may need to be developed for assisting freshman males to accept more realistic academic expectations and aspirations. From the comparison of male and female responses to the SSHA and the EST, it was evident that the differences in self-reported academic attitudes are more significant than are the differences in knowledge about how to study. The important finding is the significant differences in male and female motivation to develop and use effective study procedures.

It must be remembered, of course, that the analysis of sex differences in academic orientation was based entirely on freshmen enrolled at Southwest Texas State College. Caution must therefore be exercised in generalizing the findings to other groups of students on other types of campuses. Each institution has its own unique academic and social climate, and the environmental press of a particular campus will greatly influence the value orientations of its students. Still, the research findings do suggest three tentative conclusions that may be generalized with appropriate reservations. First, male and female freshmen typically report holding different academic values and displaying different academic behaviors. Second, the differences in their academic orientations may result in females' being better prepared than males for successfully meeting collegiate academic requirements. Third, differences in the academic orientations of male and female freshmen suggest differential needs in terms of counseling, especially about academic problems and difficulties.

RATIONALE FOR A MOTIVATIONAL ORIENTATION APPROACH

Perceptive college admissions officers, personnel workers, and faculty deans have long been concerned about the poor study habits and negative study attitudes exhibited by many entering freshmen.

Surveys (24) reveal that college deans and counselors estimate that 80 percent, or four out of five, beginning freshmen do not possess study skills adequate for handling college assignments, and that 90 percent, or nine out of ten, beginning freshmen blame their deficient study skills upon inadequate high school preparation.

Failure by high schools to provide effective study skills instruction has forced many colleges to introduce systematic instructional programs for correcting inefficient study behavior. These programs have concentrated on correcting deficient reading and writing skills, with some attention being given to note taking, time budgeting, library usage, and test taking skills. Little, if any, attention has been given to examining negative academic attitudes,

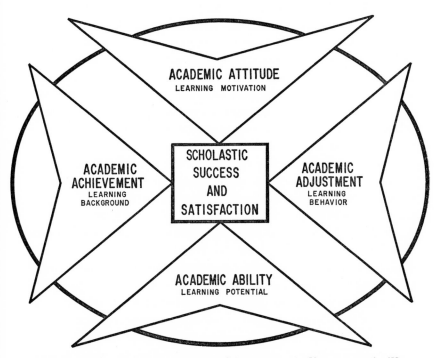

1. Factors Influencing Academic Achievement. A diagrammatic illustration of the four-factor approach to predicting scholastic success and satisfaction.

their underlying basis, and their probable influence upon scholastic success.

As reported earlier in this chapter, a series of coordinated investigations into the relationship between motivational orientations and scholastic success was conducted at various Texas colleges between 1952 and 1966. The cumulative findings from these studies indicate that at least four factors interact to influence initial success or failure in college. In addition to academic ability, three other factors—academic achievement, academic adjustment, and academic attitude—combine to determine whether or not academic performance will be high, average, or low. Figure 1 illustrates the interaction of these four factors in influencing scholastic success and satisfaction.

Academic ability, or learning potential, refers to the student's intellectual capacity for learning the materials presented in his courses. People differ greatly in their capability for learning. In fact, two individuals having identical total scores on an intelligence test will often show appreciable variance when they are compared on the various specific aptitudes being evaluated. It is obvious, of course, that a student will probably find greater success and satisfaction performing operations maximizing the use of his highest aptitudes and minimizing the use of his lowest aptitudes. Consequently, it is very important that the student know his potential strengths and weaknesses for academic learning and that he plan his educational program accordingly.

Academic achievement, or learning background, refers to the foundation of knowledge that the student has already acquired. While a poor foundation may be a consequence of disadvantaged opportunity or inadequate instruction, it is more likely to be due to insufficient study. For the beginning freshman, effective reading and writing skills are the two essential requirements for success in all college courses. Because reading and writing activities are so important, the student should make every effort to correct quickly any deficiencies in his reading speed and comprehension or in his writing mechanics and effectiveness.

Academic adjustment, or learning behavior, refers to the student's mastery of basic study skills and his efficiency in performing academic activities. Most beginning freshmen, for example, must adjust their learning behavior in order to cope with such collegiate procedures as formal lectures, programmed instruction, final examinations, and independent research. Study skills that were good enough for high school work are seldom adequate for college assignments. The changing scene in college teaching and learning places ever greater emphasis on independent study. Thus, efficiency in doing academic assignments will largely depend upon the student's use of effective techniques for organizing and accomplishing his study activities.

Academic attitude, or motivation to learn, refers to the student's feelings and expectations about college and to his acceptance of and desire for academic learning. A student's scholastic performance is, of course, influenced by the variety of positive and negative social presses stemming from his interaction with family members, same-sex peers, opposite-sex peers, and others. Such social input affects level of scholastic success through its impact upon the student's academic attitudes. Educational values can be positive or negative and educational objectives can be long term or short range. If the student's learning motivation is indifferent or if his academic goals are undecided, these weaknesses can prove to be his undoing when the "going gets rough" and the assignments pile up. Knowing what one wants from college and why he wants it is the key to having a good academic attitude, and such insight is influenced significantly by the level of family and peer-group acceptance and support being experienced by the student.

The interactions of at least four factors thus combine to determine whether a student's scholastic success and satisfaction will be high, average, or low. A student can still act effectively to ensure his scholastic survival even though he finds himself deficient in one, two, or even all four factors. Two procedures are available for the student to employ—compensation for deficiencies and correction of deficiencies. If a student finds that his academic ability is below average for learning the materials being presented in one of his courses, the only practical solution is to compensate for his lack of ability by putting extra time and effort into his studying so that he can compete more effectively. On the other hand, a student's difficulty may stem from deficient reading, writing, or study skills. Here, his solution should be to undertake a systematic program designed to correct the deficiency as quickly as possible. Deficient learning skills can usually be corrected, provided the student is willing to do the extra work and exercise the self-discipline required to overcome the deficiency.

The student's academic attitude is the key to whether or not he will put forth the necessary effort to achieve the needed compensation and correction. The student with negative academic attitudes will likely procrastinate, criticize, and rationalize while his assignments pile up until they overwhelm him. Whether a student performs above, at, or below his measured scholastic potential is primarily the result of his motivation to learn. Consequently, it is essential that counseling on academic difficulties, either present or potential, take into account the counselee's academic attitudes and the learning motivation behind them.

Research findings have repeatedly demonstrated the importance of learning motivation as a determinant of scholastic success. Such instruments as the SSHA and the EST will efficiently and effectively identify a student's negative academic attitudes and deficient study skills. Then problem, then, is how best to utilize the information provided by such instruments in an organized guidance program designed to identify, examine, and correct motivational orientations productive of poor academic attainment. An old and often repeated maxim is that "motivation can be caught, but cannot be taught." Another is that "motivation comes from within, not from without." If there is real truth underlying these sayings, then a realistic, practical, and effective program of academic adjustment guidance for beginning college freshmen could be built around the use of carefully selected, trained, and supervised student counselors. After all, a major problem in counseling is the establishment and continuance of effective communication and, as was pointed out in Chapter 1, the advice given by student counselors possesses greater credibility because they speak the same language and share the same problems as their counselees. Thus the "big brother" or "big sister" approach should help the beginning freshman to "catch" a more positive learning motivation because the counseling is coming from within—from within his peer group, that is!

3. A Model Program of
Student-to-Student Counseling

The freshman counseling program that evolved at Southwest Texas State College goes considerably beyond using student counselors to assist in freshman orientation activities. In fact, the systematic utilization of carefully selected, trained, and supervised student counselors is the heart of the college's counseling effort for beginning freshmen. Developed to take maximum advantage of the potentialities inherent in the student-counseling-student relationship, the freshman counseling program employs peer-group discussion procedures to communicate academic survival information, to transmit standardized test results, to analyze potential problem areas, and to plan appropriate preventive action.

Types of Student Counselors

Two types of student counselors are used in the program—student residence hall counselors and student academic counselors. The college environment is, at best, confusing and, at worst, overwhelming to most newly arrived freshmen. There are new regulations to learn, new procedures to master, new values to accept, new people to meet—in short, a whole new way of life to adjust to. In many cases, home and family have been left behind, along with the sense of security that familiarity gives. Surrounded by the unfamiliar, the freshman needs a helping hand to restore his self-confidence and smooth out his personal-social adjustment. At Southwest Texas State College, student residence hall counselors provide the needed "first-echelon" assistance in adjusting to the college community. These student counselors reside in the freshman residence halls, work directly under the residence hall director, receive no payment for their services, and are trained to provide limited counseling on personal-social concerns. The work performed by the student residence hall counselors is about the same as that of their counterparts on other college campuses.

Soon after classes begin, the freshman finds that college instructional procedures and work requirements are considerably different from what he experienced in high school. In contrast to high school, lectures are used extensively, lengthy reading assignments are routine, independent study is emphasized, examinations are infrequent and comprehensive, and grading standards are more rigid. The freshman also finds that time budgeting is solely his responsibility—nobody reminds him to prepare assignments or to study for examinations. Student academic counselors provide the needed assistance in adjusting to new teaching methods and expanded study requirements. These student counselors are employed by the Testing and Counseling Center, are supervised by the director of counseling, are paid at an hourly rate for their counseling services, and receive forty clock hours of systematic counseling training.

OVERVIEW OF PROGRAM COMPONENTS AND OBJECTIVES

The freshman counseling program consists of an organized series of interrelated counseling activities, each with its own objectives and procedures. The counseling activity sequence provided for beginning freshmen is outlined in Table 12. The personal-social orientation is provided by student residence hall counselors for all

TABLE 12

Activity Sequence for Organized Freshman Counseling Program

Environment Orientation Activities

General Purpose: To facilitate individual orientation to the college community

A. Personal-Social Orientation by Student Residence Hall Counselors
   1. Survey common personal-social adjustment problems faced by freshmen
   2. Explain regulations and procedures related to college residence hall living
   3. Discuss behavioral variables influencing peer-group acceptance
   4. Explain activities scheduled during freshman orientation period

Specific Objective: To help each resident freshman adjust to the college environment

B. Curriculum Orientation by Faculty Advisors
   1. Explain regulations and procedures related to college academic life
   2. Explain graduation requirements and the college curricula
   3. Review registration problems and procedures

Specific Objective: To help each freshman understand the college's academic program

---

Academic Adjustment Activities

General Purpose: To facilitate individual adjustment to scholastic requirements and procedures

A. Survival Orientation by Student Academic Counselors
   1. Survey common academic adjustment problems faced by freshmen
   2. Advise on efficient time management procedures
   3. Advise on efficient note taking procedures
   4. Examine rewards and frustrations of college attendance
   5. Report student assistance resources available to freshmen

Specific Objective: To provide each freshman with academic survival information

B. Test Interpretation by Student Academic Counselors
   1. Explain factors influencing scholastic success or failure
   2. Interpret results of standardized ability and achievement tests
   3. Survey current study behavior and scholastic motivation
   4. Survey proven procedures for effective college-level studying
   5. Discuss appropriate corrective measures for identified academic weaknesses

Specific Objective: To help each freshman understand his potential academic problems

C. Study Habits Evaluation by Student Academic Counselors
   1. Discuss causes and cures for residual study problems
   2. Report unsatisfactory mid-semester grades received

3. Analyze probable causes of scholastic difficulties

Specific Objective: To help each failing freshman identify and correct his remaining study deficiencies

---

Academic Improvement Activities

General Purpose: To facilitate individual correction of deficient study skills

A. Study Skills Counseling by Student Academic Counselors
   1. Advise on effective methods for organizing time
   2. Advise on effective methods for reading textbooks
   3. Advise on effective methods for taking lecture notes
   4. Advise on effective methods for writing themes and reports
   5. Advise on effective methods for improving memory
   6. Advise on effective methods for passing examinations

Specific Objective: To help each freshman develop an efficient study program

B. Reading Improvement Instruction by Student Academic Counselors
   1. Assess current reading speed and reading comprehension levels
   2. Guide systematic activities for improvement of reading comprehension
   3. Guide systematic activities for improvement of reading speed
   4. Advise on progress of reading improvement efforts

Specific Objective: To help each freshman improve his competency for reading college-level material

C. Subject Matter Tutoring by Student Tutor-Counselors
   1. Explain unclear materials presented in lectures and reading assignments
   2. Advise on preparation of outside written assignments
   3. Demonstrate use of efficient methods for studying subject matter
   4. Guide studying activities for expected examinations

Specific Objective: To help each freshman cope with the specific subject matter content of his difficult courses

---

Educational Planning Activities

General Purpose: To facilitate individual determination of educational and vocational reality

A. Vocational Counseling by Student and Professional Vocational Counselors
   1. Assess occupational aptitudes and interests
   2. Survey characteristics of the world of work
   3. Relate occupational potential to the world of work
   4. Relate aptitudes and interests to college curricula

Specific Objective: To help each undecided freshman make the wisest possible educational and vocational choices

B. Educational Advising by Faculty Advisors
   1. Provide information about degree plans and course requirements

Table 12 (continued)

---

2. Discuss occupational opportunities for departmental majors
3. Assist with preparation of appropriate educational program

Specific Objective: To provide each freshman with departmental information and assistance

---

NOTE: Student Residence Hall Counselors, Student Academic Counselors, Student Tutor-Counselors, and Student Vocational Counselors utilized the student-counseling-student approach to provide different services for freshmen. Although many student counselors served in more than one capacity, the training received and the duties performed by the four types of student counselors differed according to the services to be provided within their respective roles.

freshmen residing in college-owned dormitories. Curriculum orientation and educational guidance are provided by thirty-two faculty advisors assigned to work with the Testing and Counseling Center. Vocational counseling is provided by two professional counselors, with uncomplicated cases being routinely assigned to specially trained student academic counselors. The other six organized counseling activities are provided by a team of twenty-four part-time student academic counselors.

The student academic counselors thus provide the academic adjustment and academic improvement counseling, which is the original aspect of the freshman counseling program. The overall goal for this student-to-student counseling effort is to increase the probability of scholastic survival by beginning freshmen. In a very real sense, the concepts and materials developed for these counseling activities have evolved through necessity. A freshman attrition rate of nearly 35 percent had focused attention on the need for improving the college's academic counseling effort. Concern had also been voiced about the indifferent study behavior of many incoming freshmen. The recognized desirability of expanding counseling facilities and activities was, however, attenuated by financial restrictions and personnel shortages. Meanwhile, freshmen were routinely turning to upperclassmen to obtain information and advice that was not readily available elsewhere on campus.

To meet this problem, a program was developed that used student-counseling-student procedures to provide systematic academic counseling for beginning freshmen. Expanded and improved over a five-year period, the final program incorporated the following characteristics: (*a*) utilization of the *peer approach*, in that academic adjustment counseling is accomplished by carefully selected, trained, and supervised upperclassmen; (*b*) utilization of the *group approach*, in that most of the counseling by student counselors is accomplished with groups of three to five or twenty-five to thirty counselees; (*c*) utilization of the *motivation approach*, in that each freshman's study behavior and academic values are systematically examined; and (*d*) utilization of the *prevention approach*, in that emphasis is given to identifying potential academic problems and planning appropriate corrective measures.

A variety of published materials are routinely used by the student academic counselors in the performance of their counseling duties. Table 13 lists the materials that are regularly used in each

TABLE 13
Published Materials Routinely Used
in Organized Counseling Activities

Personal-Social Orientation by Student Residence Hall Counselors:
  Freshman handbook
Curriculum Orientation by Faculty Advisors:
  College catalog
Survival Orientation by Student Academic Counselors:
  Effective Study Guide: College Edition[a]
  Effective Study Test: College Level[a]
  Daily Activity Schedule[a]
  Student-to-Student Tips[a]
  Sample Lecture Notes[a]
Test Interpretation by Student Academic Counselors:
  Survey of Study Habits and Attitudes: College Form[b]
  American College Test[c]
  Davis Reading Test: Form 1A[b]
  Daily Activity Schedule[a]
  Student-to-Student Tips[a]

[a] Published by Effective Study Materials, San Marcos, Texas.
[b] Published by The Psychological Corporation, New York, New York.
[c] Published by American College Testing Program, Iowa City, Iowa.

Table 13 (continued)

Reading and Remembering Guide[a]

Study Habits Evaluation by Student Academic Counselors:
Study Skills Surveys[a]

Study Skills Counseling by Student Academic Counselors:
Student's Guides to Effective Study[a]
  1. *Guide to Managing Time*
  2. *Guide to Reading Textbooks*
  3. *Guide to Taking Lecture Notes*
  4. *Guide to Writing Themes and Reports*
  5. *Guide to Improving Memory*
  6. *Guide to Passing Examinations*
Guide to Writing Research Papers[a]

Reading Improvement Instruction by Student Academic Counselors:
Davis Reading Test: Forms 1B, 1C, and 1D[b]
SRA Reading Laboratory IVa[e]
Student Record Book: SRA Reading Laboratory IVa[e]

Subject Matter Tutoring by Student Tutor-Counselors:
Effective Study Guide: College Edition[a]
Scriptographic Booklets[d]
  1. *About Words*
  2. *About Punctuation*
  3. *About Grammar*
  4. *About Writing*
Guide to Writing Research Papers[a]

Vocational Counseling by Student and Professional Vocational Counselors:
Differential Aptitude Tests[b]
Educational Interest Inventory[f]
Kuder Preference Record: Vocational[e]
California Short-Form Test of Mental Maturity: Secondary[g]
American College Test[c]
Handbook of Job Facts[e]
SRA Occupational Briefs[e]

Educational Advising by Faculty Advisor:
College catalog
SRA Occupational Briefs[e]

---

[a] Published by Effective Study Materials, San Marcos, Texas.
[b] Published by The Psychological Corporation, New York, New York.
[c] Published by American College Testing Program, Iowa City, Iowa.
[d] Published by Channing L. Bete Co., Inc., Greenfield, Massachusetts.
[e] Published by Science Research Associates, Inc., Chicago, Illinois.
[f] Published by Educational Guidance, Inc., Dearborn, Michigan.
[g] Published by California Test Bureau, Monterey, California.

TABLE 14
Level of Freshman Participation in Organized Counseling Activities
Provided by Testing and Counseling Center in Fall, 1964

| Counseling Activity | Type Counselor | When Offered | % Participation[a] | | Counselor-Counselee Ratio[b] |
			Commuter Students	Resident Students	
Personal-social orientation	Student residence hall counselor	Orientation week	0.0	100.0	2:12–20
Curriculum orientation[c]	Faculty advisor	Orientation week	70.0	95.0	1:25–30
Survival orientation[c]	Student academic counselor	Orientation week	86.4	98.6	2:25–35
Test interpretation	Student academic counselor	1–6 weeks	41.7	84.3	1:3–5
Study habits evaluation[d]	Student academic counselor	10 weeks	8.2	8.7	1:1
Study skills counseling	Student academic counselor	3–12 weeks	24.3	57.3	1:1
Reading improvement instruction	Student academic counselor	3–15 weeks	3.4	12.9	1:8–12
Subject matter tutoring	Student tutor-counselor	4–18 weeks	1.6	7.9	1:1–5
Vocational counseling	Student or professional vocational counselor	3–15 weeks	13.1	32.6	1:1
Educational advising	Faculty advisor	3–15 weeks	34.1	68.7	1:1

[a] Computation of percent participation is based upon an enrollment of 1,187 first-semester freshmen as of the twelfth class day of the 1964 fall semester.

[b] Counselor-counselee ratio refers to the usual number of counselors and counselees participating in a single counseling session.

[c] Participation in counseling activity was scheduled for all beginning freshmen but attendance was not absolutely mandatory.

[d] Participation in counseling activity was required of all freshmen accepting test interpretation and receiving two or more mid-semester unsatisfactory reports.

of the ten organized counseling activities outlined in Table 12. Each student academic counselor is carefully trained in the proper use of all materials that he will employ in any counseling activity to which he is assigned. The special materials employed to provide vocational counseling and reading instruction are restricted to experienced student academic counselors receiving appropriate additional training.

Freshman participation in the various organized counseling activities is reported in Table 14. The data presented are for the fall semester of 1964, the first year when all ten elements were in routine operation. At that time, approximately 72 percent of the freshman class resided in college-owned housing, with the remaining 28 percent commuting to college from their homes. Inspection of this table indicates that the participation of resident students was much higher than that for commuter students and that the participation rate for resident students was at a consistently high level for all components of the freshman counseling program. The differences in the participation rates for resident and commuter freshmen is, of course, consistent with the low level of commuter involvement in noncurricular activities found on almost all campuses.

SELECTION AND TRAINING OF PEER COUNSELORS

The selection, training, and supervision of those students given counseling responsibilities are important factors in the success or failure of student-to-student counseling. The selection standards, training programs, and supervision requirements for student residence hall counselors and student academic counselors are largely determined by the different duties performed by each type of student counselor. Student residence hall counselors serve as "big brothers" or "big sisters" in helping beginning freshmen adjust to living in a college residence hall; student academic counselors help incoming freshmen adjust to new instructional procedures and expanded study requirements by providing appropriate academic adjustment counseling. The selection, training, and supervision of these two types of student counselors reflect the differences in their counseling responsibilities.

Selection and Training of Student Residence Hall Counselors

Student residence hall counselors reside in the freshman residence halls, work directly under the residence hall director, and provide "first-echelon" counseling on personal-social concerns. Although they receive no pay or allowances for their work, the job is much sought after because it carries considerable peer prestige and provides a satisfying outlet for service motives. In addition to meeting exacting personal and academic standards, students selected for this job must complete satisfactorily a special eight-hour training program. The selection and training of student residence hall counselors is accomplished during the spring.

In March, residence hall directors invite qualified upperclassmen to apply for training. The list of volunteers is then forwarded to the Division of Student Personnel Services for screening by a selection committee consisting of the dean of students, director of men's housing, director of women's housing, director of student life, and director of counseling. Selection of potential residence hall counselors is based upon the following variables: (*a*) academic history, (*b*) peer acceptance, (*c*) leadership experience, and (*d*) personality characteristics. Specifically, each student must meet the following criteria to be eligible for counseling assignment. First, the student's grade average must be "C" or above, with no failing grades. Second, the student must be rated average or above on each of seven variables by his residence hall director and by a faculty member of his choice. The seven variables on which ratings are made are as follows: (*a*) judgment and common sense, (*b*) personal morals and behavior, (*c*) emotional stability, (*d*) friendliness and tactfulness, (*e*) sense of responsibility, (*f*) peer acceptance, and (*g*) study habits and attitudes. Finally, the student must have demonstrated effective leadership experience as revealed by the Personal Data Form completed by each applicant.

Training of potential residence hall counselors is accomplished through a program of four weekly, two-hour meetings sponsored by the Division of Student Personnel Services. Lectures, demonstrations, and group discussions are employed to provide instruction in the following five areas: (*a*) philosophy and operation of the student personnel program; (*b*) counseling goals, responsibilities, and limitations of student residence hall counselors; (*c*) effective interview procedures and group discussion techniques; (*d*) academic and social policies, regulations, and procedures; and (*e*) student assistance facilities and appropriate referral procedures. Trainees are rated on their attendance at and participation in the four training sessions. Shortly after training is completed, the final selection of student residence hall counselors for the following year is made by the selection committee and announced by the dean of students. The number of student residence hall counselors selected is sufficient to provide a counselor-counselee ratio of one to eight. These student counselors are under the jurisdiction of the dean of men or dean of women and are directly responsible to the director of the residence hall in which they reside.

Selection and Training of Student Academic Counselors

Experience has established that one student academic counselor will be needed for every sixty freshmen to be counseled. Thus a college having an anticipated fall enrollment of twelve hundred entering freshmen would require twenty such student counselors. Since approximately one-half of these student counselors will be lost each year through graduation, the selection and training of replacements is an annual affair.

At Southwest Texas State College, twelve to sixteen counselor trainees are selected from the freshman class during February and complete thirty clock hours of intensive training during March and April. Another ten hours of review are provided in September for those trainees chosen to fill existing vacancies. Needless to say, the selection and training process must be given careful attention, for the success or failure of the entire program rests primarily upon the student academic counselors themselves.

Because of the demanding nature of the job, students selected for training as student academic counselors are required to meet high standards. Scholastic ability, study orientation, academic history, leadership experience, peer acceptance, and conversational effectiveness are variables that are systematically evaluated during the selection process. The first three attributes may be measured objectively; the other three can only be assessed subjectively.

Scholastic ability is determined from scores on the American College Test, which had been administered previously to all entering freshmen. Study orientation is assessed with the Brown-Holtzman *Survey of Study Habits and Attitudes*. The high school transcript and the college permanent record card provide objective data for evaluating the student's academic history. Each counselor trainee is expected to be in the upper third of his class on each of these criteria of scholastic success.

Leadership experience is evaluated by having applicants complete a Personal Data Form or write an autobiographical sketch. Peer acceptance is determined from ratings prepared by the applicant's residence hall director and house council, supplemented by information obtained from the Division of Student Personnel Services. Conversational effectiveness is judged through personal interview. In assessing leadership experience and peer acceptance, it is essential that these variables be examined from two viewpoints. First, the student should have demonstrated his or her capacity to provide leadership within the peer group. Second, the student must not be so involved with social and extracurricular activities as to restrict unduly his or her participation in the counseling program.

Counselor trainees are systematically recruited through an eight-step screening process. The names of likely freshmen are routinely obtained from four major sources: (*a*) the dean of students and his professional staff, (*b*) faculty advisors working with beginning freshmen, (*c*) directors of freshman residence halls, and (*d*) experienced student academic counselors. Additional names may be suggested by other faculty members or by part-time clerical workers employed by the Testing and Counseling Center. Recommended students are listed alphabetically and all receive equal consideration during the selection procedure summarized in Table 15. A copy of the Student Counselor Evaluation Form completed by appropriate faculty members and residence hall directors is included as Appendix D.

If the selection procedure appears thorough or the selection criteria seem severe, it must be remembered that the duties to be performed are equally demanding. The student academic counselors

TABLE 15

Selection Procedure for Student Academic Counselor Trainees

Step	Activity	Action*
1.	Check scholastic ability as measured by the American College Test	Separate if composite score is below sixty-sixth centile on local norms
2.	Check study orientation as measured by the Survey of Study Habits and Attitudes	Separate if total score is below sixty-sixth centile on local norms
3.	Check academic history as reported on high school transcript and college permanent record card	Separate if college grade average is below "B" or high school quarter rank is below top quarter
4.	Request peer acceptance evaluation from residence hall director and house council	Eliminate if negative or doubtful rating is given
5.	Request personal behavior evaluation from appropriate dean	Eliminate if negative or doubtful rating is given
6.	Evaluate conversational effectiveness through interviews with selected student academic counselors and the director of counseling	Eliminate if oral communication skills are judged inadequate for performance of job duties
7.	Evaluate leadership experience through Personal Data Form completed by applicant	Separate if leadership activities appear to be either too limited or too involved for effective performance of job duties
8.	Request scholastic and social achievement evaluation from faculty member named by applicant	Separate if negative or doubtful evaluation is received

*Elimination terminates further consideration of applicant; separation permits further consideration provided evaluation on other variables merits same. Separation on two or more variables is tantamount to elimination.

operate in a working environment that demands social skill, assumes mature responsibility, forbids careless performance, and requires subtle perseverance. Obviously, the selection procedure must assure that only capable students are selected.

Each student academic counselor must be trained to handle his duties in a competent, confident, and effective manner. The training program requires appropriate instructional materials and effective teaching procedures. A systematic training schedule must be set up and followed, with all instruction being given by competent personnel.

A 102-page *Student Counselor's Handbook* (21) and a sound filmstrip, *Student-to-Student Counseling to Aid Academic Adjustment* (34), have been developed to facilitate the training of student academic counselors. Specimen sets of the Survey of Study Habits and Attitudes: Form C (43), Effective Study Test: College Level (13), and Study Skills Surveys (16) are also utilized during counselor training. In addition to their *Student Counselor's Handbook*, the trainees are also issued the following materials: *Effective Study Guide: College Edition* (42), *Student-to-Student Tips* (29), and *Student's Guides to Effective Study* (19). These materials are issued at the appropriate time and remain in the student's possession until his employment is terminated. Throughout the training period, counselor trainees are encouraged to underline or write on all materials issued to them.

Tape recordings and live demonstrations of counseling sessions are also utilized to facilitate the instructional process. Tape recorders permit the trainees to examine critically both counselor and counselee behavior during the counseling period. Furthermore, they can listen to their own counseling sessions and obtain the reactions of more experienced student academic counselors to specific counseling problems and procedures. The use of a tape recorder for self-evaluation of counseling skills and the use of an observation-demonstration facility for demonstrating the counseling process are illustrated in the picture section following page 114. A one-way vision screen and public address system permit those in the observation room to see and hear everything occurring in the demonstration room, without themselves being seen or heard by those being observed. Both observation of the experienced and evaluation of the inexperienced are permitted by such an arrangement.

The interchange of ideas and the opportunity for evaluation afforded by these mechanical aids are of proven value in the training of counselors. The acquisition of requisite knowledges and skills is greatly facilitated through their use. Of course, these training aids should be employed to assist instructional personnel, not to replace them or to make up for their inadequacies.

Training the initial group of student academic counselors requires the active participation of a competent professional person throughout the training program's duration. Subsequently, experienced student academic counselors can provide effective assistance in training replacements through use of the "buddy system." As the term suggests, the buddy system is a training method wherein an experienced student counselor explains and demonstrates requisite materials and procedures to an inexperienced student counselor. Thus each student counselor trainee is assigned an experienced "buddy" who shows him what to do and how to do it.

In addition to appropriate training and experience, all persons giving instruction to student academic counselors should possess comprehensive knowledge in the following areas:

1. Understanding of group counseling processes and related leadership dynamics

2. Understanding of the interaction of factors influencing scholastic success and satisfaction

3. Understanding of the academic, social, and personal adjustment problems faced by male and female college freshmen

4. Understanding of the nature and nurture of effective study skills and positive academic attitudes and their influence upon scholastic success

5. Understanding of psychometric procedures, with special reference to questionnaires and their effective use in counseling

The training program utilizes lectures, demonstrations, discussion periods, and role-playing activities, as appropriate, to assure the acquisition of requisite knowledges and skills. Training is continued until each counselor trainee has developed the following proficiencies:

1. Ability to promote and lead group discussion of assigned topics through sagacious employment of counseling materials and techniques

2. Ability to achieve understanding of past scholastic performance through analysis and synthesis of available ability, achievement, adjustment, and attitude data

3. Ability to utilize test and questionnaire data in identifying potential academic problems and planning appropriate corrective actions for same

4. Ability to interpret test and questionnaire results objectively and realistically to counselees having low, average, or high scores

5. Ability to discuss, without criticism or emotionality, negative study attitudes, their underlying basis, and their probable influence upon scholastic success

6. Ability to explain and illustrate, quickly and accurately, all study tools and techniques described in the materials distributed to counselees

7. Ability to recognize adjustmental problems requiring professional attention and to make competent referral of same to the program director

The training of student academic counselors is accomplished through a forty-hour instructional program provided by the Testing and Counseling Center. Trainees receive no pay for participating in this training activity. Discussion guides, activity sequence check lists, and overhead transparencies have been developed to facilitate instruction. Whenever possible, the buddy system is employed to permit experienced student counselors to assist in the training of selectees. A conference room, a demonstration-observation facility, and several counseling offices are utilized during the training process. Figure 2 shows the location of these facilities and the equipment provided in each.

Table 16 outlines the activity sequence that is usually followed for training new student academic counselors. During the spring, thirty clock hours of training are provided through fifteen two-

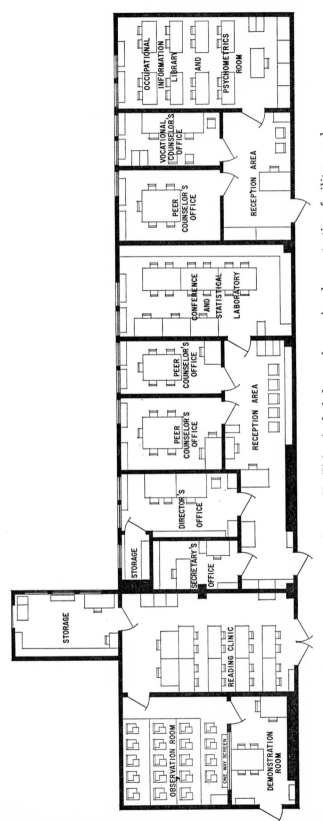

2. Testing and Counseling Center. Facilities included an observation-demonstration facility, reading clinic, two storerooms, six private offices, conference room, statistics laboratory, psychometrics room, and occupational information library.

TABLE 16
Student Academic Counselor Training Sequence

Spring Session	*Activity*

1. Orientation Briefing: Overview of guidance objectives, procedures, and results[a]
2. Lecture #1: Counseling materials familiarization and counseling dynamics analysis[a]
3. Lecture #2: Scholastic success factors and scholastic motivation analysis[a]
4. Lecture #3: Effective Study Test and Survey of Study Habits and Attitudes familiarization[a]
5. Discussion #1: Survival Orientation demonstration and analysis[b]
6. Simulation #1: Survival Orientation role playing and critique[b]
7. Discussion #2: Test Interpretation demonstration and analysis[b]
8. Simulation #2: Test Interpretation role playing and critique[b]
9. Discussion #3: Study Skills Counseling demonstration and analysis[b]
10. Simulation #3: Study Skills Counseling role playing and critique[b]
11. Discussion #4: Study Habits Evaluation demonstration and analysis[b]
12. Simulation #4: Study Habits Evaluation role playing and critique[b]
13. Lecture #4: Report on materials and procedures used for reading improvement instruction and subject matter tutoring[b]
14. Lecture #5: Report on materials and procedures used in vocational counseling and educational advising[a]
15. Question and Answer Period: Student counselor's duties, responsibilities, and limitations[a]

Fall Session
16. Lecture #6: Review of program objectives, procedures, and materials[a]
17. Discussion #6: Review of Survival Orientation activities and materials[b]
18. Discussion #7: Review of Test Interpretation activities and materials[b]
19. Discussion #8: Review of Study Skills Counseling activities and materials[b]
20. Discussion #9: Review of Study Habits Evaluation activities and materials[b]

NOTE: Total training time=40 hours (30 hours in the spring and 10 hours in the fall).

[a] Provided by professional staff of the Testing and Counseling Center.

[b] Provided by experienced student academic counselors.

hour training periods scheduled between 7 P.M. and 9 P.M. each Monday, Wednesday, and Friday for one month. In September, five two-hour review sessions are provided prior to the beginning of active counseling.

DESCRIPTION OF ORGANIZED COUNSELING ACTIVITIES

The organized counseling program for entering freshmen is divided into four major components—environment orientation, academic adjustment, academic improvement, and educational planning. As indicated in Tables 12, 13, and 14, each of these four major components is further subdivided, with each subdivision having its own counseling objectives, materials, and procedures. Freshmen are required to attend the organized testing and counseling activities scheduled during orientation week. However, this required participation is not backed up by any type of enforcement procedure other than special make-up periods scheduled for absentees. Freshman participation is completely voluntary for all organized counseling activities offered after the orientation-week period.

Environment Orientation Counseling

To facilitate their orientation to the college community, freshmen are scheduled to arrive on campus five days prior to the reporting date for other students. A variety of activities are planned during this period, all designed to provide assistance in adjusting to college life. Scheduled activities include orientation assemblies, testing periods, group meetings, registration, and the president's reception. Unscheduled activities include informal discussion sessions, social visitations, and campus tours. The objectives of these various activities are to initiate the freshman's adjustment to the personal-social-academic demands of college life.

During the five-day orientation period, freshmen are systematically greeted, lectured, tested, and registered, in addition to receiving informal counseling on personal, social, and academic adjustment problems. Freshmen are welcomed by the college administration at an "introductory assembly" and greeted by the student body leadership at a "student life assembly." At still another assembly, a visiting dignitary lectures the new students on their academic responsibilities to the nation, to their parents, and to themselves. Special testing periods are scheduled for the measurement of academic ability, reading performance, speech performance, and study behavior. Registration of freshmen is accomplished on the fifth day, followed that evening by the president's reception honoring all new students.

All these activities are both desirable and necessary, but they are not the focus of this report. Responsibility for smoothing initial personal-social orientation is assigned to the student residence hall counselors; responsibility for assuring initial curriculum orientation is delegated to the faculty advisors. Small group meetings and informal discussion sessions are the media utilized to achieve these counseling objectives.

PERSONAL-SOCIAL ORIENTATION

Two student residence hall counselors are normally assigned to provide "first-echelon" counseling for the twelve to eighteen freshmen housed in each wing of a freshman residence hall. These counselors arrive on campus two days before the freshmen are scheduled to report. The two days are spent in study and planning for their orientation duties. General counseling responsibilities are spelled out in an initial meeting with the residence hall director; specific orientation duties are determined in a series of planning sessions directed by the house council president.

After their general and specific duties have been explained, the counselors assemble necessary materials, review pertinent publications, and otherwise prepare to meet the freshmen assigned to their wing. For each assigned freshman, the counselors are provided with a Personal Data Sheet containing the student's picture, home address, and information about high school experiences and personal preferences. The counselors carefully study the personal data on each freshman and utilize this information in filling out required admittance forms prior to the student's arrival. The counselors also review and discuss pertinent information contained in the various student handbooks to be distributed soon after the freshmen arrive.

The orientation duties performed by the student residence hall counselor are best described in this excerpt from a report prepared by the director of a freshman residence hall.

On the day the freshmen arrive, the counselors are waiting in the living room, and someone greets each freshman as she enters. Many times the counselors recognize their counselees on sight. Finding that someone expects and already knows something about them definitely helps the freshmen to feel welcome and accepted. Each freshman is then introduced to other counselors seated in the living room, to the head resident if she is present at the time, and to the secretaries who check her in officially. The checking-in routine begins with the fresh-man presenting her admittance card, filled out earlier by her coun-selor. The secretary then tells the freshman her room number, room-mate's name, and mail box number, and gives her a temporary meal ticket and her room key. The freshman is then escorted to her room by one of her wing counselors. As a matter of course, numerous introduc-tions are made in the process.

For the first meal the counselors usually take the freshmen in their wing to the cafeteria as a group. On this occasion, the counselors usu-ally conduct the freshmen on a tour of the campus, pointing out the various classroom buildings and the other dormitories. Needless to say, they are usually kept busy introducing the freshmen to friends encoun-tered in route.

After all freshmen have arrived, the counselors conduct an informal orientation tour of the residence hall. Operation of the intercom sys-tem and telephones receives particular attention, since these are the first and most frequently used items. The location of laundry rooms, and the use of the washing and drying machines installed therein, are likewise demonstrated.

A house meeting is usually held the first evening the freshmen are in the residence hall. The house council president welcomes the new students, introduces the counselors and head resident, and reviews the orientation procedures for the next day. Two booklets, the *Association of Women Students' Handbook* and *Getting Acquainted with Your Dorm*, are distributed and discussed during this meeting.

Prior to registration, the counselors help the freshmen in arranging schedules and explain the general registration procedure. The counselors also make certain that the freshmen attend the assemblies, testing periods, and other required meetings listed in the *Orientation Program for New Students*. During this first week, the counselors also spend quite a bit of time interpreting residence hall regulations and procedures, such as quiet hours, signing out and in, closing hours, housekeeping, roomcheck at night, and dress for various occasions. *Hill Hints*, a handbook of college regulations and activities distributed at the introductory assembly, is likewise discussed and interpreted during the informal wing meetings held by the student residence hall counselors.

After orientation week and registration, the counselors' duties become less strenuous. In addition to working with the house council to maintain acceptable standards of order and cleanliness on their wing, the counselors occasionally discuss personal or social problems with the freshmen. Homesickness, friction with roommate, problems with boy friends, friction with family, and difficulty with studies are the problems most often discussed. If the problem seems to be acute, or in cases of illness, the counselors notify the head resident so that proper referral may be made.[1]

Although the above description reports the ongoing counseling activities in a women's residence hall, the procedures followed in a men's residence hall are very similar. The student residence hall counselors' responsibilities continue beyond the orientation period, of course, although the pace of their activities is usually more relaxed than during the freshman's initial week on campus. These ongoing counseling duties may be organized under ten problem areas as follows: extracurricular, social, academic, health, financial, vocational, housing, home, emotional, and religious. Observable problem symptoms, recommended counselor actions, and appropriate referral agencies for each problem area are summarized in Table 17. As may be seen from this summary of counseling activities, the role of the student residence hall counselor is to provide limited counseling on minor personal and social concerns and to

[1] From a report, "The Dormitory Counselor's Duties," prepared by Miss Jewell Posey, Head Resident, Retama Hall, Southwest Texas State College, July, 1962.

TABLE 17
Summary of Student Residence Hall Counselor's Ongoing Duties and Activities

Area	Things to Look for	Things to Do	Places to Refer t
Extracurricular	Restlessness or home-sickness Lack of information Indifference or failure to participate	Discuss problem with student Take to organization meetings Talk to organization leaders	Residence hall director Organization office and sponsors
Social	No dates Not making friends Being shy and with-drawn Refusal to participate Uncooperativeness Nonsocial behavior Bad manners	Discuss social behav-ior with student Help to make contacts Take to social gatherings	Residence hall director
Academic	Low grades on tests Dissatisfaction with courses Inability to manage time properly Poor reading or writing skills Being overwhelmed by outside assign-ments Dissatisfaction with teachers	Urge conference with teachers or with faculty advisor Check study habits Discuss college goals	Course instructors Faculty advisor Testing and Coun seling Center Reading clinic English laborator
Health	Frequent colds Chronic fatigue Nervousness, irrita-bility, constant worry Headaches Insomnia Evidence of eyestrain	Urge student to re-port to infirmary Check on eating and sleeping habits Discuss problem with residence hall director	Residence hall director Infirmary
Financial	Worrying about money Borrowing money Talking about having to drop out and go to work Excessive spending	Discuss spending habits with group Advise how to apply for student employment Advise on sources of student loans	Student Employ-ment Office Student Loan Of

ocational	Inability to decide on major	Urge conference with vocational	Testing and Counseling Center
	No vocational interests	counselor or faculty advisor	Faculty advisor
	Ignorance of job requirements	Suggest visit to Occupational	
	Unrealistic career choice	Information Library	
	Education not adding up to anything		
	Too many interests		
Housing	Disliking roommate	Discuss problem with roommate	Residence hall director
	Finding residence hall too noisy	Discuss "quiet hours" with group	
	Room not satisfactory	Discuss problem with residence hall director	
	Wanting to change residence halls		
Home	Receiving letter from home every day	Encourage writing home once a week	Residence hall director
	Writing home every day	Discuss home relations with group	Minister
	Delaying all decisions until parents have ruled	Encourage making own decisions as needed	Testing and Counseling Center
	Rarely hearing from home		
	Rarely writing home		
	Worrying about home situation		
Emotional	Extreme nervousness	Encourage talking out problems	Residence hall director
	Extreme indecision	Don't diagnose, don't prejudge, and don't pry	Testing and Counseling Center
	Crying and outbursts		Infirmary
	Moodiness		
	Unpopularity	Don't get too emotionally involved	
	Extreme unhappiness	Be patient	
	Antisocial behavior		
Religious	Ignoring religious activities	Encourage a church connection if it seems appropriate	Minister
	Scoffing at religion		
	Excessive piety		

make appropriate referral on major personal-social adjustment problems.

CURRICULUM ORIENTATION

Responsibility for facilitating the freshman's initial academic orientation is delegated to the faculty advisor. Prior to registration, a required meeting with academic advisors is scheduled for all freshmen. For this meeting, decided freshmen are assigned to faculty advisors on the basis of their stated academic major. Assignment of undecided freshmen is made on an alphabetical basis to special faculty advisors for nonmajors. The meeting's objective is to explain the college's scholastic regulations, curriculum requirements, and registration procedure.

The faculty advisor usually begins the meeting by reviewing college policies and services. College regulations are reported and discussed, as appropriate, for each of the following: (*a*) course numbering and credit, (*b*) academic load, (*c*) majors and minors, (*d*) mid-semester grades, (*e*) quality points, (*f*) minimum standard of work, (*g*) scholastic probation, (*h*) scholastic honors, and (*i*) class attendance. Operation of the college's counseling service, reading clinic, English laboratory, and other service facilities are also described and their use encouraged.

For students decided upon their academic major, the faculty advisor outlines the curriculum leading to the appropriate bachelor's degree. Courses to be taken during the freshman, sophomore, junior, and senior years are delineated, with special attention being given to arranging a class schedule for the freshman-year courses. Where appropriate, the faculty advisor also reports the certification requirements for teaching areas related to the student's chosen major. For students as yet undecided about a major, the faculty advisor surveys the college curricula, outlines the graduation requirements in general education, and helps the freshman plan an appropriate class schedule from these required courses.

Finally, the faculty advisor explains the registration procedure and assists the freshman in preparing for this activity. In addition to preparing a class schedule for courses to be taken, the student is required to fill out all forms routinely used during registration. A step-by-step review of the registration process is then given, including a description of the procedure for changing courses.

Academic Adjustment Counseling

The overall goal for academic adjustment counseling is to facilitate adaptation to unfamiliar instructional procedures and expanded study requirements. The student-to-student approach is employed for Survival Orientation, Test Interpretation, and Study Habits Evaluation—the three sequential counseling activities comprising this program component. Freshman participation in Survival Orientation is required; participation in Test Interpretation and Study Habits Evaluation is entirely voluntary. The motivational orientations approach is employed in all three counseling activities, in that the importance of efficient study behavior and positive study attitudes is continually stressed by the student academic counselors.

SURVIVAL ORIENTATION

Survival Orientation, first of the three academic adjustment counseling activities, is provided by student academic counselors during freshman orientation week, or the week before classes actually begin. Survival Orientation is a briefing session designed to acquaint all freshmen with their new learning environment, to present information about college academic life, and to give advice on effective study procedures. Attendance at this session is required of all entering freshmen and transfer students with less than fifteen semester hours of college credit. Two student academic counselors meet with approximately thirty freshmen in a two-hour session. The session must be well organized so that all material can be covered, but the counseling climate is informal and freshmen are urged to ask questions at any time. The student academic counselors do not give a lecture, but rather they talk *with* the freshmen about their future college life.

The purpose of the two-hour meeting is to provide each freshman with academic survival information. Specifically, the session's objectives are to emphasize the necessary adjustment to college instructional procedures, to survey the major factors contributing to academic failure, to stimulate interest in developing effective study skills, and to report where and how freshmen may obtain help with their problems. The facts are presented, not as a threat or warning, but as a challenge to be understood and faced realistically.

A comprehensive Activity Sequence Check List for the two-hour Survival Orientation session may be found in Appendix E. This check list is used for training purposes only and is *not* rigidly followed during actual counseling sessions. To do so would undermine the program's effectiveness by destroying the relaxed, informal, personal touch given to the contents by the student academic counselors. A list of the materials utilized during Survival Orientation is given in Table 13. An outline of activities to be accomplished during Survival Orientation is given in Table 18, together with a suggested time allotment for each topic to be covered. The alloted times are suggestive only, and the student academic counselors make no effort to observe them rigidly. A typical counselor-counselee arrangement in a Survival Orientation session is illustrated in the picture section.

TEST INTERPRETATION

Test Interpretation, second of the three academic adjustment counseling activities, is offered during the first six weeks of the semester following the beginning of classes. Test Interpretation is a student-to-student counseling session designed to provide interested freshmen with a meaningful interpretation of their test results and a systematic review of proven techniques for effective study. Student participation is entirely voluntary, with interested freshmen being given the opportunity to sign up at the close of Survival Orientation. A student academic counselor meets with a small group of three to five freshmen for a two-hour session that is both highly organized in content and highly informal in climate. For the counseling period to achieve maximum effectiveness, the

TABLE 18
Outline of Academic Adjustment Counseling Activities
Performed by Student Academic Counselors

Activity	Suggested Amount of Time (mins.)
Survival Orientation Session	
1. Establish group rapport	4–6
2. Report college survival facts	8–12
3. Interpret Effective Study Test results	8–12
4. Analyze time budgeting problems	15–25
5. Analyze note taking problems	15–25
6. Analyze scholastic motivation problems	15–25
7. Answer questions about college life	10–20
8. Inventory college rewards	8–12
9. Inventory sources of student assistance	4–6
10. Explain available counseling services	4–6
Test Interpretation Session	
1. Establish group rapport	4–6
2. Explain college success factors	4–6
3. Interpret American College Test scores	8–12
4. Interpret Survey of Study Habits and Attitudes scores	25–35
5. Analyze textbook reading problems	15–25
6. Analyze theme and report writing problems	15–25
7. Analyze examination taking problems	15–25
8. Offer additional counseling	4–6
9. Evaluate comprehension of counseling content	4–6

student academic counselor must continually strive to lead a meaningful discussion in which all counselees participate to the maximum extent possible.

A comprehensive Activity Sequence Check List for the two-hour Test Interpretation session is included as Appendix F. Again, this check list is utilized only for training purposes. A list of the materials utilized during Test Interpretation is provided in Table 13. An outline of activities to be accomplished during Test Interpretation is given in Table 18, together with a suggested time allotment for each topic to be covered. The normal counselor-counselee seating arrangement for a Test Interpretation session is illustrated in the picture section.

Prior to the counseling session, the student academic counselor pulls each counselee's Information Form and reviews the following items of personal information recorded thereon: high school quarter rank; high school size; most liked and least liked high school subjects; academic, social, or athletic awards and honors received during high school; and employment history during high school. A copy of the Information Form is included in Appendix G. Next, the counselor verifies the accuracy of all centiles recorded on each counselee's Test Results Report Form and SSHA Diagnostic Profile. Finally, the student counselor uses the SSHA Counseling Stencil to circle negative answers on each counselee's SSHA Answer Sheet.

Test Interpretation sessions are initiated immediately following the final Survival Orientation briefing. The program remains in operation until all freshmen filling out the Test Interpretation Request Form have been scheduled for this additional guidance. The operational characteristics of the counseling effort are as follows: (*a*) the counseling is accomplished through a peer-group discussion process, (*b*) each counselee group consists of three to five same-sex freshmen previously matched on their ability test scores, (*c*) the student academic counselor is of the same sex as the counselees, and (*d*) each student academic counselor holds only one such counseling session per day. These operational features permit the counseling of about twenty counselees per week per counselor, for a total of approximately eighty freshmen counseled by each student academic counselor during the first four weeks of the semester.

The purpose of the two-hour counseling period is to help each freshman develop an efficient study program. Specifically, the session's objectives are as follows: (*a*) to report the results of standardized ability, achievement, and attitude tests administered previously; (*b*) to identify potential academic difficulties due to deficient academic preparation; (*c*) to survey current study behavior and identify deficient study skills; (*d*) to examine present scholastic objectives and discuss related motivational problems; (*e*) to provide assistance in planning appropriate corrective action for academic weaknesses thus identified; and (f) to provide the opportunity to obtain such follow-up counseling as is deemed desirable.

The two-hour counseling session is normally scheduled to begin at 1 P.M. or at 3 P.M., with scheduled freshmen being excused from classes, labs, and extracurricular activities conflicting with their counseling appointment. To minimize conflict with the instructional program, however, students are scheduled only at times reported as free on their Test Interpretation Request Form. Counseling is accomplished in one of the three identically equipped offices designated for student academic counselors.

The scheduling of counseling appointments, with its prerequisite construction of same-sex counselee groups matched on ability test scores, is a somewhat exacting and time-consuming operation. All required scheduling information is recorded upon the Test Interpretation Request Form. A spread of three points in the composite score on the American College Test is considered to be an acceptable tolerance limit for matching purposes. Within this tolerance limit, groups of three to five same-sex counselees are constructed in accordance with their self-reported free time. Counseling assignments are usually made for two weeks at a time, with the student academic counselor being briefed by the program director on the appropriate counseling tempo and content emphasis for each counselee group.

The student academic counselor employs a structured discussion-demonstration procedure to communicate standardized test results, to delineate potential problem areas, and to initiate improvement in study skills. Subscale scores on the Survey of Study Habits and Attitudes are employed to alert each counselee to potential scholastic difficulties stemming from deficient study behavior or negative academic values. Discussion of items identified with the SSHA Counseling Key will also permit analysis of each counselee's specific behavioral and attitudinal problems. In order to illustrate the procedures employed by peer counselors in using the Survey of Study Habits and Attitudes, the complete transcription of a tape-recorded Test Interpretation session has been included in Appendix H.

STUDY HABITS EVALUATION

Study Habits Evaluation, last of the three academic adjustment counseling activities, is provided when the mid-semester unsatisfactory progress reports are sent to students. Study Habits Evaluation provides student-to-student counseling on the probable causes for failing grades and the appropriate corrective actions for residual study problems. A list of first-semester freshmen receiving two or more unsatisfactory grades at mid-semester is obtained from the college's Data Processing Center. The list is checked to identify those freshmen who attended a Test Interpretation session. These students are then notified to report to the Testing and Counseling Center to pick up their mid-semester grades. Upon reporting, they meet individually with a student academic counselor for a one-hour analysis of the probable causes and possible cures for their unsatisfactory academic progress.

A comprehensive Activity Sequence Check List for the one-hour counseling period is included in Appendix I. The check list is not followed rigidly, however, for success or failure depends upon the counselor's skill in providing the counselee with a comprehensive, meaningful, realistic, permissive discussion of his scholastic difficulties, the reasons for them, and appropriate measures to correct them. Typical counselor-counselee interaction during Study Habits Evaluation is illustrated in the picture section. The Scholastic Difficulty Analysis Form completed jointly by counselor and counselee has been included in Appendix J.

Academic Improvement Counseling

The overall goal for academic improvement counseling is to facilitate correction of deficient study skills. The student-counseling-student approach is employed for all three guidance activities comprising this program component. Freshman participation in each activity is entirely voluntary. The importance of positive academic attitudes is stressed whenever and wherever possible.

STUDY SKILLS COUNSELING

Study Skills Counseling, first of the three academic improvement counseling activities, is offered any time after the third week of classes. Study Skills Counseling provides a student-to-student counseling activity designed to provide interested freshmen with individualized assistance in one or more of the following areas: (*a*) managing time, (*b*) taking notes, (*c*) reading textbooks, (*d*) writing themes and reports, (*e*) improving memory, and (*f*) passing exams. The purpose of Study Skills Counseling is to provide additional help in these six areas for freshmen expecting or experiencing academic difficulties and wanting to improve their study methods.

Student participation is entirely voluntary, with interested freshmen being given an opportunity to sign up following Test Interpretation. The student academic counselor meets with counselees individually to discuss the student's specific problems in a particular study skills area. Table 19 describes the typical steps to be followed in such a one-to-one counseling situation. The counseling process must be both highly individualized in approach and highly informal in climate. There should be much less formal structuring of counseling activities than was the case for Survival Orientation and Test Interpretation, for the aim is to provide counseling suited to each student's individual needs. Accordingly, the time involved may vary from a single half-hour session to many hours of student-to-student counseling spread over several weeks. The amount of time consumed will depend upon the counselee's initial study skills development and subsequent study skills improvement, as well as upon the counselor's initial diagnostic insight and subsequent counseling effectiveness.

Because the counseling process and content must be individualized and, therefore, relatively less structured, activity sequence check lists cannot be formulated for the six study skills areas. In

TABLE 19
Typical Steps in Study Skills Counseling

Things to Be Accomplished	What to Do to Accomplish Them
1. Help the counselee feel at ease	Begin in an interested and friendly way. Be natural and sincere. Take it easy. Discuss topics of mutual interest. Ensure privacy. Follow counselee's lead in getting into the problem. Provide comfortable setting.
2. Win the counselee's confidence	Show a sincere interest. Recognize and respect his attitudes and ideas. Stress his strengths. Increase his self-respect. Do not violate confidential materials of other counselees. Don't be hurried. Let him talk. Do not pry. Try to understand *his* point of view. Do not sermonize.
3. Try to make the interview helpful	Encourage counselee to express himself frankly and freely. Encourage an analysis of the *real* problems. Observe reactions, mannerisms, and tensions to locate key spots. Listen and observe. Listen for counselee's "theme song." Stimulate self-examination and self-therapy. Try to help counselee identify, analyze, and suggest solutions for own problems. Don't monopolize the conversation.
4. Keep the interview going	Try to move into helpful action. Don't get too far afield. Stop and summarize. Emphasize decisions and plans made by counselee. Restate counselee's ideas occasionally. Try to explore all desirable angles.
5. Guard against yourself	Don't take over the responsibility for the problem. Watch your own biases, attitudes, and values. Be sure you are talking a language both understand. Don't push, coerce, or decide.
6. Close the interview carefully	Plan some next steps. Don't drag on too long. Use other resources as referral aids. Make it possible for person to return. Observe counselee to determine time to stop. Stress plans involving action.

NOTE: Adapted from *A Manual for Faculty Counselors*, Morgan State College, Baltimore, Maryland, 1955, pp. 26–27.

order to maximize counseling productivity, however, the following six-step sequence is normally utilized for the *initial* counseling session: (*a*) question the counselee's experiences and expectations, (*b*) report the difficulties most commonly experienced by freshmen,

(c) review the study procedures recommended previously, (d) analyze examples of the counselee's current work, (e) discuss appropriate corrective steps for identified deficiencies, and (f) decide upon appropriate follow-up actions.

Table 13 lists guidance materials available for use in providing instruction on effective study skills. Many of these items are also used in Survival Orientation and Test Interpretation, while others are specific to Study Skills Counseling. The student academic counselor is instructed to be particularly careful that he does *not* allow these materials to limit the scope of his counseling effort. They are useful for stimulating discussion, but, more often than not, the really significant counseling results will stem from consideration of problems and procedures apart from those covered in these materials.

Appendix K outlines a possible sequence of activities for the initial hour of counseling on taking lecture notes. The outline is not intended to serve as a check list to be followed, but rather as one example of what might be done during the initial counseling period. Similar outlines could readily be prepared for the other five study skills areas. This has not been done, so as to minimize the possibility that they might become a counseling "crutch," with a consequent perfunctory formalization of the counseling process and content. The emphasis of Study Skills Counseling is upon the identification of scholastic difficulties through careful analysis of the counselee's lecture notes, textbook underlining, returned themes, returned tests, and other materials. This emphasis upon analysis of the counselee's own work is illustrated in the picture section.

READING IMPROVEMENT INSTRUCTION

Reading Improvement Instruction is another student-to-student counseling service offered by the Testing and Counseling Center to help freshmen make a more efficient and effective adjustment to college academic requirements. The program is operated as a self-help activity and provides instruction in two areas: reading comprehension improvement and reading speed improvement. Materials utilized for improving reading comprehension and reading speed, respectively, are the SRA Reading Laboratories and the SRA Reading Accelerators developed by Science Research Associates.

The reading clinic is operated by two experienced student academic counselors who receive additional training in remedial reading instruction. Selection of these student counselors is made by the program director on the basis of judged effectiveness in student-to-student counseling, and the additional training consists of twenty-four clock hours of specialized instruction given by a remedial reading specialist. Following their training, the two student counselors are given complete responsibility for the scheduling, instructing, assisting, and testing of students, as appropriate, to assure progress in the improvement of reading skills. They also determine, through testing, the appropriate level for each student to begin his reading improvement effort.

During Test Interpretation, all freshmen scoring below the thirty-third percentile on the Davis Reading Test: Form 1A are encouraged to sign up for Reading Improvement Instruction. Applicants are contacted immediately by the student counselors assigned to the reading clinic and groups of eight to twelve students are scheduled to begin instruction as soon as possible. The reason for thus organizing students into groups is primarily to economize on the amount of staff time required to operate the reading clinic. Once a group has been tested and the clinic operation has been explained, instruction is then individualized, and a student can change his scheduled reporting time if he so desires. The reading clinic is basically a voluntary "do-it-yourself" program, with the assigned student counselors providing a minimum of supervision and a maximum of encouragement. However, the students are encouraged to be consistent and regular in their attendance in order that they may obtain maximum value from the course. Each student is scheduled to attend either two ninety-minute sessions or three one-hour sessions per week. A minimum of six weeks' participation is most strongly recommended, with a full fifteen-week program being available each semester. Each student records his own daily progress in a Student Record Book, and periodic testing with different forms of the Davis Reading Test provides additional evidence of the student's progress.

SUBJECT MATTER TUTORING

Not infrequently, a student encounters difficulty in a specific course due to an inadequate background in the subject matter area. The Testing and Counseling Center offers a limited tutoring service as the third counseling activity aimed at individual improvement of academic skills. Subject Matter Tutoring is a highly individualized service. Consequently, the tutoring service is restricted to those students who demonstrate a deficient background or lack of proficiency in one or more academic fields and whose college careers may be jeopardized by the resulting academic difficulties.

The need for an organized, systematic tutoring service became apparent when freshmen, as a direct result of the student-counseling-student approach, began to attach greater significance to academic success in college. Motivated freshmen began applying for tutoring assistance in the basic freshman courses—English, history, mathematics, biology, chemistry, and foreign languages. The Testing and Counseling Center, at the request of the Student Senate, undertook the sponsorship of a tutoring program in cooperation with appropriate department chairmen.

Most often, students already involved in student-to-student counseling are utilized to provide tutoring. Additional qualified tutors are obtained through recommendations made by departmental chairmen and faculty advisors. All students providing tutoring for freshmen must first be approved by the appropriate department chairman.

Tutors are notified of tutoring assignments by the Testing and Counseling Center. As tutoring requests are received, tutors are assigned according to the appearance of names on a master roster of approved tutors. When a tutor is notified of a tutoring assignment, he contacts the student to be tutored and arranges the time and place for the initial tutoring session.

Tutoring may be given individually or to small groups of two to four students. The initial tutoring session is always individual, with subsequent tutoring sessions being group or individual at the discretion of the tutor. The rates for individual and group tutoring are $2.50 per hour and $1.50 per hour, respectively.

Each tutor is responsible for collecting his tutoring fees. If a student fails to keep a tutoring appointment, he is still charged one-half the regular rate. If a tutor encounters excessive difficulty in collecting his fees, he may notify the dean of students, and appropriate assistance will be provided.

The tutor is charged with maintaining records on his tutoring activities. After each tutoring session, he is required to complete a report on what was done during the meeting. These reports are turned in to the Testing and Counseling Center at the end of the third session and following termination of tutoring for each student. The reports are placed in the freshman's individual folder for future reference should he seek further counseling at a later date.

The tutoring objective is to help the freshman cope with the subject matter content of his difficult courses. The successful tutor, therefore, is continually striving to eliminate the need for his services by helping the student become self-sufficient in his studying. Thus the teaching of efficient study methods is often a significant aspect of the tutor's job.

Educational Planning Counseling

Uncertainty about future educational and vocational plans is characteristic of many college freshmen because they have not given sufficient thought to the factors that influence occupational success and satisfaction. Furthermore, most freshmen require help in planning an educational program that will both meet college graduation requirements and fit their own individual needs. The work of the student academic counselors stimulates freshmen to seek counseling on their educational and vocational plans. A systematic procedure for obtaining counseling on these problems is thus an essential follow-up to the student academic counselor's work. This follow-up counseling is provided by thirty-two faculty advisors and two professional counselors, with student participation in either activity being entirely voluntary.

During Test Interpretation, freshmen are invited to request vocational and educational guidance if they feel that this additional counseling would be of value. Freshmen having definite educational plans are referred directly to the faculty advisor for their major department; students undecided about an academic major are encouraged to seek vocational counseling prior to their assignment to a faculty advisor. However, to prevent an undeserved premium being placed upon the immediate selection of a major, special faculty advisors are provided for nonmajors unwilling or unready to make occupational decisions. Where an undecided freshman is referred directly to a faculty advisor, vocational counseling may be given at a later date if the student should decide to request this service.

VOCATIONAL COUNSELING

Systematic vocational counseling is provided by the Testing and Counseling Center to interested freshmen on a voluntary participation basis. Approximately 65 percent of this vocational counseling is handled by four student academic counselors under the direct and close supervision of the Center's two professional counselors. These experienced student academic counselors, usually seniors or beginning graduate students, are given appropriate additional training so that they can handle the relatively uncomplicated cases. Complicated cases are, of course, always handled by one of the professional counselors.

The importance of providing the opportunity for vocational counseling is underscored by the results of a longitudinal study of the class of 1962 at Southwest Texas State College. Analysis of the students' stated educational objectives at time of college entrance revealed that 39.8 percent were undecided about their major, that another 29.4 percent changed their major one or more times prior to graduation, while the remaining 30.8 percent remained firmly committed to their originally stated college major. Furthermore, when their first-semester grade averages were compared, it was found that the decided freshmen averaged .6 of a letter grade higher than did the undecided freshmen. Analysis of the academic records of all freshmen enrolled during the fall semester of 1958 revealed that the scholastic probation and drop-out rates for undecided freshmen greatly exceeded those for decided freshmen. Specifically, the drop-out ratio for undecided and decided freshmen was 4.1:1 and the scholastic probation ratio was 3.4:1. As a consequence of these findings, undecided freshmen are encouraged to request vocational counseling, provided they feel ready to act upon the information received through such counseling.

Vocational counseling seeks to provide the student with realistic information about his own occupational potentialities and about the world of work. Its objective is to help each student make the wisest possible educational and vocational plans. To accomplish this objective, the vocational counselor assists the student in the examination of his own abilities, experiences, interests, needs, and expectations; the exploration of the job duties, training requirements, and working conditions for appropriate career fields; and the consideration of the limitations, alternatives, and consequences of possible vocational choices. The vocational counselor *does not* make educational or vocational decisions for a counselee, but allows the student complete freedom in making his own decisions after examining all significant facets of the problem. No action of the counselor is in any way binding upon the counselee, and counseling can be terminated by the student at any time.

The vocational counseling process consists of a three-step sequence requiring the services of a psychometrist, a vocational counselor, and an occupational information librarian. In addition to the four student academic counselors assigned to provide vocational counseling, the psychometrist and occupational information librarian are also upperclassmen employed by the Testing and Counseling Center. All these student employees are carefully trained and supervised in the performance of their job duties by the Center's professional counselors.

The three-phase vocational guidance sequence is outlined in Table 20. The initial step, obtaining required biographical and psychometric data, requires about five hours and is handled by the student psychometrist. This first meeting is held in the psychometrics laboratory, with as many as sixteen freshmen being briefed about the program and tested as a group. After the tests have been scored, each student meets with a vocational counselor to discuss his test results and to consider possible educational and vocational choices. If, during this second step, the student is able to select a tentative academic major, he is then scheduled for the third step, obtaining occupational information, and is instructed in the use of the Occupational Information Library. If a student is unable to select a tentative academic major, he will normally bypass the third step and go directly to a faculty advisor for nonmajors. Students selecting an academic major will, of course, be referred to the faculty advisor for their major department.

Several forms are employed in the vocational guidance program. Each student completes a Personal Data Form during the first meeting. A copy of this form, together with directions for filling it out, is included as Appendix L. Appendix M contains a copy of the Occupational Analysis Form used during the third session, and the Counseling Summary Form prepared by the vocational counselor after vocational guidance is completed is included as Appendix N.

Effective vocational counseling is a complex process that cannot be performed in an automatic, routine manner. During the course of vocational counseling, it may become necessary to obtain additional psychometric data or to make referral to individuals able to provide needed career or curriculum information. Also, personal adjustment and family acceptance problems are often involved in the decision-making process. Several counseling periods may thus be required before the counselee can make meaningful decisions. Consequently, the activities outlined in Table 20 are suggestive only, and the actual counseling process will vary with each counselee's needs and problems. For this reason, a detailed step-by-step description of the vocational counseling process is neither possible nor desirable.

TABLE 20
Vocational Counseling Activity Sequence

Step 1. Obtain Biographical and Psychometric Data

Explain vocational counseling goals and objectives
Prepare Personal Data Form
Administer Differential Aptitude Test
Administer Kuder Preference Record: Vocational
Administer Educational Interest Inventory
Schedule appointment with vocational counselor

Step 2. Survey Occupational Potential

A. Preparation Period
Study personal history data
Examine test results

B. Counseling Period
Review vocational counseling approach
Confirm significant biographical data
Discuss current and past academic achievement
Report aptitude test results
Report interest inventory results
Summarize counselee's strengths and weaknesses
Examine possible occupational fields
Discuss appropriate academic majors and minors[a]
Explain occupational analysis procedure
Schedule appointment with occupational information librarian
Assign appropriate faculty advisor[b]

C. Termination Period
Prepare Counseling Summary Form

Step 3. Obtain Occupational Information

Examine appropriate occupational folders[c]
Prepare appropriate Occupational Analysis Form[d]

---

[a] If the student is unable or unwilling to select a tentative major, vocational counseling is terminated and the student is transferred to a special faculty advisor for nonmajors.

[b] Faculty advisor assignment is determined by the counselee's major department.

[c] The counselee examines occupational folders to find those career fields for which his academic major provides training.

[d] Counselee prepares Occupational Analysis Form for career fields of special interest only.

EDUCATIONAL ADVISING

The faculty member's traditional role as friend and confidant of the student has become increasingly difficult to maintain as a consequence of the trend toward larger classes, busier schedules, and more formalized instruction. One of the objectives of educational advising is to delegate certain counseling duties to carefully selected and trained faculty members, thereby restoring the personal contact between faculty and students, which is generally recognized as desirable and beneficial for both. Consequently, the counseling responsibilities assigned to faculty advisors involve a good deal more than merely advising on curriculum matters. Specifically, the faculty advisor is expected to continue the process of *assisting* the student to develop understanding of his capacities and interests, to make an intelligent choice of educational and vocational objectives, to develop an effective program for achieving maximum benefit from his college experiences, and to review and evaluate his progress toward the achievement of selected goals.

A counselee is assigned to a faculty advisor by the Testing and Counseling Center upon the student's request for such additional counseling following Test Interpretation. Students with definite educational plans automatically proceed directly into educational counseling with the faculty advisor for their major department; students undecided about their educational objectives are invited to seek vocational counseling prior to contacting a faculty advisor. However, since many undecided students are unwilling or unready to make vocational decisions, special faculty advisors are provided for these nonmajors, thereby preventing an undeserved premium's being placed upon the immediate choice of an academic major.

The student's request for an appointment is sent to the appropriate faculty advisor, together with a Test Results Report Form giving the student's scores on the American College Test and the Davis Reading Test. If the student has received vocational counseling prior to his assignment for educational advisement, his Personal Data Form and Profile Sheet for the Kuder Preference Record: Vocational are also forwarded to the faculty advisor. The faculty advisor then decides when to schedule the counseling appointment, enters the necessary data on an Appointment Notification Card, and mails the card to the student at least three days prior to the appointed time.

Each departmental chairman is asked to recommend appropriate faculty members to serve as faculty advisors for his department. The department's advisors are then selected jointly by the dean of the college and the director of counseling. New faculty members will not be asked to serve as advisors until they have had sufficient opportunity to become familiar with the organization and operation of the college. The customary term of appointment as a faculty advisor is for three years, with appropriate reduction in other committee activities during the appointment period.

Faculty members invited to serve as advisors should be interested in assuming counseling responsibilities and willing to work to acquire some skill in counseling. With reference to the criteria for selection of faculty advisors, Hardee (74) has this to say:

> The least useful criterion is the one occasionally voiced by an academic dean or department head, "Well, Professor Drydock might as well counsel. We can't seem to fill his classes and he ought to have something to take up his time." The allocation of Drydock to either a newly established or an old-line program of counseling bodes no good. Students get the word about the caliber of ineffective counselors much as they get the word about ineffective teachers, with the result that Drydock sits in splendid isolation as a counselor just as he did as a teacher.
>
> The only respectable criteria for use in selecting faculty for the counseling role are those concerned with (1) the interest of the faculty member in counseling, (2) the ability of the faculty member to deal effectively with students in a one-to-one relationship, and (3) the willingness of the faculty member to learn the fundamentals of his counseling responsibility.

Advising students regarding their choice of courses and the relationship of this choice to their abilities, interests, and needs is a complex operation. Since few faculty members are specifically trained in the counseling process, a program of in-service orientation is normally needed to assist the faculty advisor in meeting his counseling responsibilities. If these responsibilities are properly explained beforehand, most newly assigned faculty advisors are receptive to a reasonable amount of in-service training, provided a pragmatic approach is taken toward their counseling duties. Of course, an effective selling job is needed if the typical faculty member is to become an effective faculty advisor. Otherwise, the faculty member may resent both the counseling assignment and the in-service training.

Training for faculty advisors is provided by the director of counseling through four one-hour meetings utilizing a combination lecture-discussion-demonstration process to provide information about the following: (*a*) faculty advisor duties and limitations; (*b*) freshman problems, needs, and expectations; (*c*) interviewing and test interpretation procedures; (*d*) graduation and certification requirements; and (*e*) student assistance facilities and referral mechanics. In addition to the current college catalog, each new faculty advisor is provided with a *Faculty Advisor's Guide* (22), *Effective Study Guide* (42), and *Occupational Briefs* (114) for appropriate career fields.

Faculty advisors are selected and trained to provide follow-up educational counseling for beginning freshmen. To be effective, they must recognize that each student has different abilities, interests, aspirations, needs, experiences, and problems. Consequently, the giving of educational counseling cannot be a mechanical routine matter. The faculty advisor's primary responsibility is to help individual students plan the program of study that will meet college requirements and at the same time fit the student's specific needs. To accomplish this goal, the counselor must urge the student to give ample thought to the matter, he must direct him to appropriate sources of information, and he must aid him in examining all significant facets of the problem while making necessary decisions.

Although the functions of the faculty advisor will probably vary somewhat for different students, his general counseling duties are normally as follows:

1. The faculty advisor explains to the student the program of general or basic education as it relates to the first two years of college, to the major of the student, and to preparation for life pursuits generally.

2. The faculty advisor helps the student examine the course offerings in his major, relate these to appropriate minors, and understand the graduation requirements for the curriculum leading to an appropriate degree.

3. The faculty advisor helps the student explore the career fields for which his major provides training and obtain related vocational information and survey job opportunities.

4. The faculty advisor serves as a link between the student and the administration by counseling the student on his scholastic problems (course scheduling, course adjustment, and academic progress) and by making appropriate referral to other assistance agencies.

5. The faculty advisor serves as a "faculty friend" to the student by demonstrating a personal interest in him and in his adjustment to college; by serving as a central contact person in obtaining information that can be used to help the student; and by allowing the student freedom to make his own choices after the limitations, alternatives, and consequences involved in a decision are pointed out.

The faculty advisor assigned to counsel undecided students has somewhat different responsibilities. Instead of helping the student explore his selected major, he assists the student's investigation of potential majors by referring him to the Testing and Counseling Center for vocational guidance, to the Occupational Information Library to survey career fields, and to special activities wherein interests may be explored and experiences gained. Once the undecided student has selected a major, he is then transferred to the faculty advisor for his major department.

Faculty advisors must also recognize their limitations as counselors. The restrictions placed upon faculty counselors may be stated as follows:

1. A faculty advisor cannot make decisions for a counselee, but

he can be a sympathetic listener and even offer various possible solutions to the student's problem.

2. A faculty advisor cannot increase the native ability of a counselee, but he can encourage the maximum use of the ability that the student has.

3. A faculty advisor should not attempt to solve maladjustments involving physical or mental disorders, but he should refer such cases to the proper professional agencies.

4. A faculty advisor cannot reduce the academic or employment load of a floundering counselee, but he can make recommendations that such adjustments be made.

5. A faculty advisor should not criticize a fellow teacher to a student, but he can make a friendly approach to any teacher if that teacher is involved in the student's problem.

6. A faculty advisor should not tell a counselee his raw scores on psychological tests, but he can indicate areas in which the student seems weak or strong by discussing centiles derived from local norms.

7. A faculty advisor should not betray a student's confidence on matters of a personal nature, but he can seek appropriate professional assistance in helping a student with minor personal or social adjustment problems.

A check list of general counseling duties, developed for use in the faculty advisor orientation program, is presented in Table 21. As may be seen from this table, several of the listed activities are to be accomplished only if they are appropriate to the student's needs. Likewise, it may be necessary to refer the student to another faculty member for specific information or to have him obtain the needed information from external sources. It will also be noted that students are assisted in completing an Educational Analysis Form. A copy of this form may be found in Appendix P.

Although the duties delineated in Table 21 are specific to the initial contact between faculty advisor and student, it should be recognized that the student may request additional help as new problems are encountered. Normally, educational counseling is

TABLE 21
Educational Advising Check List

A. Preparation Period
   1. Schedule counseling appointment
   2. Survey psychometric and biographical data
B. Counseling Period
   1. Explain counseling objectives
   2. Review student's educational and vocational plans
   3. Discuss general educational requirements
   4. Survey course offerings in major
   5. Relate major to appropriate minors
   6. Complete Educational Analysis Form
   7. Discuss potential career fields
   8. Describe occupational information sources*
   9. Survey current and past academic performance
  10. Review student assistance agencies
  11. Discuss referral procedure*
C. Termination Period
   1. Initiate referral process*

---

* Activities to be accomplished only if appropriate to counselee's needs.

provided by the faculty advisor during the freshman and sophomore years, and by the department chairman thereafter.

Cost Effectiveness of Student-to-Student Counseling

As detailed in the preceding pages, the freshman counseling program at Southwest Texas State College provides a series of ten organized counseling activities for entering freshmen. Seven of these services are provided by student counselors, two by faculty advisors, and one by a combination of student and professional counselors. Freshman participation is required for the three organized counseling activities scheduled during orientation week. Participation in the other seven counseling services is entirely voluntary.

In the fall of 1964, the first year when all ten organized guidance activities were fully operational, the staff required to implement these services for about fourteen hundred beginning freshmen included eighty-two student residence hall counselors, twenty-four student academic counselors, thirty-two faculty advisors, and three half-time professional counselors. The counseling activities received necessary secretarial support from a full-time administrative secretary and eight part-time student clerical workers.

In 1964, the total cost for providing the environment orientation, academic adjustment, academic improvement, and educational planning programs was found to be less than $12,000 for all student-to-student counseling, supporting secretarial services, required testing and counseling materials, and maintenance and operation of the Testing and Counseling Center. This figure did not, of course, include any part of the salaries paid to the professional counseling staff and assigned faculty advisors or the original cost for constructing and equipping the Testing and Counseling Center. Exclusive of those expenses, the total program of student-to-student counseling cost slightly more than $8 per freshman—a very reasonable price indeed if the counseling effort was achieving its stated objectives.

Some indication of the effectiveness of the total freshman counseling effort at Southwest Texas State College is provided by a report on freshman-to-sophomore attrition rates prepared by the Coordinating Board, Texas College and University System (117).[2] The reported attrition rate for the twenty-two state-supported senior colleges and universities in Texas averaged 36.5 percent for 1964–65, with all but one of the twenty-two institutions reporting a first-year attrition rate greater than 25 percent. The lone exception was Southwest Texas State College with an attrition rate of 15.6 percent for the 1,462 freshmen enrolled in the fall semester of 1964.

It has been estimated that each college dropout represents a financial loss of about $1,000 to the typical state-supported institution (24, 57). The freshman-to-sophomore attrition rate at Southwest Texas State College was approximately 20 percent below the 1964–65 average for the twenty-two state-supported senior colleges and

[2] As used in this report, attrition rate simply means the percentage of students classified as freshmen in one fall semester who were not classified as sophomores in the next succeeding fall semester.

universities in Texas. This 20 percent difference thus represents 290 students retained at an approximate saving of $290,000. Of course, the student-to-student counseling effort cannot claim all the credit for the comparatively high retention rate at Southwest Texas State College. Still, the freshman-to-sophomore attrition rate was estimated to be almost 35 percent before the program became operational. It is, therefore, reasonable to assume that the student-counseling-student approach, backed up by the other organized freshman counseling services, did make a significant contribution to the 19 percent drop in the freshman-to-sophomore attrition rate at Southwest Texas State College between the 1959–60 and 1964–65 academic years.

4. Evaluation of the
Student-Counseling-Student Approach

The organized counseling program at Southwest Texas State College was specifically designed to increase the probability of scholastic success during the first semester of the freshman year. The student-counseling-student and motivational orientation approaches were employed to achieve this objective. The validity of the motivational orientation approach had been established through earlier research with the Survey of Study Habits and Attitudes (4, 37, 38, 39, 40, 41, 43, 56, 64, 83, 84, 85, 92, 99, 100). Consequently, a comprehensive program of research was undertaken in order to evaluate critical aspects of the student-counseling-student approach and to determine whether or not the various student-to-student counseling activities were achieving their stated objectives.

Between September, 1959, and June, 1968, a series of six investigations was carried out in order to assess the effectiveness and acceptability of student-to-student counseling at Southwest Texas State College. The focus of these investigations was on the student academic counselors, since their efforts provided the unique element in the college's freshman counseling program. During the 1959–60 and 1960–61 academic years, research was undertaken to assess the effectiveness and acceptability of the counseling being done by student academic counselors. Once the approach had been demonstrated to be both effective and accepted, the research focus turned to specific problem areas associated with the operation of such a student-to-student counseling program. During the 1961–62 and 1962–63 academic years, research focused on the comparative effectiveness and acceptability of male and female student academic counselors. Research undertaken during the 1963–64 academic year was designed to compare the effectiveness and acceptability of students and professionals as academic adjustment counselors. Finally, research undertaken during the 1967–68 academic year was designed to assess the student counselor's effectiveness and acceptability with freshmen identified as potential dropouts.

Three types of criteria—test scores, course grades, and questionnaire responses—have been employed to assess freshman reaction to student-to-student counseling. Precounseling and postcounseling scores on three standardized tests—the Survey of Study Habits and Attitudes, the Effective Study Test, and the Study Skills Surveys— were utilized to evaluate the student academic counselor's effectiveness in teaching efficient study skills and in communicating positive academic attitudes. The point-hour grade ratio and quality-point total were employed to determine the program's influence upon subsequent academic performance.[1] Finally, counselee acceptance of the student-counseling-student approach was determined through anonymous responses to a sixty-item Counseling Evaluation Questionnaire and a ten-item Sentence Completion Survey.[2]

---

[1] The point-hour ratio was computed by assigning numerical values of 4, 3, 2, 1, and 0 to grades of *A*, *B*, *C*, *D*, and *F*, respectively; multiplying each value by its corresponding number of credit hours; and obtaining the weighted average for all courses carried by the student. The quality-point total was computed exactly like the point-hour ratio except that the student's point-hour values were summed instead of averaged.

[2] The anonymous response procedure was followed whenever the Counseling Evaluation Questionnaire or the Sentence Completion Survey was employed for research purposes. This was done in order to minimize a student's possible con-

EFFECTIVENESS AND ACCEPTABILITY
OF STUDENT-TO-STUDENT COUNSELING

Matching groups of experimental (counseled) and control (uncounseled) students were utilized to evaluate the effectiveness of student-to-student counseling. Improvement in first-semester academic adjustment was inferred through comparison of precounseling and postcounseling test scores for the two groups and through comparison of the academic achievement records made by the two groups. Counselee acceptance of student-to-student counseling was assessed through anonymous responses obtained through questionnaire and sentence completion procedures. Detailed reports of these evaluation studies may be found elsewhere (17, 18, 20, 25).

Two samples of 108 students, each containing 54 males and 54 females, were selected from the 731 freshmen entering Southwest Texas State College in the fall of 1959. Students in the control sample were individually matched on the following eight variables with those in the experimental sample: chronological age, sex, high school quarter rank, high school size, scholastic ability score, study orientation score, residency, and employment status.[3] Students in the experimental sample received academic adjustment counseling from student academic counselors; students in the control sample were not given such academic adjustment counseling. Six student academic counselors, three males and three females, were randomly assigned as counselors to same-sex counselees.

Data for assessing immediate counseling effectiveness were obtained through precounseling and postcounseling administrations of the Survey of Study Habits and Attitudes and the Effective Study Test. Initial testing was accomplished on September 17–18, 1959; retesting was accomplished on December 3–4, 1959. Table 22 reports the comparative performance of experimental and control

cern about the personal consequences of reporting his true feelings about the counseling he had received.

[3] Scholastic ability and study orientation were assessed, respectively, by the Cooperative School and College Ability Test and the Survey of Study Habits and Attitudes.

TABLE 22
Comparative Performance of Matched Experimental (Counseled)
and Control (Uncounseled) Samples on Two Immediate
Criteria of Counseling Effectiveness

Group	Sex	N	Survey of Study Habits and Attitudes		Effective Study Test	
			Test[a]	Retest[b]	Test[a]	Retest[b]
Counseled	Male	54	103.7	132.1*	94.8	101.9*
Uncounseled	Male	54	104.1	101.0	94.3	93.3
Counseled	Female	54	115.1	142.7*	97.5	109.4*
Uncounseled	Female	54	115.2	111.9	97.3	97.7

[a] Initial testing was accomplished on September 17–18, 1959.
[b] Retesting was accomplished on December 3–4, 1959.
* Counseled freshmen scored significantly higher than matching uncounseled freshmen on retest $(P = < .01)$.

samples on the two criteria. On both variables, counseled freshmen earned significantly higher scores on retest than did matching uncounseled freshmen. Specifically, counseled males gained 28.4 and 7.1 points, respectively, on the Survey of Study Habits and Attitudes and Effective Study Test, whereas uncounseled males actually lost 3.1 and 1.0 points, respectively, on retest. Counseled females likewise gained 27.6 and 11.9 points, respectively, on these two tests, while uncounseled females dropped 3.3 and gained .4 points, respectively, on retest. It may be concluded, therefore, that counseled students gained information about effective study skills that was not acquired elsewhere by uncounseled students.

The acceptability of student-to-student counseling was determined through anonymous responses to a sixty-item Counseling Evaluation Questionnaire. The 265 freshmen counseled between September 28 and October 9, 1959, completed this questionnaire immediately following their Test Interpretation session. All responses were made anonymously, in that the freshmen were specifically instructed not to sign their names. The specially constructed questionnaire provides a five-choice response continuum for the counselee to indicate the extent of his agreement or disagreement with each statement. Twenty statements are positively worded, in that agreement indicates a positive reaction toward the counseling; forty statements are negatively worded, agreement indicating a negative reaction toward the counseling. The questionnaire contains four fifteen-item scales, with each scale having a possible score range of −30 to +30, inclusive. The scales were constructed to measure the counselee's evaluation of four aspects of the counseling process: (*a*) counselor behavior, (*b*) material covered, (*c*) counseling climate, and (*d*) results achieved. A copy of the Counseling Evaluation Questionnaire may be found in Appendix Q, together with a table reporting the distribution of item responses for the 265 counselees.

Counselee responses to representative positive and negative statements drawn from each scale are reported in Table 23; response means and standard deviations for each scale are reported in Table 24. From the information presented in these two tables it is obvious that counselee reaction to all evaluated aspects of the counseling process was very favorable. It can be concluded, therefore, that the student-counseling-student approach to providing academic adjustment counseling is an acceptable counseling procedure from the counselee's viewpoint.

The fall, 1959, research was replicated in fall, 1960, with a comparison of first-semester academic grades being added as another means for assessing the counseling program's effectiveness. Two samples of 216 students, each containing 108 men and 108 women, were selected from the 670 full-time freshmen entering Southwest Texas State College in fall, 1960. Students in the control (uncounseled) sample were individually matched with those in the experimental (counseled) sample on sex, chronological age, high school quarter rank, high school size, scholastic ability, and study orientation.[4] Experimental subjects were organized into fifty-four counselee groups, with the four freshmen in each group being carefully matched on sex, scholastic ability, study orientation, and high

[4] Scholastic ability and study orientation were assessed, respectively, by the Cooperative School and College Ability Test and the Survey of Study Habits and Attitudes.

TABLE 23
Counselee Responses to Representative Positively and Negatively Worded
Statements from the Counseling Evaluation Questionnaire

	Distribution of Counselee Responses*				
	SA	A	U	D	SD
Scale I. Counselor Evaluation					
40. The counselor was well prepared to discuss the problems a student encounters in adjusting to college.	44.5%	43.4%	7.9%	2.6%	1.5%
34. The counselor appeared to lack understanding of the needs and interests of students.	0.8	0.4	6.0	50.6	42.3
Scale II. Content Evaluation					
7. The discussion of attitudes toward school and teachers was time well spent.	26.4	46.4	13.6	9.4	4.1
21. Too much time was spent in telling us how to study.	2.6	6.8	13.6	57.4	19.6
Scale III. Climate Evaluation					
5. I benefited from hearing the views of other students on the problems that were discussed.	27.5	53.2	12.8	4.5	1.9
26. I would prefer to discuss my test scores with the counselor individually instead of in a student group.	4.9	3.8	15.5	47.9	27.9
Scale IV. Achievement Evaluation					
2. Discussing my test scores helped me to better understand my academic adjustment problems.	41.1	44.5	11.3	2.6	0.4
52. I didn't get enough useful information from the counseling to make any real decisions.	3.8	6.0	17.7	55.1	17.4

* Responses are reported in terms of the percentage of 265 freshmen marking Strongly Agree (SA), Agree (A), Undecided or Uncertain (U), Disagree (D), and Strongly Disagree (SD).

school quarter rank. Six student academic counselors, three men and three women, were randomly assigned to counsel same-sex counselee groups.

The Survey of Study Habits and Attitudes and the Effective Study Test were employed to evaluate the program's effectiveness in communicating information about efficient study procedures. Table 25 reports the comparative test-retest differential for coun-

TABLE 24

Scale Means and Standard Deviations for Counseling Evaluation
Questionnaires Completed Anonymously by 265 Freshmen
Counseled during October, 1959

Questionnaire Scale	Mean	Standard Deviation*
Counselor evaluation	18.36	6.16
Content evaluation	14.67	5.42
Climate evaluation	18.39	5.55
Achievement evaluation	15.31	6.29

* For positively worded statements, values of $+2$, $+1$, 0, -1, and -2 are assigned, respectively, to Strongly Agree, Agree, Undecided or Uncertain, Disagree, and Strongly Disagree. These scoring weights are reversed for negatively worded statements. The possible score range for each fifteen-item scale is thus $+30$ to -30, inclusive.

TABLE 25

Comparative Performance of Matched Experimental (Counseled)
and Control (Uncounseled) Samples on Two Immediate
Criteria of Counseling Effectiveness

Group	Sex	N	Survey of Study Habits and Attitudes		Effective Study Test	
			Test[a]	Retest[b]	Test[a]	Retest[b]
Counseled	Male	108	102.8	134.1*	94.3	104.8*
Uncounseled	Male	108	104.0	101.8	93.8	93.5
Counseled	Female	108	115.6	143.8*	98.8	111.4*
Uncounseled	Female	108	116.3	113.8	99.2	97.9

[a] Initial testing was accomplished on September 14–15, 1960.
[b] Retesting was accomplished on December 7–8, 1960.
* Counseled freshmen scored significantly higher than matching uncounseled freshmen on retest $(P = <.01)$.

seled and uncounseled freshmen on both measures of study behavior. From this table it may be noted that counseled men gained an average of 31.3 points on the Survey of Study Habits and Attitudes, while uncounseled men lost an average of 3.2 points over the same time period. On the same instrument, the 108 counseled women averaged a gain of 28.2 points, while the matching group of 108 uncounseled women averaged a loss of 2.5 points. Similar results are found when precounseling and postcounseling scores on the Effective Study Test are compared. From the data reported in Table 25 it may be concluded that the student academic counselors were successful in communicating information about effective study skills.

The impact of academic adjustment counseling on subsequent scholastic achievement was assessed by employing the first-semester point-hour ratio and quality-point total as criteria. The results of these analyses are reported in Table 26. Inspection of this table shows that counseled men earned semester grades averaging .4 letter-grade and 6.4 quality points higher than those earned by uncounseled men. The results for women were even more striking. Girls who were counseled averaged .6 letter-grade and 10.3 quality points higher than did those who were not counseled. From the data reported in Table 26 it may be concluded that the academic adjustment counseling produced significant improvement in the subsequent scholastic achievement of counseled freshmen.

The results of a different evaluation study are presented in Table 27. In this analysis, forty-one freshmen who missed the Survival Orientation briefing were individually paired with forty-one students present at the meeting. Students were carefully

TABLE 26

Comparative Performance of Matched Experimental (Counseled)
and Control (Uncounseled) Samples on Two Delayed
Criteria of Counseling Effectiveness

Group	Sex	N	Point-Hour Grade Average	Quality-Point Total
Counseled	Male	108	2.27*	21.2*
Uncounseled	Male	108	1.88	14.8
Counseled	Female	108	2.69*	28.0*
Uncounseled	Female	108	2.06	17.7

* Counseled freshmen earned significantly higher grades than did matching uncounseled freshmen ($P = <.01$).

TABLE 27
Significance of Differences between Total Score Means Obtained
for Matched Samples and Repeated Administrations
of the Effective Study Test

Testing Date	Absentee Sample (N=41)		Attending Sample (N=41)		P*
	Mean	S.D.	Mean	S.D.	
September 14–15, 1960	97.0	10.2	96.4	10.4	.80
October 18–19, 1960	95.8	10.4	115.5	8.9	<.001
P*		.60		<.001	

* Significance of difference between means was computed by the t-test.

matched on the following four variables: (*a*) age, (*b*) sex, (*c*) place of residence, and (*d*) total score on the Effective Study Test administered September 14–15, 1960. On December 7–8, 1960, the Effective Study Test was readministered to these students. Students attending the survival briefing scored 19.1 points higher on retest; absent students actually scored 1.2 points lower on retest. Clearly the student academic counselors succeeded in communicating to students present at the briefing information that was not acquired elsewhere by those who missed the meeting.

All freshmen receiving Survival Orientation briefings on September 28, 1960, were asked to complete the ten introductory phrases on a specially prepared Sentence Completion Survey. All responses were made anonymously, in that the freshmen were specifically instructed not to sign their names. The 108 completed blanks thus obtained were subsequently evaluated by a team of five graduate students. Each counselee's set of responses was evaluated as revealing a positive, ambivalent, or negative feeling tone toward the procedures and contents of the survival briefing. Typical examples of positively, ambivalently, and negatively completed sentences are given in Table 28. Of the 108 forms thus evaluated, 94, or 87.0 percent, were judged positive in feeling tone; 10, or 9.3 percent, were deemed ambivalent; and 4, or 3.7 percent, were rated negative. As revealed by the sentence-completion technique, the students' anonymous reaction to the Survival Orientation component would appear to be very favorable.

Finally, freshman acceptance of the two-hour Survival Orientation briefings by student academic counselors must be judged high on the basis of their response to the opportunity for further coun-

TABLE 28
Typical Positive, Ambivalent, and Negative Responses
Received on the Sentence Completion Survey

Positive Feeling Tone

1. The survival briefing *was just what we needed to wake us up.*
2. The survival facts *really shook my complacency.*
3. My study motivation *is probably below average and should be discussed with a counselor.*
4. My study skills *are terrible and must be improved quickly.*
5. The Effective Study Test *really showed me how poor my study habits are.*
6. The "Effective Study Guide" *should really help me improve my study habits.*
7. Time budgeting *is one of the keys to survival in college.*
8. Additional counseling *is something I really need to help me get straightened out.*
9. My future plans *are confused and I need help in working them out.*
10. Student counselors *are a wonderful idea because they know our problems better.*

Ambivalent Feeling Tone

1. The survival briefing *was well planned.*
2. The survival facts *are something to think about.*
3. My study motivation *is at least average.*
4. My study skills *are about average but could be improved.*
5. The Effective Study Test *showed about what I expected.*
6. The "Effective Study Guide" *ought to be interesting and helpful.*
7. Time budgeting *sounds terribly dull.*
8. Additional counseling *is probably a good idea for most freshmen.*
9. My future plans *are to get married next June.*
10. Student counselors *are a good idea I guess.*

Negative Feeling Tone

1. The survival briefing *was just a waste of time.*
2. The survival facts *are a lot of hot air.*

3. My study motivation *isn't as important as was made out.*
4. My study skills *are good enough to get by.*
5. The Effective Study Test *was a lot of nonsense.*
6. The "Effective Study Guide" *might be worth looking at.*
7. Time budgeting *is a waste of time.*
8. Additional counseling *is something I can very well do without.*
9. My future plans *are my own business.*
10. Student counselors *think they know it all.*

NOTE: The three sets of responses are reported exactly as received from the counselees.

seling by these counselors. At the conclusion of the meeting, freshmen were invited to sign up for Test Interpretation if they desired further counseling on their academic adjustment problems. Despite the admonition not to sign up unless seriously motivated, 83.2 percent of the freshmen in attendance did request this further counseling.

The research findings from these various investigations may be summarized as follows: (*a*) the student-counseling-student approach produced significant improvement in the study skills and academic attitudes of most counseled freshmen, (*b*) the counseled freshmen usually earned significantly better first-semester grades than did matched uncounseled students, (*c*) the anonymously obtained reactions of the majority of counseled freshmen were decisively positive to all evaluated aspects of the peer counseling program. It may be concluded, therefore, that student-to-student counseling to aid academic adjustment is an effective and acceptable counseling procedure for beginning college freshmen.

COMPARATIVE EFFECTIVENESS OF MALE
AND FEMALE STUDENT COUNSELORS

Findings from factorial investigations into the relationship between motivational orientation and scholastic success (5, 9, 45) had revealed characteristic differences in the role behavior of male and female freshmen. The factor analysis results suggested that motivational orientations should be interpreted in keeping with the disparity of experiences and expectations acquired in male and female sex roles. Research with the Survey of Study Habits and Attitudes (8, 47, 107) confirmed that freshman males and females exhibited significantly different beliefs, values, and expectations about academic activities. The response differences of men and women to the SSHA items indicated the likelihood of strong sex differences in such attributes as attitude, set, and motivation in the academic situation.

The identified differences in male and female scholastic motivation strongly suggested that the counseling process should take greater cognizance of the academic orientations of the two sexes. Consequently, it seemed desirable that male and female freshmen should be counseled by same-sex peer counselors and that the composition of counselee groups should be all male or all female. The logical basis for this arrangement, of course, was the belief that the initial academic adjustment problems of male and female freshmen differed significantly and that these problems were best understood and discussed by same-sex peer counselors. Numerous scheduling problems were created by this approach, however, so research was undertaken during the 1961–62 and 1962–63 academic years to evaluate systematically the success of male and female student academic counselors in counseling male and female freshmen. Specifically, the research project was designed to assess the comparative effectiveness and acceptability of male and female student academic counselors with stratified random samples of same-sex, opposite-sex, and mixed-sex counselees.

The 1961–62 and 1962–63 freshman classes at Southwest Texas State College furnished the research population for the investigation. The project utilized six stratified random samples of 120 beginning freshmen each, with half of each sample being drawn from each of the two freshman classes. During Survival Orientation, about one-third of the male and female counselees were counseled in mixed-sex groups, while the other two-thirds were counseled in all-male or all-female groups. Half of the all-male counselee groups received their counseling from same-sex student academic counselors and the other half were counseled by student academic counselors of the opposite sex. The same assignment of student academic counselors was also employed for the all-female counselee groups. Thus six categories of counselees were formed through random assignment: (*a*) male counselees with male counselors, (*b*) male counselees with female counselors, (*c*) female counselees with male counselors, (*d*) female counselees with female counselors, (*e*) mixed-sex counselees with male counselors, and (*f*) mixed-sex counselees with female counselors.

All freshmen in each category who signed up for Test Interpretation were ranked according to their composite scores on the American College Test. Six samples of 60 freshmen each were drawn each year, with one-third of each group having high ACT scores (22 or above), one-third having average ACT scores (19–21), and one-third having low ACT scores (18 or below). Freshmen in each of the six counselee samples were thus organized into counselee groups for Test Interpretation, with the four freshmen in each group being approximately matched on scholastic ability and study orientation.[5] Six student academic counselors, three men and three women, were each assigned to counsel five same-sex, five opposite-sex, and five mixed-sex counselee groups. Thus a stratified random sampling design was employed to provide six samples of approximately 120 counselees each over the two-year period.

Precounseling and postcounseling scores on the Survey of Study Habits and Attitudes and the Effective Study Test were employed to assess the comparative effectiveness of male and female student academic counselors. Table 29 reports these scores for all six counselee samples, together with the score gains on retest for both tests. Inspection of the data presented in this table reveals that the least effective counselor-counselee combination was the all-male counselee group with a female student academic counselor. On the other hand, male student academic counselors proved to be equally effective with all-male and all-female counselee groups. For both male and female student academic counselors, the most effective

[5] Scholastic ability and study orientation were assessed, respectively, by the American College Test and the Survey of Study Habits and Attitudes.

TABLE 29

Comparative Effectiveness of Male and Female Student Academic
Counselors with Stratified Random Samples of Same-Sex,
Opposite-Sex, and Mixed-Sex Counselees

Counselor Sex	Counselee Sex	N[a]	Survey of Study Habits and Attitudes			Effective Study Test		
			Test	Retest[b]	Gain	Test	Retest[b]	Gain
Female	Female	116	113.7	139.4	+25.7*	97.1	106.9	+ 9.8*
Female	Male	113	102.1	110.0	+ 7.9	92.9	98.9	+ 6.0*
Female	Mixed	117	109.0	135.2	+26.2*	95.3	105.6	+10.3*
Male	Female	119	114.0	142.5	+28.5*	97.3	107.4	+10.1*
Male	Male	116	101.2	128.0	+26.8*	93.1	102.8	+ 9.7*
Male	Mixed	114	108.4	139.8	+31.4*	96.0	108.2	+12.2*

[a] Number out of stratified random sample of 120 freshmen who completed required retesting as scheduled.
[b] Retesting was accomplished approximately ninety days following the initial testing of beginning freshmen.
* Counselees averaged significantly higher scores on retest $(P<.01)$.

counseling results were obtained with mixed-sex counselee groups.

Counselee reactions to the student-to-student counseling were obtained through postcounseling administration of the sixty-item Counseling Evaluation Questionnaire. A comparison of the evaluations made by each of the six counselee samples is given in Table 30. Examination of the data presented in this table reveals that the all-male counselee groups showed a significant preference for male counselors over female counselors, while the all-female and mixed-sex counselee groups did not show a meaningful counselor preference.

The research findings suggest two conclusions about the comparative effectiveness and acceptability of male and female student academic counselors. First, female student counselors are significantly less effective and less accepted than male student counselors in giving academic adjustment guidance to opposite-sex counselee groups. Second, male and female student counselors are equally effective with, and accepted by, either same-sex or mixed-sex counselee groups. These findings suggest that female student counselors

TABLE 30
Comparison of Counseling Evaluation Questionnaire Scores
for Male and Female Student Academic Counselors
Evaluated by Stratified Random Samples of Same-Sex,
Opposite-Sex, and Mixed-Sex Counselees

| | Sex Composition of Counselee Groups | | | | | |
| | Male Counselees | | Female Counselees | | Mixed Counselees | |
	Male Counselor	Female Counselor	Male Counselor	Female Counselor	Male Counselor	Female Counselor
N	116	113	119	116	114	117
$\bar{x}$	55.4	33.2	63.6	60.9	57.1	54.7
σ	25.1	30.7	28.3	29.6	26.9	27.8
$D\bar{x}$	22.2		2.7		2.4	
t	5.93		.75		.60	
P	<.01		>.10		>.10	

should not be assigned to give academic adjustment guidance to male freshman counselees, while no such restriction is indicated for male student counselors.

In view of the research findings reported earlier, it is not surprising that female student counselors were less effective than male student counselors in counseling all-male groups of freshmen about their academic adjustment problems. Significant sex-related differences in the academic beliefs, values, and expectations of freshmen enrolling at Southwest Texas State College had strongly suggested that the freshman counseling program should take cognizance of the different motivational orientations of the two sexes toward academic activities.

Since females were typically found to be more positive than males in their self-reported orientation toward all aspects of the academic environment, it logically follows that female student counselors would find it more difficult than male student counselors to understand and accept the negative attitudes displayed by many freshman males. Thus, the female student academic counselors could be expected to encounter difficulty in establishing and maintaining effective rapport with male freshmen because of their difficulty in empathizing with the male viewpoint about academic activities. In the absence of effective rapport, meaningful communication would be more difficult, with a consequent reduction in counselee acceptance of the suggestions offered during counseling.

The male student academic counselor is much less likely to experience such difficulties simply because he has had much more experience in understanding the masculine viewpoint. Furthermore, his greater experience in dealing with masculine behavior makes him better prepared to respond effectively to the typical masculine manner of expressing one's beliefs, values, and attitudes. In most cases, the female student academic counselor's difficulties are increased when counseling an all-male counselee group because the male counselees are likely to reinforce each other in the expression of negative views. In the mixed-sex counselee group, however, these problems are likely decreased because she finds support for her counseling efforts from the positive views expressed by the typical female counselees within the group. Thus, when counseling a mixed-sex group, the female student academic counselor is less likely to be pushed into a defensive position as a consequence of being outnumbered by counselees sharing a motivational orientation that is significantly different from her own.

Although this interpretation of the research results is not the only one that might be ventured, it does have the advantage of explaining the research findings in a meaningful way. In any event, the investigation suggests that it is probably unwise to assign female student counselors to counsel with all-male freshman groups on their academic adjustment problems.

COMPARATIVE EFFECTIVENESS OF STUDENT AND PROFESSIONAL COUNSELORS

Another approach to assessing the effectiveness and acceptability of student-to-student counseling was undertaken during the 1963–64 academic year. The purpose of this further research was to determine if student academic counselors were as effective and accepted as professional counselors in providing academic adjustment counseling to beginning college freshmen. Specifically, comparative evaluations were made on the following: effectiveness of

Recording Counseling Session. The counseling session is tape recorded to permit subsequent analysis of the trainee's counseling performance.

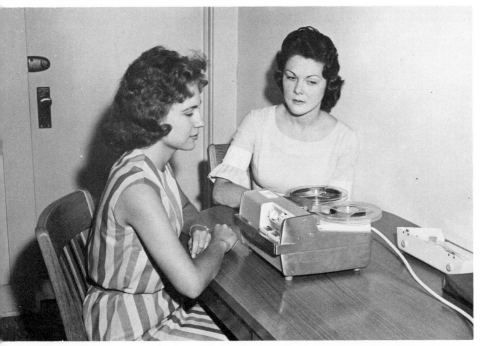

Evaluating Counseling Session. The trainee and an experienced student academic counselor listen together to the tape recording and discuss the trainee's counseling performance.

Demonstration Room. From the demonstration-room side, the one-way screen appears to be a mirror. Counselee concern about being observed is thus quickly dispelled because the observers remain invisible and anonymous.

Observation Room. From the observation-room side, the one-way screen serves as a window. Observers are thus able to see and hear everything occurring in the demonstration room without themselves being seen or heard by those being observed.

Survival Orientation Briefing. A friendly, informal atmosphere characterizes the two-hour discussion of academic survival problems faced by freshmen.

Test Interpretation Session. The seating arrangement is designed to both maximize group interaction and facilitate counselor control.

Study Habits Evaluation. Reporting of unsatisfactory mid-semester grades is accompanied by a thorough review of the counselee's residual study problems.

Study Skills Counseling. Samples of the counselee's own academic work provide the focus for an analysis of his scholastic difficulties.

the counseling in communicating information about academic adjustment problems and solutions, impact of the counseling upon subsequent academic achievement, and acceptability of such counseling by the counselees. A more detailed report of this investigation may be found elsewhere (130, 131).

Two female and two male professional counselors were selected and trained for the research project. Each of the four professional counselors met the following selection criteria: (*a*) certified as a secondary school counselor by the Texas Education Agency, (*b*) at least ten years older than the typical entering college freshman, (*c*) recommended by two professors who were primarily responsible for directing their professional training for counseling certification, (*d*) presently employed as a counselor with at least five years of professional teaching or counseling experience, and (*e*) advanced professionally to the master's degree level.

Eight upperclassmen, four males and four females, were selected and trained as student academic counselors for the research project. Seven of the students selected had sophomore classification, while one had junior standing. Only one of the students had experience as a student academic counselor prior to the fall semester of 1963. Both the professional counselors and the student counselors completed the regular training program for student academic counselors conducted by the Testing and Counseling Center at Southwest Texas State College. Table 16 provides a brief description of the twenty two-hour training sessions that comprise this training activity.

The total training time consisted of forty clock hours: thirty hours of initial instruction during the spring semester and ten hours of reviewing during the fall semester. Student and professional counselors were trained together for thirty-two of the forty clock hours of special training, with the remaining eight hours of segregated training consisting of practically identical reviews of the procedures and materials to be employed in Survival Orientation, Test Interpretation, Study Skills Counseling, and Study Habits Evaluation. The four professional and eight student academic counselors were thus trained by the same personnel, using the same training materials and providing the same training content.

The 1963-64 freshman class at Southwest Texas State College furnished the research population. The research utilized experimental and control samples drawn from the total freshman class. One hundred sixty entering freshmen, half males and half females, received the academic adjustment counseling from same-sex professional counselors. The 80 men and 80 women comprising this experimental sample were randomly selected from the 154 female and 187 male occupants of two selected freshman residence halls. Equivalent guidance from same-sex student academic counselors was given to all other freshmen residing in college housing. A control sample of 80 men and 80 women was subsequently drawn from those students counseled by student academic counselors. Students counseled by professional counselors were matched as closely as possible with students counseled by student counselors on the following variables: sex, chronological age, scholastic ability, study orientation, and high school quarter rank.[6] Counseling of the control and experimental groups was accomplished in the special counseling offices provided in each freshman residence hall. For all essential purposes, the residence halls and the counseling facilities were equivalent for the two groups.

The counseling activity sequence employed in this investigation was exactly the same as that reported in Table 12 except that freshman participation was required for the following four components: Survival Orientation, Test Interpretation, Study Skills Counseling, and Study Habits Evaluation. Also, both Test Interpretation and Study Skills Counseling were given in two-hour sessions to groups of four same-sex counselees. These changes are reflected in the description of required counseling activities given in Table 31.

The Effective Study Test was used to assess growth in study skills through a comparison of test-retest differential scores ob-

[6] Scholastic ability and study orientation were assessed, respectively, by the American College Test and the Survey of Study Habits and Attitudes.

TABLE 31

Counseling Activity Sequence Followed by Professional
and Student Counselors in Comparison Research

Meeting Number	Time Period	Size of Group	Length of Meeting	Activity
1	9/16/63 to 9/27/63	20	2 hours	*Survival Orientation:* Briefing session on college survival facts, academic adjustment problems, scholastic achievement standards, effective study behavior, time management principles, note taking techniques, and student assistance resources
2	9/30/63 to 10/17/63	4	2 hours	*Test Interpretation:* Counseling session on factors determining scholastic success, results of standardized ability and achievement tests, current study habits and attitudes, time budgeting problems, environmental variables influencing study efficiency, college rewards and frustrations, common personal-social adjustment problems, the give and take of dormitory life, and the factors influencing peer-group affiliation
3	10/21/63 to 11/7/63	4	2 hours	*Study Skills Counseling:* Counseling session on how to read and remember textbook material, take lecture and reading notes, write themes and reports, prepare for essay and objective examinations, and organize study time and place
4	11/25/63 to 11/27/63	1	½ hour	*Study Habits Evaluation:* Counseling session on probable causes for unsatisfactory mid-semester grade reports and appropriate corrective action for residual study organization, techniques, and motivation problems

tained through precounseling and postcounseling administrations. Comparison of scores on the Study Skills Surveys administered after all counseling was completed provided additional data for assessing changes in study organization, techniques, and motivation. Counselee reactions to critical aspects of the program were obtained from the sixty-item Counseling Evaluation Questionnaire described earlier in this chapter. Counselee retention of the information given during counseling was assessed by a specially constructed sixty-item Counseling Comprehension Test. Twenty questions—each to be answered true, undecided, or false—were provided for each of the three required two-hour counseling periods. Questions on the Counseling Comprehension Test covered material other than that included on the Effective Study Test. A copy of the Counseling Comprehension Test is included as Appendix S. Earned course grades at the end of the 1963 fall semester were used to evaluate counseling productivity. Two indices of scholastic success were computed—the point-hour grade ratio and the quality-point total. A four-point scale (A=4 and F=0) was employed in computing both measures of academic achievement.

Results of the statistical analyses are reported in Tables 32–37. Fisher's t-test for correlated means was employed in comparing differences between professional-counseled and student-counseled freshmen on the following criteria: (*a*) test-retest differential scores obtained from precounseling and postcounseling administrations of the Effective Study Test; (*b*) total scores on the Counseling Evaluation Questionnaire, Study Skills Surveys, and Counseling Comprehension Test obtained through postcounseling administrations; and (*c*) initial academic achievement as measured by first-semester point-hour ratios and quality-point totals. Each table reports the means and standard deviations for professional-counseled and student-counseled freshmen, together with the resulting t-test values and significance levels obtained when comparing the two groups. Data for each sex and for the combined group are presented in each table.

Table 32 reveals that professional and student academic counselors did not differ significantly in their ability to communicate information about effective study procedures, as measured by a comparison of test-retest differential scores from the Effective Study Test. This is the only criterion on which the hypothesis of no difference in counseling effectiveness is supported.

TABLE 32

Comparison of Test-Retest Differential Scores* Earned
by Professional-Counseled (PC) and Student-Counseled (SC)
Freshmen on the Effective Study Test

	Males		Females		Total	
	PC	SC	PC	SC	PC	SC
x̄	3.9	4.0	4.0	4.2	3.9	4.1
σ	10.3	9.4	5.6	5.4	8.2	7.6
t	.07		.30		.12	
P	>.10		>.10		>.10	

* Obtained by subtracting each counselee's precounseling score from his post-counseling score.

Table 33 indicates that student-counseled freshmen evaluated the counseling program significantly higher than did professional-counseled freshmen. Responses to items on the Counseling Evaluation Questionnaire clearly reveal that the counselees believed they received more useful information from the counseling program when the material was presented by student academic counselors.

The number of study organization, technique, and motivation problems remaining after counseling, as measured by the Study Skills Surveys, indicated that female freshmen counseled by student academic counselors made significantly better use of the study skills knowledge acquired during counseling. However, Table 34 does not show a comparable difference for male counselors.

TABLE 33

Comparison of Counseling Evaluation Questionnaire
Scores for Professional-Counseled (PC) and
Student-Counseled (SC) Freshmen

	Males		Females		Total	
	PC	SC	PC	SC	PC	SC
x̄	41.0	55.8	35.0	63.8	39.9	59.8
σ	32.5	22.6	33.0	26.1	31.0	24.7
t	2.78		6.09		5.89	
P	<.01		<.01		<.01	

TABLE 34

Comparison of Study Skills Surveys Scores for Professional-
Counseled (PC) and Student-Counseled (SC) Freshmen

	Males		Females		Total	
	PC	SC	PC	SC	PC	SC
x̄	38.4	38.2	38.9	41.8	38.7	40.1
σ	9.6	9.7	9.8	7.9	9.7	9.0
t		.11		2.04		1.16
P		>.10		<.05		>.10

From Table 35 it may be seen that student-counseled freshmen of both sexes retained significantly more of the information communicated about topics other than effective study procedures. As measured by the Counseling Comprehension Test, counselee retention of information given during the three two-hour counseling sessions was highest when the information was transmitted by student academic counselors.

Tables 36 and 37 report, respectively, a comparison of grade-point ratios and quality-point totals earned by professional-counseled and student-counseled freshmen during their first semester in college. Inspection of Table 36 reveals that the differences were not significant when grade-point ratios for males and females were analyzed separately. However, when male and female counselees are combined, a significant difference in favor of student-to-student counseling is obtained. Table 37 reveals a significant difference in

TABLE 35

Comparison of Counseling Comprehension Test Scores
for Professional-Counseled (PC) and
Student-Counseled (SC) Freshmen

	Males		Females		Total	
	PC	SC	PC	SC	PC	SC
x̄	40.3	43.1	42.7	44.5	41.7	43.8
σ	6.7	5.8	4.7	5.2	5.8	5.5
t		2.84		2.88		4.04
P		<.01		<.01		<.01

TABLE 36
Comparison of First-Semester Point-Hour Ratios
Earned by Professional-Counseled (PC) and
Student-Counseled (SC) Freshmen

	Males		Females		Total	
	PC	SC	PC	SC	PC	SC
x̄	1.77	2.06	2.30	2.47	2.04	2.27
σ	.82	.87	.84	.63	.86	.77
t		1.79		1.77		2.50
P	<.10	>.05	<.10	>.05		<.01

TABLE 37
Comparison of First-Semester Quality-Point Totals
Earned by Professional-Counseled (PC) and
Student-Counseled (SC) Freshmen

	Males		Females		Total	
	PC	SC	PC	SC	PC	SC
x̄	27.4	32.0	37.1	39.0	31.3	35.5
σ	14.1	14.8	14.0	10.6	14.7	13.2
t		2.30		1.25		2.63
P		<.02		>.10		<.01

favor of the student counselors for male counselees, but not for female counselees. However, as in the case of grade-point ratios, when the male and female counselees are combined, the significance of differences in quality-point totals is even more in favor of the student-counseled freshmen.

Three conclusions appear warranted by the research results. First, student counselors were as effective as professional counselors on all criteria of counseling productivity employed in this study. In fact, the student counselors achieved significantly better results than did the professional counselors on the majority of variables used to evaluate counseling outcome. Second, the student counselors received greater acceptance from counselees than did the professional counselors and were thus able to evoke better retention of most information communicated during counseling. Finally, freshmen counseled by student counselors made greater use of the information received during counseling, as reflected by earned grades and residual study problems.

From the findings of this study it appears reasonable to conclude that the use of carefully selected, trained, and supervised student academic counselors does provide a practical and productive addition to the college guidance program. The research results should not, however, be construed to suggest that the work of professional counselors can be replaced by student-counseling-student procedures in areas outside those in which the comparison was made. Within the constraints of the program described in the preceding chapter, however, student counselors have been found to be at least as effective and accepted as professional counselors.

SUCCESS OF STUDENT-TO-STUDENT COUNSELING
WITH LOW-ABILITY FRESHMEN

Research had demonstrated that student-to-student counseling on academic adjustment problems was both a practical and an effective means for increasing the chances of scholastic success for the average college freshman and that carefully selected and trained student counselors were as effective and as accepted as were professional counselors in providing such counseling. Of special interest, however, is the effectiveness of student-to-student counseling for freshmen identified as potential college dropouts. During the 1967–68 academic year, therefore, research was undertaken to evaluate systematically the effectiveness of student-to-student counseling upon the initial scholastic adjustment and subsequent academic survival of college freshmen identified as potential dropouts. A detailed report of this investigation may be found elsewhere (48, 125).

The research was specifically designed to evaluate the impact of the student-counseling-student approach upon the scholastic motivation, study behavior, and subsequent academic achievement of potential college dropouts. Experimental students were selected and given academic adjustment counseling, whereas an individually matched control group did not receive such counseling. Upon completion of counseling, the two matched groups were compared on four indices of counseling results—study orientation, study knowledge, study problems, and semester grade-point averages. In addition, the effectiveness and acceptability of the counseling program were evaluated by the experimental group.

Freshmen entering Southwest Texas State College with a composite standard score of eighteen or below on the American College Test were considered to be potential dropouts. Institutional research had demonstrated that freshmen who score eighteen and below have only one chance in three of continuing their second year in good standing. Experimental and control subjects were, therefore, limited to students who attained an ACT composite standard score of eighteen or below and were first-semester freshmen.

The *Student Counselor's Handbook* (21) served as a guide for the student academic counselors in using the materials and procedures developed for Survival Orientation, Test Interpretation, Study Skills Counseling, and Study Habits Evaluation. The student academic counselors were trained to accomplish the following activities during counseling: (*a*) to employ peer-group discussion procedures, (*b*) to communicate academic survival information, (*c*) to disseminate standardized test results, (*d*) to analyze potential academic and social adjustment problems, and (*e*) to initiate individualized corrective measures for identified problems. Where appropriate, the counseling approach was modified in ways that were likely to increase the acceptability of study skills counseling to beginning freshmen identified as potential college dropouts.

All entering freshmen were required to attend the two-hour Survival Orientation session as part of the college's general orientation program. Students met in groups of thirty and were counseled about general college adjustment problems by a team of two student academic counselors. At each group session all freshmen completed an information form giving their name, age, sex, high school size, high school quarter rank, enrollment classification, and college address. Student academic counselors then utilized the Testing and Counseling Center files to verify the recorded information and to add the ACT composite scores to each information form.

At the conclusion of Survival Orientation, all students with an ACT composite of eighteen or below were encouraged to register for additional academic adjustment counseling. The experimental group was selected from those potential dropouts who voluntarily participated in the postorientation activities of the counseling program. A like number of freshmen were selected from a control group of identified potential dropouts who had also volunteered for the additional counseling but who were subsequently unable or unwilling to participate in the project due to schedule conflicts or other obligations. The experimental and control subjects were individually matched on chronological age, sex, ACT composite score, high school quarter rank, and high school size. All subjects resided in college-operated residence halls. From the 124 potential dropouts receiving the additional counseling, 111 students (experimental group) were individually matched with 111 students (control group) who did not receive the additional counseling.

Students having a "D" or an "F" in a course at the end of the first nine weeks were sent an unsatisfactory progress report by their instructor. A copy of this mid-semester grade report was forwarded to the Testing and Counseling Center and the probable causes and possible cures for the failing work were discussed during the Study Habits Evaluation meeting. Table 38 provides a comparison of the mid-semester grades reported for the two matched groups of potential college dropouts. The 111 counseled freshmen received a total of 167 unsatisfactory progress reports at mid-semester; the 111 uncounseled freshmen received a total of 236 mid-semester notices of unsatisfactory grades. Uncounseled freshmen thus received 41.3 percent more unsatisfactory grade reports than did the freshmen receiving student-to-student counseling on their academic adjustment problems.

The SSHA and EST were administered to the experimental and control groups both before and after the experimental group received counseling. Comparisons of differences in precounseling and postcounseling scores provided one indication of the effectiveness of the student-to-student counseling received by the experimental group. Table 39 reports the comparative test-retest per-

TABLE 38
Comparison of Mid-Semester Grades Reported for Matched
Experimental (Counseled) and Control (Uncounseled)
Samples of Potential College Dropouts

Number of Unsatisfactory Reports Received	Counseled N	Counseled %	Uncounseled N	Uncounseled %
0	35	31.6	12	10.8
1	24	21.6	28	25.2
2	31	27.9	36	32.5
3	9	8.1	15	13.5
4	9	8.1	12	10.8
5	2	1.8	5	4.5
6	1	.9	3	2.7
Total	111	100.0	111	100.0

TABLE 39
Comparative Test-Retest Performance of Matched
Experimental (Counseled) and Control (Uncounseled)
Samples of Potential College Dropouts

Group	N	Survey of Study Habits and Attitudes Test	Survey of Study Habits and Attitudes Retest[a]	Effective Study Test Test	Effective Study Test Retest[a]
Counseled	111	98.6	112.1*	99.8	103.5*
Uncounseled	111	99.2	99.3	99.9	99.3

[a] Retesting was accomplished approximately ninety days after initial testing of beginning freshmen.
* Counseled freshmen scored significantly higher than matching uncounseled freshmen $(P < .01)$.

formance for the matched groups of counseled and uncounseled freshmen identified as potential college dropouts. Inspection of the SSHA data reveals a significant positive change in the measured study orientation of the experimental group, whereas no significant change occurred for the control group. Inspection of the EST data indicates that members of the experimental group significantly increased their knowledge about effective methods of study, whereas those in the control group remained relatively unchanged in their study-skills knowledge. Thus the additional student-to-student counseling on effective study skills and positive study attitudes produced significant improvement in these areas which are so vitally important to the academic survival of potential college dropouts.

Comparisons of postcounseling scores on the Study Skills Surveys for the experimental and control groups provided additional data for assessing changes in study organization, techniques, and motivation. Table 40 reports the means, standard deviations, t-test values, and significance levels obtained through this statistical comparison. From Table 40 it may be seen that there was a significant difference in self-reported study problems in favor of the experimental group. These results indicate that students receiving the additional academic adjustment counseling from student counselors not only improved their study procedures and increased their how-to-study knowledge, but also reported significantly fewer study skills problems than did students who did not receive this additional counseling.

The counseling program's productivity was evaluated through a comparison of first-semester grade-point averages. Grade-point averages were calculated on the basis of 4, 3, 2, 1, and 0 points for the letter grades of *A*, *B*, *C*, *D*, and *F*, respectively. Table 40 also

TABLE 40

Comparative Postcounseling Study Skills Problems and Grade-Point Averages for Matched Experimental (Counseled) and Control (Uncounseled) Samples of Potential College Dropouts

	Study Skills Survey		Grade-Point Average	
	Counseled	Uncounseled	Counseled	Uncounseled
N	111	111	111	111
$\bar{x}$	34.9	30.3	1.77	1.52
σ	9.5	8.7	.72	.70
D$\bar{x}$		4.6		.25
t		2.09		3.13
p		$<.05$		$<.01$

gives the results for the comparison of grade-point averages earned by the counseled and uncounseled samples. Again, examination of the research data reveals that there was a significant difference in earned grades in favor of the potential dropouts who received the additional student-to-student counseling.

The Counseling Evaluation Questionnaire was anonymously administered to the experimental students after completion of the counseling program. Tabulation of responses to all sixty statements indicated that the experimental students' reactions were decisively positive to *all* evaluated aspects of the program. Furthermore, the strongest aspect of the counseling program, as perceived by the counselees themselves, was the student-to-student approach, while the weakest perceived aspect of the program was the lack of sufficient time for comprehensive discussion of identified study skills problems. These two factors appear to complement each other, in that it would appear that counselees would want more time to discuss their study skills problems with student academic counselors only if such counseling was meaningful and acceptable to the counselees.

In summary, several specific conclusions appear warranted by the research results. First, potential dropouts receiving the additional student-to-student counseling showed significant positive changes in their measured study orientation and study knowledge as indicated on the SSHA and the EST, respectively, whereas potential dropouts not receiving such counseling did not show such improvement. Second, the counseled group reported fewer residual study problems, as indicated on the SSS, than did the group that received only the orientation counseling. In fact, students receiving additional counseling over and beyond the orientation counseling showed significant improvement on all variables measuring effective study procedures and scholastic motivation. Third, students receiving the additional counseling made significantly better grade averages than did matching students not receiving such help, thereby suggesting that the counselees were putting the information received during counseling to effective use. Finally, the counselee's evaluation of the counseling program, as indicated on the Counseling Evaluation Questionnaire, was decisively positive on all evaluated aspects of the counseling program.

From the findings of this study, it appears reasonable to accept the following general conclusion: Student-to-student counseling designed to improve study skills, scholastic motivation, and academic achievement is a practical and productive means of aiding the student whose measured potential for successfully completing college is questionable.

5. Adaptability of Student-to-Student Counseling

During the ten-year period between 1960 and 1969, the model program described in Chapter 4 has been adapted to fit a variety of counseling situations. Appropriate modification of counseling procedures and materials has resulted in a variety of programs for high school and college students. High school programs have included student-to-student counseling activities for the college-bound and for the educationally disadvantaged; college-level programs have included college preparation seminars and scholastic probation clinics. Finally, the counseling materials developed for the student-counseling-student approach have been translated into Spanish, and the procedure has been tried and evaluated in Mexico. Student-to-student counseling for study skills improvement has thus proven to be a procedure that is readily adaptable to a wide range of counselees and conditions.

ADAPTABILITY TO COLLEGE SITUATIONS

The student-counseling-student approach has been successfully adapted to college preparation seminars offered prior to college entrance, to college orientation courses taught subsequent to initial enrollment, and to scholastic probation clinics following an unsatisfactory first semester. In the first program, student and professional counselors worked closely together in a true teamwork approach to the counseling effort; in the other two, professional counselors and student counselors worked independently except for the necessary training and supervision of the student counselors.

College Adjustment Seminar

A twelve-hour privately operated, tuition-financed college preparation course, called College Adjustment Seminar, was initiated on the campuses of several Texas high schools and colleges in the summer of 1962. The course content was designed to better prepare the college-bound high school graduates to handle the academic and social problems that they were certain to encounter in college. The program was a logical extension of the successful student-to-student counseling program at Southwest Texas State College and employed, with appropriate modification and adaptation, most of the counseling procedures and materials that had been developed for the Survival Orientation, Test Interpretation, and Study Skills Counseling components of the freshman counseling program described in Chapter 3.

In introducing the seminar, appropriate college administrators and personnel workers at twenty-two Texas colleges and appropriate school administrators and counselors in Austin, San Antonio, Houston, Dallas, and Fort Worth were thoroughly briefed about the program and why it was needed. In almost every instance, the reaction received from college presidents, deans, and personnel workers and from school superintendents, principals, and guidance counselors was positive and cooperative in every respect. The few reservations that were expressed during more than seventy such briefings concerned the use of student-to-student counseling as a major element of the seminar operation. In every instance, these reservations were alleviated, if not eliminated, by an explanation of the procedures employed in the selection, training, and supervision of the student counselors.

The seminars were advertised by obtaining address lists of college-bound seniors from cooperative high schools and then mailing descriptive brochures to the students shortly after high school graduation. The initial brochure was mailed out about eight weeks before a seminar was scheduled and a follow-up brochure was mailed out about four weeks later. Altogether, the advertising materials were sent to approximately thirty thousand students annually, with about 7 percent of those contacted eventually enrolling in one of the sixteen College Adjustment Seminars that were offered each summer. During the eight summers between June, 1962, and September, 1969, over fifteen thousand college-bound students voluntarily enrolled in the program. Tuition for the twelve clock hours of instruction was $25.00.

All teaching and counseling activities were accomplished during eight 1½-hour units. Depending upon the local situation, these eight instructional units could be presented during two full days or four half days, whichever was more desirable. About 60 percent of the information presented during the eight sessions dealt with the development of effective study habits and the other 40 percent of the instructional content dealt with the importance of positive study attitudes. A course outline for the four instructional units is given as Table 41. A 22-minute film (35) has been developed to explain the College Adjustment Seminar. Narrated by one of the student counselors, the film provides a detailed examination of the instructional objectives, teaching techniques, and counseling materials developed for the course.

The seminars were usually held during July and August on eight or more Texas college campuses.[1] In addition to the director, the seminar staff normally included a visiting professor, four student counselors, a psychometrist, and part-time clerical help recruited locally as needed. Where necessary, additional student

[1] Seminars have been held at the following colleges: Abilene Christian College, Angelo State College, Baylor University, Del Mar College, Houston Baptist College, Incarnate Word College, McMurry College, San Antonio College, Southwest Texas State College, University of Texas at Arlington, and West Texas State University.

TABLE 41
College Adjustment Seminar Course Outline

Period	Staff	Activity

First half-day unit	Seminar director and student counselors	Examine collegiate academic demands
		  College preparation requirements
		  College survival facts
		  College success factors
		  College adjustment problems
		
		Examine collegiate social problems
		  Problems of self-reliance
		  Problems of group living
		  Problems of extracurricular participation
		  Problems of social activities
		
		Analyze your current study habits and attitudes
		  Examine your study behavior
		  Examine your study methods
		  Examine your attitudes toward teachers
		  Examine your attitudes toward learning
		
		Discuss note taking problems
		  How to improve your listening comprehension
		  How to improve content and organization of notes
		  Formula for efficient note taking

Second half-day unit	Student counselors and visiting professor	Report results from Survey of Study Habits and Attitudes
		Discuss time budgeting problems
		  How to schedule your classes and labs
		  How to schedule your studying
		  Formula for efficient time budgeting
		
		Discuss study environment problems
		  How to organize your room
		  How to use the library
		  Formula for efficient study environment
		
		Question-and-answer period on study organization
		LECTURE: "What the College Professor Expects
		  of the Student"
		  Expectations of the college administration
		  Expectations of the professors
		  Expectations of the other students
		  Practical exercise in taking lecture notes
		  Question-and-answer period on college expectations

rd	Student	Discuss textbook reading problems
f-day	counselors	How to improve your reading comprehension
t		How to reduce rate and amount of forgetting
		Formula for efficient textbook reading

Discuss report writing problems
How to collect your research materials
How to prepare your research report
Formula for efficient report writing

Discuss test taking problems
How to prepare for essay and objective tests
How to write essay and objective tests
Formula for efficient test taking

Question-and-answer period on study techniques

Evaluate your current study effectiveness
Examine your study organization
Examine your reading behavior
Examine your writing behavior
Examine your examination behavior

rth	Seminar	Survey sources where freshmen can get help
f-day	director	Course instructors
t	and	Faculty advisors
	student	Personnel services
	counselors	Private tutoring

Report results of Study Effectiveness evaluation

FILM: "I Wish I'd Known That before I Went to College"

Inventory the rewards of college
The reward of job preparation
The reward of gaining knowledge
The reward of having fun
The reward of meeting people

Summarize and evaluate seminar content

counselors were added so as to maintain a student-counselor ratio of about thirty to one. The seminar director served as the overall coordinator of program activities and was responsible for opening and closing each session and for introducing each of the various topics to be covered. The visiting professor, an experienced English instructor, gave a fifty-minute lecture, "What the College Professor Expects of the Student," which presented the faculty viewpoint about how the student could best cope with college academic requirements, especially those for the first-year English course required on almost all college campuses. A team teaching approach prevailed throughout the course with the student counselors presenting a major portion of the instruction and the seminar director and visiting professor, together, providing less than 30 percent of the instructional content.

EVALUATION OF THE 1962 SEMINARS

The 323 students attending the eighteen seminars offered during the summer of 1962 provided the research sample for the first systematic evaluation of the College Adjustment Seminar (50). Immediately following the final 1½-hour session, all seminar students were asked to complete sentence stems designed to elicit evaluations of four specific aspects of the program: (*a*) seminar personnel, (*b*) course contents, (*c*) counseling materials, and (*d*) instructional procedures. The students were mailed a follow-up evaluation questionnaire approximately forty-five days after completion of their fall semester in college. Completed follow-up questionnaires were subsequently returned by 85 percent of the college freshmen who had attended the seminars.

Specially constructed nine-point rating scales were employed to evaluate student response to the two sentence completion questionnaires. Using these rating scales as a guide, two independent evaluators read each student's sentence completions and evaluated the student's perception, before and after college attendance, of the relative value of the study habits counseling and study attitudes counseling received during the seminar. Judgments from the two independent evaluators were then pooled to provide four sets of data derived from the two sentence completion questionnaires: (*a*) immediate evaluation of study habits content, (*b*) delayed evaluation of study habits content, (*c*) immediate evaluation of study attitudes content, and (*d*) delayed evaluation of study attitudes content. Copies of the Sentence Completion Survey and the two rating scales used in the evaluation may be found in Appendices T, U, and V.

Table 42 gives the percentage of seminar students judged to be in each of the nine categories of the rating scale continua for both immediate and delayed evaluations of the seminar's study habits content and study attitudes content. Table 43 provides a statistical comparison of the four sets of data derived from the student evaluations. Inspection of Table 42 indicates a strong, positive student reaction to the study habits content and the study attitudes content both before and after college attendance. However, the statistical analysis provided in Table 43 shows a significant change in the student perceptions made before and after college attendance. Student reactions to the seminar's study habits instruction, although still highly favorable, were significantly less positive after college attendance than they were prior to attending college, while student assessments of the value of the seminar's study attitudes instruction increased somewhat after a semester of college experience. More

TABLE 42

Percentage of Students in Each Rating Scale Category for the
Initial and Follow-up Evaluations of the
College Adjustment Seminar (1962)

Rating Scale Category	Study Habits Content		Study Attitudes Content	
	Initial Evaluation[a]	Follow-up Evaluation[b]	Initial Evaluation[a]	Follow-up Evaluation[b]
9 Strongly Positive	4%	1%	3%	5%
8	20	13	14	17
7 Positive	46	43	34	36
6	26	30	27	20
5 Ambivalent	4	4	20	20
4	0	3	1	2
3 Negative	0	3	1	0
2	0	2	0	0
1 Strongly Negative	0	1	0	0
Mean Rating	6.93	6.41	6.49	6.60

[a] Initial evaluation was made by students immediately following the final 1½-hour session of the 12-hour College Adjustment Seminar.

[b] Follow-up evaluation was made by students approximately 45–60 days after completion of their fall semester at college.

TABLE 43

Comparison of Student Evaluations of College Adjustment Seminar
Study Habits Content and Study Attitudes Content Made
before and after College Attendance (1962)

	Study Habits Content Evaluation		Study Attitudes Content Evaluation	
	Before College Attendance[a]	After College Attendance[b]	Before College Attendance[a]	After College Attendance[b]
N	204	204	204	204
$\bar{x}$	6.93	6.41	6.49	6.60
σ	.89	1.37	1.14	1.27
$D\bar{x}$		− .52		.11
t		−4.81		1.18
P		$<.001$		$<.30$ $>.20$

	Evaluation before College Attendance[a]		Evaluation after College Attendance[b]	
	Study Habits Content	Study Attitudes Content	Study Habits Content	Study Attitudes Content
N	204	204	204	204
$\bar{x}$	6.93	6.49	6.41	6.60
σ	.89	1.14	1.37	1.27
$D\bar{x}$		− .44		.19
t		−5.31		2.20
P		$<.001$		$<.05$ $>.02$

[a] Initial evaluation was made by students immediately following the final 1½-hour session of the 12-hour College Adjustment Seminar.

[b] Follow-up evaluation was made by students approximately 45–60 days after completion of their fall semester at college.

specifically, evaluation of the seminar's study habits content was significantly higher before college attendance, whereas evaluation of the seminar's study attitudes content was significantly higher following college experience. A significant reversal had thus occurred in the students' evaluation of the seminar's two instructional content areas, thus demonstrating once again the importance of providing meaningful motivational orientation counseling for incoming college freshmen.

Analysis of student responses to the individual sentence completion items also revealed a strong, positive student acceptance of the student-counseling-student approach. Analysis of the question-naires completed prior to college attendance revealed that 88 percent of the comments made about the student counselors were positive or strongly positive, whereas only 2 percent were of a negative nature. Student comments made about their student counselors following college attendance were likewise overwhelmingly positive, with only three negative ratings being received.

The follow-up questionnaire provided space for the student to report the courses taken and grades earned during his initial semester in college. Analysis of this data was undertaken in order to determine the number of semester hours passed and the number of quality points earned by each seminar student. Using the standard for determining scholastic probation employed by most Texas colleges,[2] it was found that only 10.8 percent of the seminar students would have been placed on scholastic probation as a consequence of their first-semester grades. The obtained scholastic probation rate was then compared with available scholastic probation figures for the six Texas colleges attended by ten or more of the seminar students. Although concrete data on first-semester scholastic probations were very limited, the best available data reflected a typical first-semester scholastic probation rate of about 24.5 percent. While the finding must be regarded as tentative, it would thus appear that the usual scholastic probation rate for beginning college freshmen is approximately two and one-half times that found for the seminar students in the 1962 study. Furthermore, none of the seminar students withdrew from college during their first semester as compared with a 2.5 percent reported rate of freshman withdrawal during the initial semester of college attendance.

The follow-up questionnaire also provided space for the students to make additional comments about the seminar if they so desired. Over two-thirds of the responding students did make such spon-

---

2 At most Texas senior colleges, the requirement for avoiding scholastic probation is nine quality points earned and nine hours of course work passed for the semester. Thus a student is classified as being on scholastic probation if he has not passed at least nine semester hours with a grade of "D" or better and if his earned quality points do not total at least nine.

taneous comments, and all such comments were favorable to the program. So that the reader may comprehend more fully the nature of the student response to the course, two dozen of these comments are presented in Table 44. The comments cited, together with the quantitative analyses reported in Tables 42 and 43, seem to indicate that the College Adjustment Seminar did have a

TABLE 44

Typical Volunteered Student Comments about the College Adjustment Seminar Made after One Semester of College Attendance (1962)

I do not believe that I would have made it through the first semester if it were not for your course.

The techniques and methods learned at the seminar make studying much more enjoyable and often very interesting.

It is great preparation for college. It tells you the hard facts about college and what to do about them.

It provided the basis for a self-help program when I ran into academic difficulties.

The seminar shocked me into realizing that it is sink or swim in college, depending entirely on how willing you are to work.

It gave me the initiative and desire to work and study hard.

I found myself two steps ahead of most of my freshman friends because of the advice obtained from the seminar.

From the taking of notes to the taking of exams, a person learns how to better cope with college situations.

Its main value to me was in showing me what I could expect in college and in improving my attitude scholastically.

I have made some of the better grades of my educational career in college. I feel this seminar has helped me by giving me a better understanding of how to study.

The seminar made me aware of the fact that I was about to join a scholastic institution in which grades are not given, but earned through many hours of study.

The period of adjustment takes a shorter time after having the seminar because it prepares you for the initial shock of college.

Most of the methods that the seminar taught worked for me with beautiful results.

When college academic demands came up that were new to me, I was better able to take them in stride because of the guidance I had received.

The seminar gave my self-confidence a tremendous boost and made me feel that maybe college wouldn't be impossible if I was willing to put forth the effort.

Without the seminar I am sure that I would now be on scholastic probation.

The seminar has proved to be invaluable to me. I had no idea previously how poorly prepared for college I really was.

The seminar should be advertised more extensively, as everyone needs it. I think that it has been worth far more than the $25 I paid.

I liked the way you proved to me how beneficial good study habits can be. My parents have been trying to get this across to me for seventeen years.

It enabled me to view college life realistically before actually experiencing it because we were given first-hand information told like it really is.

If followed, the suggestions allow the student to make better grades, in less time, to learn more, and to have more spare time.

It prepared me psychologically by making me realize that college would be difficult but not impossible.

I think that it is about the best preparation for college that I and some of my friends have found for building the proper attitudes and being prepared.

It makes a student realize that college is not at all like high school in that it is much more competitive and a student has much more personal responsibility.

---

marked effect upon the subsequent scholastic behavior and motivation of many of the students taking the course.

EVALUATION OF THE 1966 SEMINARS

The 2,193 college-bound students attending the fourteen seminars offered during the summer of 1966 provided the research samples for a second evaluation of the program.[3] Immediately following the final 1½-hour session, all seminar students were asked to complete the fifteen sentence stems designed to elicit student reaction to critical aspects of the program. Table 45 reports the percentage of seminar students giving positive, ambivalent, and negative responses to the five sentence completion items that dealt

---

[3] College Adjustment Seminars were held on the following Texas college campuses during the summer of 1966: Abilene Christian College, Angelo State College, Arlington State College, Baylor University, Del Mar College, Houston Baptist College, McMurry College, San Antonio College, and Southwest Texas State College.

TABLE 45

Percentage of 2,193 Students Giving Positive, Ambivalent, and Negative
Responses to Selected Sentence Completion Items
on the CAS Evaluation Questionnaire (1966)

	Stem for Sentence Completion Items				
Evaluation Category	The handout materials...	The student counselors...	The professional counselors...	The information presented...	The seminar atmosphere
Strongly positive	18%	33%	18%	27%	30%
Positive	60	55	59	61	57
Ambivalent	15	10	17	8	9
Negative	5	2	4	3	4
Strongly negative	2	0	2	1	0

with seminar personnel, content, and materials. Again, the student reaction was decisively positive to all evaluated areas of the program, with the response to student-to-student counseling being the most positive of all.

In order to determine the seminar's impact upon first-semester academic achievement, 194 seminar students were individually matched with 194 students that did not receive this special pre-college instruction. All students in both samples entered Southwest Texas State College in September, 1966, and the seminar and control students were individually matched, within very narrow limits,[4] on the following variables: sex, chronological age, place of residence, composite score on the American College Test, total score on the Survey of Study Habits and Attitudes, and employment status. All students in both samples resided in freshman residence halls, and seminar students employed part-time were matched with control students holding part-time jobs during the fall semester.

Tables 46 and 47 provide a comparison of the first-semester academic achievement for the two samples. As may be seen from Table 46, students attending the College Adjustment Seminar earned

[4] Matching limits employed were as follows: chronological age within ±1 year, ACT composite score within ±2 standard score points, and SSHA total score within ±10 percentile points.

TABLE 46
Comparison of First-Semester Grade-Point Averages for Matched
Samples of Students Attending and Not Attending
the College Adjustment Seminar (1966)

	Seminar Students	Control Students
N	194	194
$\bar{x}$	2.28	1.81
σ	.74	.77
$D\bar{x}$	.47	
t	9.65	
P	<.001	

TABLE 47
Comparative First-Semester Academic Achievement Status of Matched
Samples of Students Attending and Not Attending
the College Adjustment Seminar (1966)

Group	N	Scholastic Achievement Category		
		Scholastic Honors List	Unlisted	Scholastic Probation List
Seminar students	194	16%	73%	11%
Control students	194	7	63	30

grades averaging almost one-half letter grade higher than did matching students not attending the seminar. As a result, 16 percent of the seminar students made the scholastic honors list for the fall semester, while only 7 percent of the students not attending the seminar did so. By contrast, 30 percent of the nonseminar students were placed on scholastic probation after the fall semester as compared with only 11 percent of the seminar students.

Test-retest performance on two measures of study skills likewise showed significant differences between the matching samples of students attending and not attending the College Adjustment Seminar. Whereas the retest scores for seminar students showed gains of 40 and 50 centile points, respectively, on the Survey of Study Habits and Attitudes and the Effective Study Test, the retest scores for students not attending the seminar showed a slight loss on both instruments. As may be seen from Table 48, the retest scores obtained approximately sixteen weeks following the seminar were significantly higher than the precourse scores made by the seminar students. No such test-retest difference was found for the control sample.

It might be argued that the obtained results are "suspect" or "contaminated" because the seminar students could have been a highly selected group in the sense of their having such advantages as positive parental reinforcement, better educational background, positive academic motivation, or affluent family life style. Evaluation of available data on the seminar students—college entrance examination scores, high school attended, home address, ethnic group membership, initial study skills test scores—does not support such an argument. From these data, the seminar students appear to represent a fairly typical cross-section of the beginning college freshmen enrolling in Texas junior colleges, senior colleges, and universities.

Results obtained from evaluations of the 1962 and 1966 College Adjustment Seminars appear to warrant the following conclusions:

TABLE 48
Comparative Test-Retest Performance on Two Study Skills Measures
for Matched Samples of Students Attending and Not Attending
the College Adjustment Seminar (1966)

Group	N	Survey of Study Habits and Attitudes				Effective Study Test			
		Precourse[a]		Postcourse[b]		Precourse[a]		Postcourse[b]	
		Score	Centile	Score	Centile	Score	Centile	Score	Centile
Seminar students	194	109.4	40	139.4*	80	96.4	25	108.3*	75
Control students	194	110.2	45	108.3	40	97.1	25	96.2	25

[a] Precourse administration of SSHA and EST was accomplished at beginning of initial session for seminar students and at beginning of fall semester of college academic year for control students.

[b] Postcourse administration of SSHA and EST was accomplished on December 14–15, 1966, for both seminar students and control students.

* Seminar students earned significantly higher grades than did matching control students $(P = <.01)$.

(*a*) spontaneous comments made by seminar students indicate a high degree of acceptance for all evaluated aspects of the twelve-hour program, (*b*) test-retest procedures show significant pre-course-to-postcourse increases in the measured study skills of most students attending the seminar, (*c*) the average first-semester scholastic achievement of seminar students is significantly higher than that for college students of comparable ability not attending the seminar, and (*d*) study habits instruction is likely to be more positively valued before than after college experience, while the reverse is true for study attitudes instruction.

Required Orientation Course

In an effort to correct inefficient study behavior, colleges and universities have introduced systematic programs designed to promote reading and writing skills, as well as note taking, time budgeting, library usage, and test taking facilities. For the newly arrived freshman, college academic life can be a highly confusing experience. The regulations to be learned, the study procedures to be mastered, the academic values to be accepted—all constitute a new learning environment to which the student must adjust.

At Stephen F. Austin State College, Nacogdoches, Texas, a required orientation course offered three days a week for five weeks had provided the needed assistance in adjusting to this new learning environment. However, college officials had decided that, effective with the fall semester of 1964, the orientation course would be discontinued because of the growing reluctance of the state government to appropriate funds for remedial instruction in college. Fortunately, the trend toward open admissions has subsequently led to a reversal of opinion about the need for remedial courses, especially for beginning students coming from economically and educationally disadvantaged backgrounds. The attitudes prevailing at that time, however, led to the employment, in 1963–64, of an experimental peer-group counseling approach in an attempt to develop a program of academic adjustment counseling that would replace the orientation course. It was hoped that student counselors would be able to obtain the same results as a professional staff, thereby permitting the continuation of freshman orientation by utilizing student counselors to provide all or most of the instruction. Dr. B. L. Covin, director of guidance at the college, served as project director for the experiment. A detailed report of the experimental procedures and findings is available elsewhere (54).

Nine student counselors from the 1962 sophomore and junior classes, four men and five women, were selected by the Stephen F. Austin State College Student Personnel and Guidance Committee on the recommendation of the director of guidance. Each was in the upper third of his class and was selected on the basis of three criteria: (a) academic achievement as measured by grades earned, (b) academic ability as measured by entrance examinations, and (c) peer acceptance as evaluated by the Student Personnel and Guidance Committee. Personality attributes of each prospective counselor also were taken into consideration. Each student counselor thus chosen completed a special twenty-hour training program conducted in the spring of 1963, plus five hours of refresher training given in the fall prior to the arrival of the entering freshmen. Lecture outlines, discussion guides, and the Activity Sequence Check List, as well as other training aids borrowed from the program at Southwest Texas State College, were used to facilitate this instruction of student counselors.

Two samples of 170 students, 86 men and 84 women, were taken from the 863 freshmen enrolled in the orientation course offered at Stephen F. Austin State College during the fall semester of 1963. Students in the control (uncounseled) sample were individually matched, within very narrow limits,[5] with those in the experimental (counseled) sample on the following variables: sex, chronological age, high school quarter rank, size of high school, and ACT composite score.

Two approaches to the orientation course were employed in the study. For the control group, all the fifteen one-hour meetings were taught by a full-time faculty member, and classes were held at 7

[5] The matching limits employed were as follows: chronological age within ±1 year and ACT composite score within ±2 standard score points.

A.M. each Monday, Wednesday, and Friday for five weeks. For the experimental group, nine of the fifteen meetings were taught by a full-time faculty member with classes being held at 7 A.M., while the other six classes were held at the students' convenience, either in the afternoon or at night, and academic adjustment counseling was given by one of the student counselors. Freshmen in the experimental group were organized into fifty-four counseling groups, with the four students in each group being carefully matched as to sex, academic ability, and high school quarter rank. A satisfactory matching from the control (uncounseled) sample of 647 students could not be made for 46 of the 216 students comprising the experimental (counseled) sample.

TABLE 49

Comparative Academic Achievement of Experimental and Control Samples
of Freshmen Enrolled in a Required College Orientation Course
(Stephen F. Austin State College, Nacogdoches, Texas)

Female Sample		Male Sample		Total Sample	
Experimental[a]	Control[b]	Experimental[a]	Control[b]	Experimental[a]	Control[b]
demic Achievement as Measured by Grade-Point Average					
84	84	86	86	170	170
2.21	2.11	1.60	1.71	1.90	1.91
.77	.76	.90	.90	.91	.92
	.10		− .11		−.01
	1.13		−1.18		−.07
	>.10		>.10		>.10
demic Achievement as Measured by Quality-Point Total					
84	84	86	86	170	170
33.61	31.35	23.92	24.09	28.71	27.68
12.25	13.08	14.39	13.63	14.22	13.84
	2.26		−.17		1.03
	1.49		−.25		.78
	>.10		>.10		>.10

Received nine clock hours of instruction from faculty members and six clock hours of lent-to-student counseling from student counselors.
Received fifteen clock hours of instruction from faculty members.

Grade-point averages and total quality points earned during the fall semester of the 1963–64 academic year were used to evaluate the effectiveness of the two orientation approaches. The comparative academic achievement data for the matched experimental and control samples are reported in Table 49. No significant difference between experimental and control samples was found on either of the academic achievement criteria, thereby supporting the hypothesis that student counselors and regular faculty members could present selected sections of the freshman orientation course with equal effectiveness. Thus, the research results suggested that the student-counseling-student approach could be an effective replacement for the faculty-taught orientation course that was being discontinued.

Scholastic Probation Clinic

At Arlington State College, Arlington, Texas,[6] as at most other tax-supported colleges having modest admissions requirements, academic policy requires that students with low grade-point averages be placed on scholastic probation; then if grades do not improve the students are dropped from college for a period of time. The placing of students on scholastic probation probably provides some motivation for better academic success; however, placing students on probation appears to have little, if any, influence on deficient study habits and attitudes. Consequently, the College Counseling Center had been seeking more effective ways of providing assistance to students placed on scholastic probation.

It seemed reasonable to combine the idea of student-to-student counseling with that of providing assistance to students on probation. In addition, it appeared reasonable to assume that students on the honor roll, presumably with good academic adjustment, would be excellent prospects for recruiting student counselors. Consequently, an experimental Study Skills Clinic, utilizing the student-counseling-student approach, was initiated at Arlington State College in 1963. Dr. W. J. Karraker, director of testing and counseling

[6] Now, The University of Texas at Arlington.

at the college, served as project director for the experimental guidance program. A detailed project report is available elsewhere (89).

The effectiveness of such student-to-student counseling at Arlington State College was then investigated through two research projects. The 1963–64 study featured student-to-student counseling for freshmen on scholastic probation. In 1964–65, student-to-student counseling was opened to all second-semester freshmen wishing to improve their study skills. Both projects also provided counselees with an opportunity to systematically evaluate the appropriateness of their college major.

In the spring of 1963, a letter was sent to 10 percent of the sophomores and juniors on the honor roll asking if they would be interested in participating in a student-to-student counseling program. Volunteers were carefully screened for scholastic ability, academic achievement, dependability, ability to communicate ideas, and acceptance by other students. Students selected as prospective student counselors were then paid $1.00 per hour to attend twenty two-hour training sessions on counseling techniques for developing effective study habits and positive study attitudes. Students selected to serve as student counselors were subsequently paid $1.50 per hour when counseling groups of three to four freshmen.

The "Non-Achievement Syndrome" described by Roth and Meyersburg (104, pp. 535–536) provided a ready-made frame of reference for training student counselors and planning counseling activities. Based upon their description, the following generalized constructs were used for training and planning purposes:

1. The student's poor achievement does not arise from an incapacity to achieve. Achievement is related to factors other than an inborn capacity, and any new perspective must take this into account.

2. Poor achievement is an expression of the student's choice. This construct presents achievement problems in terms of motivation toward goals which have meaning in the phenomenal world of the individual. The poor achieving student is perceived in terms which delineate his motives for choosing poor achievement.

3. The student's choice for poor achievement operates in the preparation he makes for achievement. The scrutiny of the student's prepara-

tion, including the actual amount of preparation time, the intensity of studying, the subject areas emphasized or avoided in the preparation, etc., indicates the choice for achievement that the student makes. The student that has chosen poor achievement tends to spend his "preparation time" with friends, relaxing, watching TV, etc.; he spends much time in fantasy; he prepares only partially for examinations; and when he does prepare he is not sure of what he is reading or writing.

4. Poor achievement is a function of the preparation for achievement which a student makes. It follows that successful achievement is improbable in the light of preparation for achievement described under 3 above.

5. Poor academic skills are related to poor achievement and are an outgrowth of previous choices for poor achievement. The progress of academic experiences moves from the learning of skills to the use of these skills to acquire systematic knowledge. When choices for poor achievement appear early in the life of an individual, skills, which at that time are the content of achievement, are not learned adequately. In later periods of academic life, the poor skills either support the individual's choice for poor achievement or limit the achievement of those who no longer choose poor achievement.

6. The choice for poor achievement may be expressed as overall limited achievement or as achievement in deviant channels. In "over-all limited achievement," the student's energies seem to be directed against experiencing and toward the maintenance of a status quo. In "achievement in deviant channels," the student does expand his world of experience, but he avoids those avenues specifically related to accredited study.

7. The patterns of choice for poor achievement are enduring and do not undergo spontaneous change.

8. Achievement patterns, like other enduring behavior patterns, can be considered to be related to "personality organization." We view poor achievement as an enduring behavior pattern related to a specific psychodynamic organization, a "character trait."

9. The counseling relationship can serve as the impetus to change the achievement pattern. Changes in the psychodynamic organization can result in changes in character pattern. To induce such changes would

require the use of psychodynamic techniques; the counseling relationship can be used to this end.

A thorough understanding and acceptance by the student counselors of the constructs appropriate for low-achieving students were considered to be most important. If the student counselor considers poor achievement to be due to inborn capacities, then the chance to develop satisfactory achievement is relatively hopeless. If the student counselor feels that poor achievement is mainly a result of inappropriate study habits and attitudes, then the chance to develop satisfactory achievement is a challenge. Consequently, the Study Skills Clinic operated on the premise that poor academic achievement is the result of inappropriate study habits and attitudes. The student counselors used this frame of reference in their group counseling sessions.

Roth and Meyersburg (104, p. 538) also suggested characteristics of the nonachievement syndrome that were helpful in predicting the types of problems that might be encountered by the student counselors. The student counselors were encouraged to expect characteristics of the nonachievement syndrome to appear in students on probation. In the training sessions for student counselors, each of the characteristics was examined and a suggested nondirective approach to each was discussed. Throughout these discussions, however, the student counselors were cautioned against getting in too deep prior to appropriate consultation with a member of the professional counseling staff. The student counselors were thus prepared to anticipate and understand the following characteristics of the nonachievement syndrome:

1. Poor academic achievement
2. General self-depreciation; lack of recognition of pleasure of "being"
3. No clear system of personal goals or values
4. Vulnerability to disparagement by others
5. Immature relations with parents
6. Frequent depressions

7. Lack of insight about self and others

8. Free-floating anxieties

During the training sessions the student counselors assisted in selecting, developing, and organizing the materials to be used in each of the sixteen scheduled counseling sessions. For each counseling session a planning sheet was prepared covering the following points:

1. Subject of discussion for the session

2. Materials needed for the session

3. Check for commitments (Each session the student counselors checked to see if the counselees were observing principles of effective study habits and attitudes.)

4. Check list for points to discuss

5. Summary of session activities (At the end of each counseling session, the student counselor assisted the counselees in summarizing points covered during the counseling session.)

6. Commitments for next counseling session (Each counselee was encouraged to make definite commitments to try the principles of effective study habits and attitudes discussed.)

Table 50 lists the discussion topics for each of sixteen one-hour counseling sessions. The participation of student counselors in developing these discussion topics served two purposes—to train the student counselors in using the counseling materials and to develop their interest in the student-counseling-student approach. Detailed discussion plans for the sixteen meetings may be found elsewhere (89).

1963–64 ACADEMIC YEAR RESEARCH

On January 29, 1964, a letter was mailed to each of the 294 freshmen on probation asking if they would like to participate in a counseling program designed to help them develop effective study habits and attitudes. Of the 60 freshmen responding to the letter, 50 decided to participate in the program and agreed to attend all sixteen counseling sessions. The 50 volunteers were then individually matched with 50 other freshmen on scholastic probation ac-

TABLE 50

Discussion Topics for Student-to-Student Counseling Sessions
(Arlington State College, Arlington, Texas)

Session	Discussion Topic
1	How has counseling helped other students? Why do students earn low grades?
2	How do I prepare a daily activity schedule?
3	What are the values of a college education?
4	How should I take and use classroom notes?
5	How effective are my study techniques? What are some ways to improve?
6	What grades did I earn this past semester? Why?
7	How can I improve my study motivation?
8	How can I improve my organization for study?
9	How can I improve my reading and remembering? How can I write better research papers and class reports?
10	What grades am I earning in my classes this semester? Why?
11	How should I prepare for examinations?
12	What are the most effective procedures to use in taking examinations?
13	What are the values of social and recreational activities?
14	Is my choice of a college major and an occupation appropriate?
15	What grades am I earning this semester? Why?
16	What have I learned through participating in this counseling program?

cording to their sex, scores on the CEEB Scholastic Aptitude Test, grade-point average for the first semester, and semester credit-hour load for the current semester.

Counselees reported for counseling twice weekly in small groups of three or four. The interpretation of diagnostic profiles for standardized tests and questionnaires was an important part of the student-to-student counseling project for several reasons. First, the test results provided some tangible evidence as to the characteristics of the counselees. Second, the test results pointed up counselee strengths and weaknesses for discussion. Third, the test results were helpful to counselees seeking to make more realistic decisions about future educational and occupational plans. The forty clock hours of training received by the student counselors included taking most of the tests and inventories to be used, having their scores interpreted to them by a professional counselor, role playing to provide practice in interpreting the test profiles, and discussing the problems and procedures involved in meaningful test interpretation. Scores from the following standardized tests and inventories were routinely interpreted to counselees by the student counselors: Survey of Study Habits and Attitudes, General Aptitude Test Battery, Strong Vocational Interest Blank, and Mooney Problem Check List.

Figure 3 compares the second-semester grade-point averages for the matched samples of counseled and noncounseled freshmen on probation. Although the counseled group did have a higher grade-point average, the difference was not large enough to be considered significant at the .05 level. However, 28 percent of the counseled students earned grade-point averages of 1.0 or above as compared with only 10 percent of the uncounseled group. Furthermore, all the counselees were in complete agreement that they had been

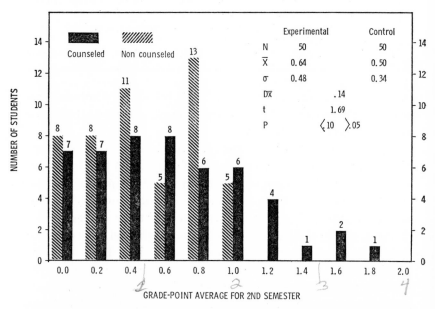

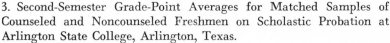

3. Second-Semester Grade-Point Averages for Matched Samples of Counseled and Noncounseled Freshmen on Scholastic Probation at Arlington State College, Arlington, Texas.

helped through student-to-student counseling, with improved study habits and attitudes being the most frequently cited benefit received. Test-retest scores on the Effective Study Test appear to confirm this belief, in that the average precounseling and postcounseling percentiles were 55 and 85, respectively, for the total Study Effectiveness score.

Many of the counselees changed their major as a result of the counseling that they received. At the beginning of the counseling sessions, 24 percent of the counselees were judged to have selected appropriate college majors, based on matching interests and abilities.[7] During the counseling program, an additional 20 percent changed to an appropriate major and another 20 percent had requested additional professional counseling in this area. Finally, a follow-up study made one year after completion of the student-to-student counseling revealed that 38 percent of the counseled group were still in college as compared with 20 percent of the uncounseled group.

Although these findings are impressive, they must be interpreted in light of the fact that only 20 percent of the freshmen on scholastic probation had bothered to respond to the invitation to participate in the study skills counseling program. However, these results do confirm the findings from research with potential college dropouts reported earlier in Chapter 4. Taken together, the studies at Southwest Texas State College and Arlington State College do indicate that student-to-student counseling is an effective approach for reaching many students encountering difficulty in meeting collegiate academic demands. This finding is of special significance in view of the trend toward open admissions policies and the growing emphasis on independent study programs, with the accompanying likelihood of higher attrition rates during the freshman year unless effective help is provided for the less capable students.

The research results also indicated that the success of student-to-

---

[7] Evaluation of the appropriateness of each student's selected college major was made by a team of three professional counselors following a detailed examination of the student's psychological test scores, academic history, and biographical data.

student counseling depends upon the careful selection, training, and supervision of the student counselors. Observation of the enthusiasm and preparation displayed by the student counselors allowed the project director, Dr. W. J. Karraker, subjectively to rank order his student counselors as to their probable effectiveness. The three counselors judged to be most effective had 81 percent of their counselees clearing probation; the three counselors judged to be least effective had only 38 percent of their counselees clearing probation. Clearly, the student counselor's attitude toward his counseling duties is an important factor in his counseling effectiveness.

1964–65 ACADEMIC YEAR RESEARCH

In the 1964–65 study, publicity materials were distributed to second-semester freshmen inviting them to visit the Study Skills Clinic if they wished to participate in a counseling program designed to develop efficient study habits and positive study attitudes. Volunteers were carefully screened to eliminate students not in need of study skills counseling, and a group of 150 freshmen were selected to participate in the program. The 150 counselees were then individually matched with 150 other freshmen according to their age, grade-point average, and total score on the CEEB Scholastic Aptitude Test.

Figure 4 provides a graphic comparison of the effectiveness of the student-to-student counseling. The counseled freshmen improved their grade-point averages by almost one-third of a letter grade, while the uncounseled freshmen showed no change between their fall-semester and spring-semester grades. The significant improvement in grade-point averages was matched by a significant increase in scores on the Effective Study Test and by a significant increase in the number of students selecting appropriate college majors, as reflected by their measured interests and abilities. Again, as in the 1963–64 study, the counseled freshmen were in 100 percent agreement that they had been helped by their student counselor and that student-to-student counseling should be continued as a permanent program available to college students on a volunteer basis. Finally, the retention rate for the 150 counseled students was 76 percent,

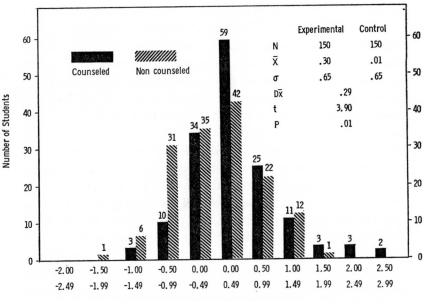

4. Influence of Student-to-Student Counseling on the Fall and Spring Semester Grade-Point Averages for Matched Experimental and Control Groups at Arlington State College, Arlington, Texas.

while that for the 150 uncounseled students was only 42 percent one year later.

The 150 counselees included a selected group of 28 students facing scholastic suspension. These students were permitted to return to college after they had agreed to participate in student-to-student counseling. The student-counseling-student approach was highly effective for these students, in that 17 out of 28, or 60 percent, cleared probation, and 11 percent made the dean's list for scholastic honors.

From this study, Karraker concluded that freshmen who have scholastic difficulty, but who also have the measured academic potential to matriculate in college, should be directed into student-to-student counseling to improve their study skills rather than terminating their educational careers.

ADAPTABILITY TO HIGH SCHOOL SITUATIONS

Educational psychologists are generally agreed that the maturation process will not, of itself, produce effective work-study habits, because such habits are a product of the learning process. However, the situation remains today, for the most part, as it has for many years. The mathematics teacher teaches math; the history teacher, history; the chemistry teacher, chemistry; and only rarely does anyone take time to teach high school students how to study. The outcome is, as one might suspect, that most high school students have not acquired the study skills required for sound scholarship. Validation research with the Survey of Study Habits and Attitudes (37, 43) and the Effective Study Test (13) indicates that the study skills and academic attitudes of most high school students leave much to be desired.

Systematic efforts aimed at improving study skills and scholastic motivation might, therefore, be even more meaningful at the high school level. Consequently, in 1959, research was initiated to explore the adaptability of student-to-student counseling to the high school campus. To date, four high-school-level studies have been completed. In two of the studies, college students counseled the high school students, while in the other two studies, the student counselors were students enrolled in a higher grade at the same high school as the counselees. Samples of high school freshmen, sophomores, and juniors have been selected to receive student-to-student counseling, with two of the investigations involving counselees from economically and educationally disadvantaged environments.

College Preparation Project

During the 1958–59 academic year, the counseling staff at San Marcos High School, San Marcos, Texas, initiated an experimental student-to-student counseling program in an effort to better prepare their college-bound students to adjust to collegiate academic procedures and requirements. The project was a logical extension of the successful student-counseling-student approach developed at

Southwest Texas State College and employed, with appropriate modification and adaptation, most of the counseling materials and procedures used in that program. Mrs. Jerlene Y. Lyle, high school guidance counselor, served as project director for the experiment.

Nine college sophomores, four boys and five girls, served as student counselors for the project. All nine student counselors were graduates of San Marcos High School, all were enrolled at Southwest Texas State College, and all ranked in the upper third of their college class in both scholastic ability and scholastic achievement. None of the student counselors were paid for their efforts, as all agreed to offer their services out of the spirit of altruism and service to their high school and community. During January, 1959, each of the student counselors completed a twenty-hour training schedule designed to achieve proficiency in the following areas:

1. To be able to synthesize aptitude, achievement, attitude, and adjustment data for forecasting potential and probable academic achievement in college

2. To be able to promote group interaction effectively while guiding group discussion into productive channels through sagacious employment of counseling materials and techniques

3. To be able to interpret all information recorded on the Test Results Report Form and to utilize same in planning a remedial program where and as appropriate

4. To be able to identify deficient study habits and to utilize accepted study techniques in planning a study skills improvement program

The 1958–59 junior class provided experimental and control samples for the investigation. The junior class was selected for the study because the students would still have another year of high school in which to correct deficient study skills. A questionnaire completed earlier by the 160 juniors had indicated that 63.1 percent planned to attend college. Using a controlled sampling procedure, three samples of 27 students each were selected from the 101 college-bound juniors. Students randomly assigned to the three samples were matched as closely as possible on the following seven variables: sex, chronological age, ethnic group, socioeconomic status, total score on the academic ability criterion, total score on the academic attitude criterion, and total score on the academic achievement criterion.[8]

Two of the three matched samples were designated as experimental samples and the third was designated as a control sample. Students in each experimental sample were systematically organized into nine counseling groups, with one group from each sample being assigned to each of the nine student counselors. The fifty-four juniors in the two experimental samples received student-to-student counseling in accordance with a carefully formulated program utilizing identical materials, procedures, and personnel to provide four hours of academic adjustment counseling. Table 51 provides an outline of the counseling activities for the four one-hour counseling sessions.

TABLE 51

Outline of Guidance Activities for the Four One-Hour
Student-to-Student Counseling Sessions

Session	Guidance Activities
1	Orient counselees to program objectives and requirements Interpret scores reported on Test Results Report Form Interpret Survey of Study Habits and Attitudes Diagnostic Profile Discuss importance of improving deficient study skills Assign reading of *Effective Study Guide* as homework
2	Review contents of *Effective Study Guide* Discuss efficient organization for effective studying Discuss proven techniques for efficient studying Assign completion of Study Skills Surveys as homework
3	Explain ability-achievement-adjustment-attitude success factors Review specific problems identified by Study Skills Surveys Discuss appropriate suggestions in *Student-to-Student Tips* Explain purpose of Effective Study Test to be administered soon
4	Report and interpret scores on Effective Study Test Discuss correction of study skills deficiencies identified by test Help counselees summarize major concepts discussed during counseling

[8] The Otis Quick-Scoring Mental Ability Test, the Survey of Study Habits and Attitudes, and the Iowa Test of Educational Development were utilized as ability, attitude, and achievement criteria, respectively.

Two criteria were employed to assess effectiveness of the experimental counseling program. Comparative test-retest performance on the Survey of Study Habits and Attitudes provided data for evaluating study skills improvement; grade-point averages for the semesters before and after study skills counseling provided data for evaluating improvement in academic achievement. The results of the data analyses are presented in Tables 52 and 53. From these tables it is apparent that the counseled students showed significant improvement in their study skills and grade averages, while data for the control students reflected no meaningful change in either criteria.

Comments made by both the student counselors and their counselees immediately following the program were of a decidedly favorable nature. Furthermore, a careful tabulation of the time expended on the project by the project director and the student counselors revealed that the time spent by the professional guidance counselor would have more than doubled if she had conducted all the counseling sessions herself.

Based upon these research findings, the project director concluded that a similar program of student-to-student counseling, presented annually if possible, would be a beneficial adjunct to the

TABLE 52

Comparative Test-Retest Performance of Matched Samples
of Counseled and Uncounseled High School Juniors
on the Survey of Study Habits and Attitudes
(San Marcos High School, San Marcos, Texas)

| | | Survey of Study Habits and Attitudes | | | |
| | | Test[a] | | Retest[b] | |
Group	N	Mean	S.D.	Mean	S.D.
Counseled	54	97.2	36.1	122.3*	37.6
Uncounseled	27	96.0	35.4	93.4	35.1

[a] Initial testing was accomplished February 5, 1959.
[b] Retesting was accomplished March 19, 1959.
* Counseled students scored significantly higher than matching uncounseled students on retest $(P = <.01)$.

TABLE 53

Comparative Academic Achievement of Matched Samples
of Counseled and Uncounseled High School Juniors
before and after Study Skills Counseling
(San Marcos High School, San Marcos, Texas)

| | | Semester Grade-Point Averages | |
Group	N	Precounseling Semester	Postcounseling Semester
Counseled	54	2.43	2.73*
Uncounseled	27	2.38	2.44

* Grade-point averages for postcounseling semester averaged significantly higher than those for precounseling semester $(P = <.01)$.

regular high school guidance program. Furthermore, where the counselor-student ratio exceeds one to four hundred, as is usually the case in Texas high schools, the guidance counselor rarely has sufficient time to provide an individualized counseling approach to each student's personal, social, and academic problems. The systematic use of student counselors to assist with appropriate group and individual guidance activities was thus seen as one promising approach to freeing the guidance counselor for individualized counseling activities.

High School Orientation Project

After three years of successful operation, the guidance department at San Marcos High School decided to change the objectives of student-to-student counseling and move the program downward to the ninth grade. Instead of using successful college students to provide college preparation counseling for college-bound juniors, the revised program employed successful high school juniors and seniors to give academic orientation counseling to entering high school freshmen. This decision was the direct outgrowth of administrative concern over the alarming number of student dropouts and the conviction that something must be done to help more students succeed in high school. Studies had shown that many dropouts were the result of poor academic grades and failure to adjust to the high school learning situation. The change, therefore, was an effort to apply the student-counseling-student approach to helping students develop good study habits and attitudes so that they would have a better chance for scholastic survival (112). The revised program was jointly supervised by Mrs. Francys Houston and Mr. Bill Dibrell, the high school guidance counselors.

Ten carefully selected juniors and seniors served as orientation counselors with responsibility for providing study skills instruction for beginning freshmen. These student counselors received forty clock hours of intensive training to prepare them for their counseling duties. The selection and training program for student counselors was modeled after that employed at Southwest Texas State College. Although the student counselors received no monetary payment for their services, they were given a half unit of transferable high school credit for the work they performed.

In the spring, prior to transferring to high school, all eighth grade students took the high school editions of the Survey of Study Habits and Attitudes and the Effective Study Test during an assembly supervised by the high school guidance counselors. During the summer months, each incoming freshman reported to the high school counseling office to register for his classes. At that time, the freshman was informed about the how-to-study instruction to be offered in the fall and was encouraged to enroll in the program. Participation was on a strictly voluntary basis,[9] with the counseling being scheduled during the freshman's physical activity period.

The study skills counseling was initiated in September, during the first week of school, and was continued for six weeks. Each student counselor was assigned twenty freshmen organized into five groups of four counselees each on the basis of their scores on ability and achievement tests. The student counselors met with their counselees for one hour per week, and the materials covered

[9] Voluntary rather than required participation was decided upon in order to avoid any negative student reaction that might be associated with a mandatory requirement. However, counselor persuasion was very effective in enrolling the students who most needed the program.

during the six counseling sessions were very much like those out-lined in Table 51. In the revised program, however, the student counselors did not interpret the results of ability and achievement tests, and the study skills instruction was spread over more time in order to permit discussion of specific study methods in greater detail. The high-school-level how-to-study course developed by Brown and Holtzman (15) provided the instructional framework for the counseling on effective study skills.

During the 1966–67 academic year, research was carried out to evaluate the freshman orientation counseling. Both the Survey of Study Habits and Attitudes and the Effective Study Test were administered a second time just prior to the final counseling session. The two instruments were readministered to all freshmen, not just to students enrolled in the counseling program. This permitted the matching of a control (uncounseled) sample with an experimental (counseled) sample. Freshmen in the two samples were individually matched on the basis of intelligence quotients, standardized achievement test results, and grade-point averages for the eighth grade. Since almost two-thirds of the incoming freshmen had participated in the program, it was only possible to match control and experimental samples of forty-eight students each.

As indicated in Table 54, test results from the Survey of Study Habits and Attitudes, administered before and after student-to-student counseling, showed a 22.7 percent total score gain for the experimental sample compared to a 5.3 percent gain for the control sample. Test-retest results for the Effective Study Test are reported in Table 55. As can be seen from this table, a 5.3 percent total score gain occurred for the experimental sample, while a 6.7 percent loss occurred for the control group. All part scores on the two instruments showed similar differences.

An analysis of the grade-point averages for the experimental and control samples was also undertaken. When first-semester grade averages for the ninth grade were compared with second-semester grade averages for the eighth grade, the experimental group showed an average gain of .14, while the control group showed an average loss of .06. Thus, the average grade-point difference was

TABLE 54

Average Percent Loss or Gain on Retest for Matching Samples of Counseled
and Uncounseled High School Freshmen on the
Survey of Study Habits and Attitudes
(San Marcos High School, San Marcos, Texas)

Sample	N	Delay Avoidance	Work Methods	Study Habits	Teacher Approval	Education Acceptance	Study Attitudes	Study Orientation
Counseled	48	34.7	28.6	31.8	19.3	12.3	15.8	22.7
Uncounseled	48	18.2	6.3	12.0	− 1.4	1.5	0.0	5.3

NOTE: Percent gain or loss was calculated by subtracting the precourse mean from the postcourse mean and dividing the remainder by the precourse mean.

TABLE 55

Average Percent Loss or Gain on Retest for Matching Samples of Counseled
and Uncounseled High School Freshmen on the Effective Study Test
(San Marcos High School, San Marcos, Texas)

Sample	N	Reality Orientation	Study Organization	Writing Behavior	Reading Behavior	Examination Behavior	Study Effectiveness
Counseled	48	1.6	9.4	7.4	6.3	1.2	5.3
Uncounseled	48	−6.8	−10.3	−3.7	−5.0	−8.2	−6.7

NOTE: Percent gain or loss was calculated by subtracting the precourse mean from the postcourse mean and dividing the remainder by the precourse mean.

.20 or one-fifth of a letter grade. This difference in grade-point averages, like the test-retest differences in measured study skills, was statistically significant at the .05 level of confidence.

In a report presented elsewhere, Dibrell (80) offers the following assessment of the program:

> We are pleased at the immediate results obtained from using student counselors to assist in orientation and instruction in the how-to-study course. First, it permits us to reach a large number of freshman students during their first few weeks of high school and discuss with them, in small personalized groups, the study skills problems common to all freshmen. This, of course, helps to bring about a greater sense of unity of purpose on the part of pupils, parents, and faculty. Second, it has become apparent that freshmen receiving peer counseling have utilized the professional counselor's services at twice the rate of freshmen not receiving this assistance.
>
> We feel that we have learned quite a bit about the possible further use of students in the field of counseling. The students selected as counselors demonstrated that competent high school students can be trusted with test results and can make a significant contribution to the counseling program. However, at the high school level, more supervision for the student counselor is required than at the college level. The professional counselor must continually coordinate the counseling activities and must work closely with the student counselors at each step of the program. Plans are being considered to increase the responsibilities of the student counselor, not only for orientation activities, but also to provide a year-long tutoring service for students whose grades fall below passing.

Although the experimental students were probably more motivated to improve their study habits, as evidenced by their volunteering for the course, a review of the research literature indicates that desire without an organized plan is ineffective. Student-to-student study skills instruction provides a systematic and organized plan for quickly reaching a large number of students at a nominal cost. Based upon on-site observations, parental and student recommendations, and the present research data, the administrative and supervisory staffs of the San Marcos High School feel that peer counseling in study skills should be adopted as a routine procedure.

Finally, the acceptability of the two student-to-student counseling programs, as perceived by the high school freshmen and juniors receiving the counseling may be determined from the data presented in Table 56. The Counseling Evaluation Questionnaire was completed anonymously by both groups, the answers tabulated, and the results converted into a percentage distribution for each sample. Two conclusions may be drawn from the data: First, both samples evaluated the program very favorably. Second, there is no significant difference in the program evaluation made by the two samples. It should be noted, however, that, while not significant, the freshmen did react more favorably than the juniors, with 9 percent more freshmen giving strongly positive or positive evaluations.

Project Upward Bound

Many reasons are offered by educators for not incorporating study skills instruction into the secondary school curriculum. The dearth of instructional materials, lack of instructional time, and absence of interest are the more commonly heard excuses. In addition, many educators believe that the students who profit most from study skills instruction are those coming from college-oriented families. By contrast, the culturally and economically disadvantaged student is not generally considered to profit meaningfully from such instruction (77, 78).

In 1966, the Office of Economic Opportunity awarded a Project

TABLE 56

Percentage Distribution of Responses on the Counseling Evaluation Questionnaire Completed Anonymously by Peer-Counseled High School Freshmen and Juniors (San Marcos High School, San Marcos, Texas)

Academic Year	N	High School Rank	Counselee Evaluation of Counseling Program				
			Strongly Positive	Positive	Uncertain	Negative	Strongly Negative
1960–61	114	Junior	37.4	41.2	12.4	5.9	2.7
1962–63	204	Freshman	40.7	45.9	9.4	3.1	0.9

Upward Bound grant to Southwest Texas State College. Upward Bound is a precollege preparatory program designed to generate the skills and motivation necessary for success in higher education by students from lower socioeconomic backgrounds and with inadequate secondary school preparation. As set forth in the project guidelines (113), the primary objective of the project is to remedy poor academic preparation and develop positive scholastic motivation, thus increasing a student's potential for acceptance of and success in the college environment.

In addition to meeting the annual family income poverty criteria, students selected for Upward Bound "shall be those who have potential for success in a two or four year college, but whose present level of achievement and/or motivation would seem to preclude their acceptance in such an institution."[10] Because of his impoverished background, the typical Upward Bound student has not had the requisite motivation or preparation to demonstrate his academic potential. Typically, this student may be apathetic or even hostile because he comes from a disadvantaged environment unable to help him release his real talent, or he has shunned meaningful educational pursuits because of inadequate school experiences. Nevertheless, he is one for whom postsecondary education seems both possible and desirable, given experiences and instruction necessary to overcome earlier obstacles.

At Southwest Texas State College, the typical Upward Bound enrollee was a sixteen-year-old Latin American student from a broken home whose family speaks Spanish rather than English. His family consisted of seven members living on an annual income of $3,200. In addition, very few, if any, of his family or friends placed a very high value on academic achievement.

STUDY SKILLS COUNSELING FOR UPWARD BOUND STUDENTS

The 120 high school sophomores selected for the project lived on the college campus for six weeks during the summer of 1966. Dur-

---

[10] Student recruitment and selecting strategies are discussed on pages 4–8 of the *UPWARD BOUND Policy Guidelines and Application Instructions* published by the Office of Economic Opportunity in October, 1967.

ing this time they received academic training in communication skills, mathematics, current issues, and study skills.

Systematic research on the productivity of study skills instruction for the culturally, economically, and academically deficient student appears to be nonexistent. Thus, there was concern as to whether or not the typical Upward Bound student would profit from such instruction. Consequently, research was undertaken to determine the effectiveness and acceptability of study skills instruction for high school juniors coming from disadvantaged backgrounds.

Twenty-eight hours of how-to-study instruction were provided in efficient and proven methods of study. Classroom activities were built around the twenty lesson plans and accompanying instructional materials developed for a precollege how-to-study course by Brown and Holtzman (14). Where appropriate, minor changes were made in the lesson plans and instructional materials in order to adapt them to the needs and interests of the Upward Bound students. The course was taught by four study skills counselors,[11] and the counselor-student ratio was limited to one to fifteen in order to help maximize peer-group interaction.

The instructional package for the course included an instructor's manual and student's textbook, together with assorted illustrated handouts, discussion questionnaires, overhead transparencies, and other supportive teaching aids. Selected sound filmstrips were shown at appropriate points to explain, demonstrate, and sell the study methods and values being taught. Supervised study activities were also provided so that the students would have an opportunity to practice, under expert direction, their newly developing study skills.

The general objectives of the how-to-study course were (*a*) to provide instruction in proven how-to-study techniques and the rewards of scholastic success, (*b*) to develop a positive orientation

[11] Each of the four study skills counselors had received forty clock hours of special training in group counseling procedures and had been employed for two years as an academic adjustment counselor in the program of student-to-student counseling in operation at Southwest Texas State College.

toward the educational environment and the value of education, (c) to motivate the development of effective study habits and positive study attitudes, and (d) to narrow the gap between level of academic potential and level of academic performance. In order to help achieve these objectives, 60 percent of the course materials were directed toward development of effective study techniques and 40 percent toward development of positive study motivation.

The course provided analysis and discussion of the following academic problem areas: taking lecture notes, taking reading notes, organizing study environment, reading textbook assignments, organizing study time, writing in-class themes, preparing outside reports, giving oral reports, remembering specific details, understanding broad concepts, using library materials, and preparing for and taking tests. Problems of motivating study, seeking assistance, facing reality, and accepting responsibility were also examined and thoroughly discussed. In addition, each student's study habits, study attitudes, and study knowledge were evaluated before and after presentation of the course content. A detailed description of the course contents and instructional procedures is available elsewhere (3, 36, 79).

All 120 Upward Bound students received the study skills instruction. Consequently, a control group of uncounseled students could not be selected to aid in the course evaluation. Furthermore, grade-point averages for the semesters before and after the 1966 summer session were not compared, because of the wide variation in grading practices at the high schools supplying students to the program and because the grades given to these students frequently reflected variables other than academic achievement.

A Course Evaluation Questionnaire was administered to the Upward Bound students upon completion of instruction in order to determine each student's reaction to counselor effectiveness, course content, and program acceptability. An anonymously answered sentence completion survey was also administered in order to determine each student's unstructured opinions of the study skills course. To ascertain the course's effect upon the student's study skills, the

Survey of Study Habits and Attitudes and the Effective Study Test were administered before and after instruction, and the resulting test-retest scores were compared.

Anonymous responses to the specially constructed sixty-item Course Evaluation Questionnaire were tabulated and converted to percentages. Table 57 reports the students' responses to representative positively and negatively worded statements from the questionnaire. Tabulation of responses to all sixty statements indicated that student reactions were decisively positive to all evaluated aspects of the how-to-study course.

Table 58 reports typical anonymous responses to the Sentence Completion Survey. These responses were selected as representative of the students' evaluation of their study skills instruction. Analysis of all of the responses indicated that the students regarded the study skills course as one of the most beneficial and popular courses they had ever taken. In fact, it was their general consensus that all high school students would benefit meaningfully from receiving how-to-study instruction, especially if such instruction was provided by student counselors.

Precourse and postcourse administrations of the Survey of Study Habits and Attitudes were employed to assess each student's study orientation before and after instruction on how to study. Since the SSHA yields separate study habits and attitudes scores, its value lies in identifying, for each student, specific areas of deficient academic behavior and scholastic motivation that may handicap future school achievement. Table 59 reports the precourse and postcourse average scores and percentiles, along with the percentage of gain on retest, for each of the seven SSHA scales. From this table, it may be noted that each of the scales indicates a significant improvement in the enrollees' self-reported study habits and attitudes.

Precourse and postcourse administrations of the Effective Study Test were employed to determine the course's contribution to knowledge about efficient study methods and the factors influencing their development. Table 60 reports the precourse and postcourse average scores and percentiles along with percentage gain

TABLE 57

Distribution of Student Responses to Representative Positively and Negatively
Worded Statements from the Course Evaluation Questionnaire
(Project Upward Bound, Southwest Texas State College, San Marcos, Texas)

	Percentage of Students Responding				
	Strongly Agree	Agree	Undecided	Disagree	Strongly Disagree
Scale 1. Counselor Effectiveness					
4. My counselor appeared to really believe in the value of the study methods being suggested.	80.5	17.0	1.7	0.8	0.0
7. My counselor seemed well informed about the problems confronting high school students.	55.1	39.0	5.1	0.0	0.8
19. My counselor didn't really seem to care whether or not we understood the material.	0.0	2.6	0.0	17.7	79.7
Scale 2. Course Content					
21. Discussing problems in student-teacher relations was time well spent.	43.2	44.1	8.5	4.2	0.0
23. Discussing the rewards of a high school education made me more aware of the importance of finishing high school.	74.6	22.0	0.0	3.4	0.0
38. The problems discussed during the class were not those that trouble students the most.	0.0	3.4	10.2	48.3	38.1
Scale 3. Program Acceptability					
42. The Effective Study Class has increased my ambition to be a successful high school student.	71.2	27.1	1.7	0.0	0.0
45. I doubt that this class is really effective in helping students adjust to high school life.	1.7	0.8	5.1	31.4	61.0
49. I'm glad that we had the opportunity to find out our study faults.	80.5	17.8	0.0	0.8	0.8

TABLE 58
Typical Anonymous Responses to Selected Items
on the Sentence Completion Survey
(Project Upward Bound, Southwest Texas
State College, San Marcos, Texas)

The study skills course ...
... was good because our counselor talked to us about the problems that we all have.
... is a course that all students should have a chance to take because many students have problems that can best be solved by this kind of class.
... was very practical and I feel that I have really learned something from it.
... helped me a great deal by helping me understand the need for working hard in high school.
... was one of the most beneficial courses I have had in my entire school life.
... was very beneficial in helping us become more effective students and gave us a deeper appreciation of our opportunities for an education.

My study habits ...
... have definitely improved and will help me throughout high school and afterwards.
... were very poor until I took this study skills course and now I like to study because I know how.
... have improved over 200 percent because this course pointed out my weaknesses in studying.

My study attitudes ...
... have changed and now I am really looking forward to going on to college after high school.
... have improved because now I don't get angry when I have to study.
... are much better and now I study because I know how important it is and because I want to.

for each of the six EST scales. Inspection of this table shows that the students' knowledge about effective study methods improved significantly in each measured area.

Using Fisher's t-test for correlated means, the differences between precourse and postcourse scores on all SSHA and EST scales were found to be significant at the .001 level of confidence. Thus it is possible to state that the study skills course taught by student counselors produced a significant improvement in the measured study habits, study attitudes, and study knowledge of the Upward Bound students. Furthermore, student responses to the anonymous-

TABLE 59

Comparison of the Precourse and Postcourse Average Scores and
Centiles Obtained on the Survey of Study Habits and Attitudes
(Project Upward Bound, Southwest Texas
State College, San Marcos, Texas)

SSHA Scale	Precourse		Postcourse		% Gain*
	Score	Centile	Score	Centile	
Delay avoidance	22.3	56	34.0	88	52.5
Work methods	25.5	63	35.1	89	37.6
Study habits	47.8	61	69.1	92	44.6
Teacher approval	31.7	63	39.4	87	24.3
Educational acceptance	31.8	67	38.4	89	20.8
Study attitudes	63.5	67	77.8	91	22.5
Study orientation	111.3	64	146.9	93	32.0

* Percentage gain for all scales was calculated by dividing the precourse score into the postcourse score, multiplying the obtained quotient by 100 to convert to percentage, and subtracting 100 percent to determine the percentage of gain or loss on retest.

TABLE 60

Comparison of the Precourse and Postcourse Average Scores
and Centiles Obtained on the Effective Study Test
(Project Upward Bound, Southwest Texas
State College, San Marcos, Texas)

EST Scale	Precourse		Postcourse		% Gain*
	Score	Centile	Score	Centile	
Reality orientation	19.4	46	22.1	81	13.9
Study organization	16.0	37	19.9	93	24.4
Writing behavior	18.0	37	20.5	75	13.9
Reading behavior	17.7	34	21.5	80	21.5
Examination behavior	17.4	43	18.9	63	8.6
Total study effectiveness	88.4	40	103.0	86	16.5

* Percentage gain for all scales was calculated by dividing the precourse score into the postcourse score, multiplying the obtained quotient by 100 to convert to percentage, and subtracting 100 percent to determine the percentage of gain or loss on retest.

ly answered Sentence Completion Survey and Course Evaluation Questionnaire clearly established that these students reacted in a decisively positive manner to all evaluated aspects of the how-to-study course.

In the summer of 1968, 96 of the original 120 Upward Bound students were enrolled in freshman courses at Southwest Texas State College. Numerous factors undoubtedly contributed to this high rate of college enrollment. However, it is reasonable to assume that the student-to-student study skills instruction was a contributing factor by helping to stimulate the necessary motivation for higher education. Although the reported investigation is restricted to a limited number of students and a specific academic situation, there is evidence that strongly suggests that students from an economically, culturally, and academically disadvantaged background can profit from receiving how-to-study instruction within a guidance-oriented program employing the student-counseling-student approach.

STUDY SKILLS COUNSELING BY UPWARD BOUND STUDENTS

The original group of 120 disadvantaged students enrolled in the Upward Bound Project at Southwest Texas State College included 9 sophomores from Phillis Wheatley High School, a public secondary school in San Antonio, Texas, having a 99 percent Negro enrollment at the time the project was conducted. All 9 students had received study skills instruction as part of the 1966 summer program, and observation of these students during the 1966–67 academic year revealed a significant improvement in their academic progress and a meaningful increase in their own self-concepts and expectations. The high school administration concluded that the peer-delivered study skills instruction received the previous summer was, in large measure, directly responsible for this improvement in study skills, scholastic motivation, and self-confidence. Consequently, it was decided to conduct an experimental student-to-student counseling program at the high school during the 1967–68 academic year.

Mrs. Dorothy Mae Pickett, dean of girls at the high school, was assigned as project director for the study. Six of the nine Upward Bound students from Wheatley High School were selected to serve as student counselors, and arrangements were made for them to be trained during the 1967 summer session by the regular student counselors assigned to teach the study skills course to new Upward Bound students. Whereas the six prospective student counselors had participated in the study skills class as students during the previous summer, they now participated as observers and as student counselor trainees helping to provide the twenty-eight hours of classroom instruction. Each of the six student counselor trainees was responsible for teaching segments of various lesson plans, and each was responsible for teaching one entire lesson plan by himself. The regularly assigned student counselors, trained and experienced college students, supervised the six trainees at all times, offering appropriate criticisms of their group counseling procedures and, in general, helping them to improve their instructional techniques. The Upward Bound student counselors would also meet with the student counselor trainees at regularly scheduled times and explain the instructional objectives, counseling methods, and guidance materials to be used with each lesson plan.

Student-to-student study skills counseling was introduced at Phillis Wheatley High School in an attempt to develop a more positive attitude toward higher education among all the students and, more specifically, to motivate the entering sophomores to improve their study habits and attitudes. The high-school-level Effective Study Course developed by Brown and Holtzman (15) provided the instructional framework for the project. The lesson plans and instructional materials developed for the course were used as recommended in the *Instructor's Manual*, but the teaching methods were adapted so that senior students, trained in the methods of student-to-student counseling, could communicate the proven techniques of effective study to their counselees.

The course was developed to provide a special instructional program for students prior to, or immediately following, high school entrance. The student counselor's role was to serve as a program moderator or discussion leader rather than as a lecturer on the subject matter. The student counselor was expected to encourage maximum student participation in the learning process in order to achieve the following course objectives: (*a*) to motivate each student toward developing more effective study habits, (*b*) to improve each student's study efficiency through better utilization of his study time, (*c*) to improve each student's study efficiency through improved organization of his study environment, (*d*) to improve each student's study efficiency through improved reading and writing techniques, (*e*) to improve each student's efficiency in preparing for and taking examinations, (*f*) to improve the self-direction of each student through the development of meaningful and realistic academic goals, and (*g*) to help each student develop a realistic understanding of high school life and peer acceptance problems.

Of the 200 students enrolled in the program, 180 were tenth graders and the remainder were college-bound juniors and seniors who requested that they be allowed to receive the study skills instruction. Sophomore enrollment, for the most part, was also on a volunteer basis. A majority of the students receiving the study skills instruction were from economically and culturally deprived backgrounds, and all but one of the students were of the Negro race.

The six student counselors taught the study skills course during their study-hall periods. Announcements about the course and its proven effectiveness were made at the beginning of the school year to the first-, third-, and fifth-period study halls. At each session, the project director explained the course in detail, answered the students' questions, and furnished interested students with letters of explanation to be taken home to their parents. The first series of study skills classes began during the first week of September and terminated the first week of October. Classes met for fifty-five minutes each day for twenty school days of instruction. Students that volunteered for the course met as a group for study skills instruction instead of attending their regularly scheduled study hall. The second series of classes began during the second week of October and terminated the second week of December. Two sections were taught during this time period—one section during first period and one section during third period. Two hours of study skills instruction per week were provided in lieu of the regularly scheduled sophomore English classes.

The third series of study skills instruction was offered during the sixth period and lasted from the first week of February to the first week of March. This section was composed of football athletes and consisted of a mixture of tenth-, eleventh-, and twelfth-grade boys. The section met for fifty-five minutes per day for twenty school days.

During the study skills session, the student counselors met periodically with each counselee's teachers. They discussed the student's academic strengths and weaknesses, his progress in the classroom, and, in general, how best to help the student adjust to the learning environment at Wheatley High School.

A comparison of precourse and postcourse scores on the Survey of Study Habits and Attitudes and the Effective Study Test was planned as one way to assess the project's impact on student study skills. Precourse tests were administered as planned; however, it was not possible to administer the tests a second time because of time limitations. Therefore, the primary criteria for evaluating the effectiveness of the project must be the observed behavioral and attitudinal changes in the participating students.

In May, 1968, several teachers of participating sophomores were asked to write briefly and anonymously their subjective feelings about the course. Their representative remarks are as follows:

Comparing my students that received the instruction to those that did not, I would say that the how-to-study students learned to interpret and understand their reading assignments better. They also were better in note taking.

All students in my English II class showed considerable improvement after being assisted by the teachers of the study skills course.

They became more involved in class discussion.

I didn't find any great grade change, but I did notice improvement in their classroom behavior.

I believe all our students should be taught study skills.

The students' notebooks were much neater and better organized than were those of students that didn't have the course.

The school's administration wrote the following statement about the how-to-study course:

It is my sincere opinion that the students voluntarily involved, as well as the tutors in the study skills program, seemed to find themselves becoming more engrossed in the total school program. Their newly acquired skills in how to study made the availability of the library facilities more meaningful to them. Their improved conduct, self-confidence, and pride were clearly evident. The need for this type of training at Wheatley is significant enough to warrant a professional full-time staff person to coordinate the program.

After the student counselors had taught the how-to-study course, they were asked to write their opinions about the program. Some of their statements follow:

I enjoyed teaching the study skills class mainly because I found that I would like to make teaching my profession. This experience gave me an idea as to what responsibilities a teacher has. The students were very cooperative and eager to learn more about how to study effectively. Not only did the students learn a lot from this course, but I learned just as they learned.

Teaching a study skills class at Phillis Wheatley High School was a very enjoyable experience for me. The greatest pleasure in my life was showing the students how they could make better grades and improve their lives. This program gave me confidence and pride in my own ability to help others.

One of the most exciting opportunities I have had was when I taught study skills. The students were very cooperative and showed a great deal of enthusiasm and interest. I felt as though I was really contributing something to their advantage. My students were very willing to help perfect their academic weaknesses, which we helped them find by testing. Because of their feelings about the course, they influenced many of their friends to become part of the class. This definitely showed me that they wanted to learn and wanted others to learn as well.

Upon completion of the course, several of the student counselors had their counselees complete anonymously an open-ended Sentence Completion Survey. Typical student completions to selected items are given in Table 61.

Although the investigation was restricted to a limited number of students, there is subjective evidence that suggests that the Wheatley High School sophomores did profit meaningfully from receiving student-to-student study skills instruction. Subjective evaluations made by the teachers at Wheatley High School indicated that they felt the how-to-study course was highly beneficial to their students

TABLE 61

Typical Anonymous Responses to Selected Items
on the Sentence Completion Survey
(Phillis Wheatley High School,
San Antonio, Texas)

My student counselor was . . .
    . . . very helpful and made me realize how much an education is worth.
    . . . understanding and knew what she was saying.
    . . . a football player and showed me studying was something I could do.
The study skills course was . . .
    . . . wonderful and something I would like to teach to others.
    . . . simply wonderful because it really helped us.
    . . . something that showed me how to get ahead.
The thing I liked most was . . .
    . . . taking tests that showed me my study weaknesses and how to change them.
    . . . somebody helping me make better grades.
    . . . having someone like ourselves teach us.
The thing I disliked most was . . .
    . . . the course didn't last long enough.
    . . . it made me sorry I didn't have it sooner.
    . . . nothing.
I believe that . . .
    . . . this course should be taught to everyone.
    . . . I can study and make good grades now.
    . . . I will work hard and try to go to college.
The course helped me . . .
    . . . by showing me how and why to be a better student.
    . . . by making me want to do better.
    . . . in organization and getting along with teachers.

—especially in the areas of organization, motivation, classroom behavior, and reading skills. The school administration felt that the course helped create a more positive attitude toward education in general and, more specifically, a more positive attitude toward themselves. The student counselors' reactions to the course were decisively positive. As a result of having taught the course, the student counselors seem to "grow" in self-confidence, in pride, and in wanting to help others help themselves. With few exceptions, students receiving the how-to-study instruction evaluated the course most favorably. The majority of students seem to think that the course helped them most in motivating them to become better students. The research report prepared by the project director recommended that the program be continued because it was a definite "asset to the local learning environment" (98).

The Wheatley High School project also added a new dimension to the student-counseling-student approach. Three levels of students were involved in the project—college-level student counselors trained high school seniors to provide student-to-student counseling for high school sophomores. Furthermore, supervision by responsible school officials was kept to the absolute minimum required for efficient coordination and scheduling of counseling activities. Thus the project results, though limited and subjective, do further suggest that student-to-student *training* can and should be employed in implementing the student-counseling-student approach, especially with students from minority groups or disadvantaged backgrounds.

ADAPTABILITY TO A DIFFERENT CULTURE

A comprehensive report (23) on the student-to-student counseling program at Southwest Texas State College was presented at the Congreso Interamericano de Psicología held in Mexico City in December, 1967. In addition to reporting the results achieved by the student-counseling-student approach, the 2½-hour presentation featured a 25-minute Spanish-language film (32) describing the counseling objectives, materials, and procedures developed for the academic adjustment and academic improvement components of the program. Shortly thereafter, Sr. Jorge Llanes B., assistant secretary for the Colegio de Psicología at the Universidad Nacional Autónoma de México, wrote to request more information about the counseling program and how it was implemented. After an exchange of correspondence, a group of Mexican psychology professors visited the campus of Southwest Texas State College in order to observe live student-to-student counseling sessions and to discuss the feasibility of adapting the approach to their own needs. After returning to Mexico, the visiting professors reported their favorable reaction to the student-counseling-student approach, and plans were formulated for setting up an experimental program of their own. Two counseling-oriented professors, Sr. Eduardo García H. and Sr. Fernando García C., were assigned to direct the counseling experiment.[12]

Assisted by a group of interested graduate students, the two professors implemented a four-step project designed to adapt the Southwest Texas State College program to the needs and conditions prevailing at the Universidad Nacional Autónoma de México. First, the counseling materials and study skills tests were translated into Spanish and the translations were carefully double-checked for content accuracy. Second, the program objectives were revised and the instructional contents were adapted to make them appropriate to the local situation. Third, a group of twelve third-year psychology students were selected and trained to provide academic orientation guidance for incoming psychology students. Finally, a sample of 171 first-year psychology majors, 63 men and 108 women, were selected to receive the student-to-student counseling.

The translation of testing and guidance materials required approximately three months to complete. Before final printing, the Spanish translations of the Survey of Study Habits and Attitudes (44), Effective Study Test (27), and Study Skills Surveys (26) were systematically rechecked by two independent teams and carefully field tested on a sample of forty-four students from fourteen Spanish-speaking nations.

[12] The investigation was financed by a research grant received from the ESSO Education Foundation.

The activities scheduled for each of the four two-hour counseling sessions are reported in Table 62. The major study skills topics covered by the student counselors were scheduling time, taking notes, reading textbooks, writing reports, and passing examinations. As indicated in Table 62, Spanish translations of the Survey of Study Habits and Attitudes, Effective Study Test, and Study Skills Surveys were administered to participating counselees at the beginning and at the end of the eight-hour counseling program. The total testing time for the two testing periods was about two and one-half hours, leaving approximately five and one-half hours of instructional time for presenting the college orientation and study skills materials. The counselees received no information about their test results until the test and retest scores were reported to them by their psychology professors about one month after the completion of student-to-student counseling. A comprehensive description of the total program, including the testing and guidance activities of the student counselors, is given in a twenty-four–minute film reporting the experimental project from inception through evaluation (33). Detailed descriptions of the research procedures and findings have been published and are available elsewhere (66, 67).

Comparisons of precounseling and postcounseling scores on the three study skills tests are presented in Tables 63, 64, and 65. Test results for all three instruments show a highly significant gain in measured study skills for the 63 men and 108 women receiving the student-to-student counseling. Unfortunately, local conditions prevailing at the time of the experiment made it impractical to try to obtain a matching group of uncounseled students to serve as a control sample.[13] Consequently, grade-point averages could not be used as a criterion for evaluating the program's effectiveness. The test-

[13] As a consequence of continuing student disorders, units of the Mexican army had occupied the campus of the Universidad Nacional Autónoma de México for ten days about three months before the experiment was conducted. The resulting disruption in normal information collecting and record keeping procedures made it impractical to attempt the matching of experimental and control samples on the basis of previous academic records or ability test scores. Likewise, it was impractical to try to collect test-retest data for the 150–200 uncounseled first-year psychology students.

TABLE 62
Outline of Counseling Activities for Four
Two-Hour Counseling Sessions
(Colegio de Psicología, Universidad Nacional
Autónoma de México, México, D.F.)

Session	Activity
1	Explain student-to-student counseling objectives and procedures Review growth and organization of the Colegio de Psicología Survey typical problems experienced by beginning psychology majors Report required courses and elective subjects for first-year students Explain need for testing and the planned use of test results Administer the three study skills tests Announce activities scheduled for second session
2	Analyze need for effective time utilization Report proper organization of available time Explain proven principles for efficient time management Direct student preparation of own daily activity schedule Analyze need for taking good lecture notes Report proven note taking procedures Demonstrate organizational characteristics of good lecture notes Compare differences between good and bad lecture notes Distribute and discuss sample lecture notes Announce activities scheduled for third session
3	Survey common textbook reading problems Explain the SQ3R approach to textbook reading Distribute and discuss the *Reading and Remembering Guide* Illustrate effective textbook underlining Analyze role of testing in the learning process Survey types of examinations favored by psychology professors Distribute and survey *Student-to-Student Tips* Discuss specific suggestions about preparing for tests Discuss specific suggestions about taking tests Discuss usual criteria for grading essay tests Describe role of effective time management during a test Analyze role of report writing in the learning process Explain proven procedures for effective report writing Discuss usual basis for grading written reports Announce activities scheduled for fourth session
4	Review study procedures presented earlier Explain test-retest methodology in psychological research Explain procedure for obtaining test results at a later date Readminister the three study skills tests Conduct a question-and-answer session on academic adjustment problems Appeal for immediate use of efficient study methods

NOTE: All sessions are of two hours' duration.

TABLE 63

Comparison of Precounseling and Postcounseling Scores on the
Survey of Study Habits and Attitudes: Spanish Edition
(Colegio de Psicología, Universidad Nacional
Autónoma de México, México, D.F.)

	Male Freshmen		Female Freshmen	
	Test	Retest	Test	Retest
N	63	63	108	108
$\bar{x}$	92.4	137.3	96.9	152.5
σ	27.9	36.5	22.4	28.8
D$\bar{x}$		44.9		55.6
t		9.05		18.28
P		$<.001$		$<.001$

TABLE 64

Comparison of Precounseling and Postcounseling Scores
on the Effective Study Test: Spanish Edition
(Colegio de Psicología, Universidad Nacional
Autónoma de México, México, D.F.)

	Male Freshmen		Female Freshmen	
	Test	Retest	Test	Retest
N	63	63	108	108
$\bar{x}$	82.7	93.1	87.3	96.8
σ	7.6	7.1	7.6	6.4
D$\bar{x}$		10.4		9.5
t		7.76		9.31
P		$<.001$		$<.001$

retest results, however, offer convincing evidence that the cross-culture research project has been successful in demonstrating the effectiveness of student-to-student counseling for students from another culture and speaking a different language.

During the spring semester of 1969, the ongoing program at the Universidad Nacional Autónoma de México was replicated, as nearly as possible, at Our Lady of the Lake College in San Antonio, Texas. The replication project used the Spanish version of the testing and counseling materials, and all instruction was given in

TABLE 65
Comparison of Precounseling and Postcounseling Scores
on the Study Skills Survey: Spanish Edition
(Colegio de Psicología, Universidad Nacional
Autónoma de México, México, D.F.)

	Male Freshmen		Female Freshmen	
	Test	Retest	Test	Retest
N	63	63	108	108
$\bar{x}$	33.3	51.0	40.6	55.1
σ	11.3	11.7	9.6	5.8
D$\bar{x}$		17.7		14.5
t		8.85		11.10
P		<.001		<.001

Spanish by two Spanish-speaking upperclassmen. Students receiving the instruction were 41 Spanish-speaking citizens of fourteen Latin American nations, whose average age and education level were almost identical to those reported for the 171 counselees in the Mexico City project. In fact, the counseling objectives, instructional contents, and counseling procedures for the two projects were almost identical in every important respect.

Precounseling and postcounseling scores were obtained for the Survey of Study Habits and Attitudes and the Effective Study Test. Test-retest results for the two projects were very similar, with the students at Our Lady of the Lake College also showing highly significant gains in their measured study skills and academic attitudes. Thus the results for the replication study confirmed those obtained for the Mexico City project. From the results obtained for the two groups of counselees, it would appear that the student-counseling-student approach might provide a practical and effective academic orientation procedure for Latin American students and institutions.

Assessment of Student-to-Student
Counseling Adaptability

The program of student-to-student counseling initiated at Southwest Texas State College in 1959 has since been adapted to a vari-

TABLE 66

Comparison of Test-Retest Scores on the Survey of Study Habits and Attitudes for Eight Peer Counseling Research Projects and Two Reliability Studies

Study	Year	N	Test-Retest Interval	Total Score Means		Difference between Means
				Test	Retest	
Repeat Reliability Research	1959	144	4 weeks	113.7	113.4	−0.3
Repeat Reliability Research	1962	51	14 weeks	117.1	115.9	−1.2
Southwest Texas State College	1960	216	12 weeks	109.2	139.0	29.8*
Southwest Texas State College	1961–62	695	12 weeks	108.1	132.7	24.6*
San Marcos High School	1959	54	6 weeks	97.2	122.3	25.1*
[a] San Marcos High School	1966	192	20 weeks	98.1	120.8	22.7*
[a] Project Upward Bound	1966	120	6 weeks	111.3	146.9	35.6*
[a] College Adjustment Seminar	1966	194	16 weeks	109.3	139.2	29.9*
[b] Universidad Nacional Autónoma de México	1969	171	4 days	95.2	146.9	51.7*
[b] Our Lady of the Lake College	1969	41	5 weeks	95.8	130.6	34.8*

* Counselees averaged significantly higher scores on retest ($P = <.01$).

[a] Survey of Study Habits and Attitudes scores reported to counselees during counseling without accompanying discussion of items identified by the counseling key.

[b] Survey of Study Habits and Attitudes scores not reported to counselees during counseling.

ety of guidance situations at the high school and college levels. The effectiveness and acceptability of the student-counseling-student approach, as evaluated by a variety of research strategies, has been consistently impressive for all reported investigations. The reaction of counselees to student-to-student counseling, as measured by both structured and unstructured approaches, has been decisively positive in every instance.

As reported in Table 66, precounseling and postcounseling scores on the Survey of Study Habits and Attitudes have consistently confirmed a highly significant improvement in the study skills and academic attitudes of students receiving how-to-study guidance from peer counselors. The test-retest results on these eight studies are especially meaningful in light of the established repeat reliability for this instrument, as reported in the same table. Comparable test-retest results have also been obtained with the Effective Study Test in all projects where such test data were obtained.

Where available, the grade-point averages for matching samples of counseled and uncounseled students have usually shown significant differences in academic performance favoring the peer-counseled samples. Thus, the counseled freshmen appear to be using the information acquired through their peer counseling experience.

In fact, the research results show student-to-student counseling to be a reasonably successful counseling procedure, whether the counseling effort be aimed at the prevention or the correction of academic difficulties, whether the counselees be from affluent or poverty backgrounds, or whether the language spoken be English or Spanish. The impressive evidence confirming the adaptability of student-to-student counseling thus suggests that a wide variety of educational institutions—high schools, junior colleges, senior colleges, universities—should consider adding the student-counseling-student approach to their mix of available counseling services. The real question, then, centers around the needs and conditions that are prerequisite to a meaningful program of student-to-student counseling.

6. Student-to-Student Counseling in Perspective

The counseling squeeze of higher education is already a fact. The explosive increase in student enrollment during the decade of the sixties, combined with limited resources available for counseling purposes, has placed a severe strain on the freshman counseling services available on many campuses. However, the urgent requirement for more and better freshman counseling, as evidenced by the high attrition rates reported for the freshman year (55, 86, 94, 117), has not gone unrecognized by the trustees and administrators at our institutions of higher learning. They are beginning to realize that each early leaver almost always represents a significant financial loss to their institution. Furthermore, they are coming to recognize that an effective counseling program is an important variable related to student retention (57), especially in view of the growing trend toward lowering the admissions requirements for disadvantaged students.

Kronovet (91) states that 92 percent of the 1,378 colleges and universities completing a 1966 questionnaire reported having some type of orientation program for their incoming freshmen. While varying in approach, content, and duration, most of these freshman orientation programs were provided during the week prior to the beginning of classes. After that, the incoming freshmen were usually left to their own resources in adjusting to the college community and to collegiate academic demands. However, about 15 percent of the reported orientation programs consisted of a required course lasting a semester or longer, with students receiving credit for satisfactory completion of course requirements. Some colleges and universities are thus reversing the trend and expanding their freshman orientation activities from what used to be fairly simple, brief, and inexpensive efforts to what are now much more elaborate, extensive, and costly programs.

Although the widespread use of brief and simple orientation programs is slowly being replaced by more elaborate efforts, the results reported for most freshman orientation activities suggest that a better definition of goals, contents, and procedures is badly needed. A systematic review of reports published during the past twenty years indicates that three major approaches to the freshman adjustment problem have been tried: (*a*) a precollege orientation program consisting of between two and five days of briefings and conferences offered during the summer or during the week before classes begin, (*b*) a first-semester orientation course consisting of a series of regularly scheduled classes lasting for between six and thirty-six weeks, and (*c*) a program of group or individual counseling sessions offered to predicted low achievers during their initial semester or to probationary students subsequent to their failing semester.

Published evaluations of precollege freshman orientation programs indicate that there is little or no evidence to support the contention that such programs help incoming freshmen to relate themselves more effectively to the academic community. Data analyzed by Cole and Ivey (53) clearly demonstrated that attendance at the precollege orientation program offered at Colorado State University made little difference in student attitudes toward academic achievement or in their subsequent academic success. Foxley (65) evaluated the precollege orientation program at the University of Utah and concluded that, instead of being oriented to meet specific program objectives, the participating freshmen were really being disoriented by the orientation experience. Furthermore, student responses to criterion instruments indicated that a "fun-and-games" type of orientation does not meet the academic and intellectual expectations and needs of incoming freshmen. Ivey (87) reported essentially negative results for a three-year evaluation of the freshman-week program at Bucknell 'University. Jessep (88) reported that students attending the precollege orientation conferences at the University of Wyoming were not helped to improve their academic performance, although conference attendance was positively related to enrollment in study skills classes, use of the counseling center, and persistence in college attendance. These findings are in basic agreement with the results reported for Auburn University by Griffin and Donnan (72) and for Kent State University by Pappas (97). Thus, the available research results indicate that the conventional precollege orientation program is not meeting the academic adjustment needs of beginning freshmen, although most of the students do enjoy and approve of such precollege activities.

Whereas the research findings are consistent in demonstrating the failure of most precollege orientation programs, the available evidence concerning the value of required college orientation courses for first-semester freshmen is inconsistent and inconclusive. Entwisle (63) surveyed the literature prior to 1960 and found eighteen reports evaluating the effectiveness of study skills courses for college students. The research results indicated that some academic improvement usually followed a study skills course, with the amount of improvement being positively related to the length of the course, the motivation of the students, and the emphasis given to supervised studying. Furthermore, all the voluntary-participation college-level courses reported substantial grade improvement, while the required-participation courses for students on scholastic probation showed only slight improvement in academic performance. These conclusions are in essential agreement with those reported by Blake (2) following a 1953 survey that revealed that about one out of ten colleges in the United States was requiring all freshmen to take a study skills course.

Research reported since 1960 has largely confirmed the positive results obtained with voluntary-enrollment how-to-study courses and the lack of results for required-participation freshman orientation courses. For example, Rothman and Leonard (105), in a carefully designed investigation, found no significant differences in the mean grade-point averages, attrition rates, and value orientations for experimental students participating in a semester-long orientation course and control students receiving no orientation instruction. The available research results thus indicate freshman orientation courses to be of limited effectiveness except where student participation is voluntary and study skills instruction is emphasized. The importance of both course content and student motivation is further confirmed by Berg and Rentel (1). They found that students who were motivated to improve and who voluntarily enrolled in a study skills course did raise their grade-point averages, whereas students who were similarly motivated, but did not receive study skills instruction, failed to make the same gains.

In recent years, numerous investigators have studied the effects of various group and individual counseling approaches upon the academic achievement of counselees. Of twenty-six studies reported during the past twenty years, only nine produced significant changes in academic performance. Investigations by Sheldon and Landsman (109), Klingelhofer (90), De Weese (59), Goodstein and Crites (71), Maroney (93), Speegle (110), Winborn and Schmidt (128), Duncan (61), Northman (96), and Hill and Grieneeks (82) all report little or no success in improving the academic achievement of counselees experiencing scholastic difficulty. Furthermore, Goodstein (70) reports that a five-year follow-up of counseling effectiveness with probationary students at the University of Iowa indicated the counseled group to have a greater percentage of students dismissed for academic failure while a comparison uncounseled group had a greater percentage of students who graduated.

By contrast, studies completed by Spielberger, Weitz and Denny (111), Hart (76), Hendrix (81), Chestnut (52), Dickenson and Truax (60), Pappas (97), Gilbreath (69), Roth, Mauksch, and Peiser (103), and Thelen and Harris (119) all produced significant improvement in the academic performance of counselees. In all of the nine studies reporting success, student participation in the counseling program was on a voluntary basis. Comparison of the successful and unsuccessful counseling projects further suggests that, in addition to being somewhat longer in duration, the successful programs were characterized by a more client-centered approach and a more motivation-oriented content.

Although there is a dearth of literature reporting the successful treatment of underachievers, the successful programs appear to have several characteristics in common. First, the successful approaches have recognized that the psychodynamics underlying underachievement are not the same for all students. Consequently, it is inappropriate to adhere to one therapeutic position offering a given therapeutic experience regardless of diagnosis. Second, the successful approaches have recognized that underachievers usually are reluctant to seek individual help. Consequently, the prevention or treatment of underachievement is best accomplished in the group setting through orientation courses, study skills seminars, and other programs that reach out to the underachiever. Third, the successful programs have recognized that lack of clarification of the underlying dynamics of underachievement produces a spurious prevention or treatment approach. Consequently, a counseling program for underachievers should be based on a set of assumptions about the variety of psychodynamics underlying underachievement and appropriate treatment approaches based on these assumptions. Finally, the successful programs have recognized that treatment approaches not directly related to motivational variables are unlikely to be successful. Consequently, the prevention or treatment of underachievement requires the inclusion of motivational correlates if maladaptive achievement behavior is to be reversed.

One other characteristic is common to all the successful programs. If implemented on a widespread basis, any one of them would require the investment of considerable financial and personnel resources. It is the thesis of this book, however, that freshmen do not have to be without adequate academic adjustment counseling simply because of such economic considerations. The research results reported in Chapters 4 and 5 have repeatedly demonstrated that the needed counseling can be provided, meaningfully and economically, through the expanded use of carefully selected and trained student counselors.

The model student-to-student counseling program described in Chapter 3 possesses all four of the features common to the successful approaches reported in the literature. First, the student counselors did seek to identify and deal with each counselee's specific dynamics of underachievement. Second, the counseling program did utilize the group setting to provide guidance activities that reached out to involve the potential underachiever. Third, the counseling program was based upon a carefully formulated set of assumptions about the psychodynamics of underachievement. Finally, the analysis of motivational correlates of underachievement was central to the student-counseling-student approach.

Thus, despite the group structuring activities associated with the formation of counselee groups, the student academic counselors did attempt to recognize and provide for individual differences in the needs of their counselees. Even during the large group counseling sessions, each counselee counseled by a student academic counselor received some individual attention. During the counseling sessions with small groups or individual counselees, the student academic counselors gave particular attention to helping each student achieve an understanding of his academic problems and how he might most effectively cope with them.

Chapter 1 reports the results of a survey made by Brown and Zunker (49) on the use of student-to-student counseling at senior colleges and universities during the 1963–64 academic year. Analysis of survey responses indicated that student counselors were already being widely used, with a developing trend toward using them to provide systematic counseling on academic adjustment problems. The survey questionnaire also included five questions designed to evaluate the acceptability and productivity of the student-counseling-student approach as perceived by the director of counseling at the responding institutions. Table 67 summarizes the answers to these five questions for the institutions of higher learning that were reported to be using student counselors.

For these 118 institutions, 83.9 percent of the respondents felt that student counselors do make an effective and positive contribution to the total counseling program. Likewise, 94.9 percent of the respondents planned to continue the use of student counselors on their campus. The respondents were divided, however, on whether or not the counseling activities of student counselors should be expanded beyond those now performed. Whereas 40 percent of the respondents thought that expansion should be made, the remaining 60 percent were evenly divided between uncertainty about such expansion and rejection of expansion in student counselor functions. Negative faculty reaction to student-to-student counseling was reported in only 3.4 percent of the institutions, with 80.5 percent of the respondents reporting little or no negative reaction from faculty members. Finally, 77.1 percent of the respondents believed that the use of student counselors was likely to increase during the next ten years. Only 2.5 percent of the respondents thought an increased use of student counselors to be unlikely.

Some differences were noted between the evaluations of respondents from smaller and larger institutions. More respondents from the large colleges and universities believed that the use of student counselors would be expanded during the next ten years, that they were making an effective and a positive counseling contribution, and that their counseling activities should be expanded. Although these percentage differences are small, in that they average only about 10 percent, they do reflect a greater acceptance of student-to-student counseling by professional personnel workers at the larger institutions of higher learning.

About 65 percent of the respondents made spontaneous comments in the space provided on the back of the questionnaire. Several of these comments have been selected for quotation because of the insight they offer into the effectiveness and acceptability of student-to-student counseling. However, quotations will be identified only by the size and regional location of the quoted institu-

TABLE 67
Evaluation of Student Counselors as Reported by Responding Institutions in a National Sample

Question	Response	Enrollment under 2,000		Enrollment over 2,000		Total	
		No.	%[a]	No.	%[b]	No.	%[c]
1. Do you feel that the student counselors make an effective and positive contribution to your institution's total guidance program?	Yes	62	80.5	37	90.2	99	83.9
	Uncertain	13	16.9	4	9.8	17	14.4
	No	2	2.6	0	0.0	2	1.7
2. Do you plan to continue the use of student counselors at your institution?	Yes	72	93.5	40	97.6	112	94.9
	Uncertain	4	5.2	1	2.4	5	4.2
	No	1	1.3	0	0.0	1	0.8
3. Do you feel that the guidance activities of your student counselors should be expanded beyond those they now perform?	Yes	29	37.7	18	43.9	47	39.8
	Uncertain	22	28.6	13	31.7	35	29.7
	No	26	33.8	10	24.4	36	30.5
4. Do a significant number (5 percent or more) of your faculty members react negatively to the use of student counselors?	Yes	3	3.9	1	2.4	4	3.4
	Uncertain	13	16.9	6	14.6	19	16.1
	No	61	79.2	34	82.9	95	80.5
5. Do you believe that the use of student counselors by colleges is likely to increase during the next ten years?	Yes	56	72.7	35	85.4	91	77.1
	Uncertain	18	23.4	6	14.6	24	20.3
	No	3	3.9	0	0.0	3	2.5

[a] Percentage is based on 77 responding institutions.
[b] Percentage is based on 41 responding institutions.
[c] Percentage is based on 118 responding institutions.

tions because respondents were assured that all responses would be considered confidential.

The respondent from a college in the Middle Atlantic Region with an enrollment of approximately 2,700 made the following comment: "Freshmen on this campus have expressed strong approval of student counselors as 'Big Brothers' and 'Big Sisters.' Then, too, these students have been very effective in counseling with freshmen relative to rules and regulations of the school, faculty-student relationships, college and community facilities, and the use of efficient study procedures. This school is making a definite effort to increase the use of student counselors."

The respondent from an institution in the Western Region having an enrollment of about 800 made this comment: "We have used students in the position of resident advisor in our dormitories for about twenty years. We have no other supervision in our dormitories and no adult residents, so that the student staff is directly responsible to the deans. Most of what could be called training goes on in group meetings with one of the deans; these meetings are more frequent at the beginning of the year, but continue during the whole year. Our system is not highly structured or particularly formal, but the contact is close and regular. It continues to seem impressive to me what student advisors can accomplish and I would not give them up for anything!"

The respondent from an institution in the Southwestern Region with an enrollment of about 600 made the following comment: "Our program could be improved with a greater emphasis upon training. An effort is being made to encourage enrollment in workshops in addition to the in-service training. I believe student counselors can be used more than they are and that effort should be extended toward greater utilization of their service."

The following statement was made by the respondent for a university from the Southwestern Region having an enrollment of approximately 10,000: "My 'yes' grows out of a feeling that student counselors represent the most expandable and cheapest resource colleges will have when they face the increased needs of the future."

The respondent from a college in the Midwestern Region having an enrollment of about 600 students had this comment: "I am very pleased with the results of our student counseling program. We have gradually expanded their responsibilities. Our student counselors are in reality policemen. They maintain law and order in the freshman dormitories. I personally feel that the student counselors could be used and trained in such a way that their contributions would be much more significant."

The following comment comes from the respondent for a college of about 2,000 students located in the Southwestern Region: "The student counseling program at our university is still in the 'budding' stage. With more concentration, we visualize a very worthwhile program here—particularly in our residence halls. In fact, as we continue to grow, I feel that much of our best and most effective counseling will be done with these resources."

Finally, the following statement was made by the respondent for a college from the Southwestern Region having an enrollment of about 700 students: "May I attest also that the parents of our students have expressed on several occasions their appreciation for this counseling program offered by our college. The student-to-student relationship through counseling has enlarged the vision of all students as to what Christian higher education is all about. The counseling program has made the quest for learning a significant and meaningful one and has given the college a smoother working operation to accomplish our academic objectives. This has been very good, and we are deeply appreciative of it."

From the evaluative answers and the spontaneous comments given by the 118 directors of counseling, it is apparent that there is a great deal of interest in expanding the use of student-to-student counseling. It is essential, however, that the strengths and weaknesses inherent in this approach be fully recognized by anyone planning to set up a program of student-to-student counseling.

To begin with, it must be recognized that each institution has its own unique set of characteristics and that the student-counseling-student approach described in Chapter 3 is generalizable to another campus only to the extent that its operational, philosophical, and environmental context is similar to that of Southwest Texas State College. For example, the mere size of the institution is a significant factor that must be taken into account. The larger the university, the more complex the organizational structure, the more attenuated the administrative control over student behavior, and the more divided and conflicting the sources of influence on students. Whereas a program of student-to-student counseling can be operated readily out of the counseling center at a small college, such a program might be better located in the various colleges at a large university—that is, engineering, education, arts and sciences.

The problems connected with the proper location of the program, as well as those of program objectives and contents, must, of course, be decided on the basis of carefully defined local needs. The unique characteristics of each institution—educational purpose, organizational structure, learning climate, student subculture—must be carefully considered while planning a student-to-student counseling program. To that end, it would be highly desirable for student leaders to be included in such planning from the beginning.

The proper reimbursement of student counselors is another point to be considered. In all but one of the student-to-student counseling projects described in this book, the student counselors undertook their duties as an added activity carried for financial reimbursement. Observation confirms, however, that even the most able of our undergraduates is frequently kept racing to keep up with the academic demands imposed by our tension-producing institutions of higher education. Why not, therefore, set up the program in a course context and give academic credit to the student counselors in recognition of their training and counseling activities? Such course-connected apprenticeships are common at the graduate level, so why not offer a practicum experience for undergraduate student counselors? One institution, Huston-Tillotson College in Austin, Texas, has already done so with positive results.[1] In addition to

---

[1] A description of the operational characteristics of this student-to-student counseling program may be obtained by writing directly to Dr. Carmen Lowry, Director of Counseling, Huston-Tillotson College, Austin, Texas.

financial reimbursement based on an hourly pay scale, the student counselors in their program received three semester hours of elec- tive college credit for each year's service as a student counselor. The course, which was offered only to secondary education students, is jointly conducted by the education department and the counsel- ing center. Everyone connected with the program—administrators, faculty members, and students—has consistently affirmed the posi- tive value of such apprenticeship experience for students enrolled in a teacher training program.

Furthermore, the introduction of student-to-student counseling will increase, rather than decrease, the work load of the profession- al counseling staff. It must *not* be assumed that student-counseling- student procedures can be employed to replace the work of profes- sional counselors. Student counselors require careful training and their usefulness is limited to carefully selected and defined coun- seling activities. Care must be exercised that student counselors do not get in too deep and that adequate professional staff are avail- able for consultation and referral as needed. A successful program requires the development of practical and effective strategies for the selection, training, and supervision of student counselors. Fail- ure in any one of these areas is likely to produce a group of student counselors who are uncomfortable in their roles, unconvinced about their duties, uncertain in their behaviors, and unconvincing to their counselees.

The importance of careful selection, training, and supervision of student counselors is clearly demonstrated in a report by Harren and Jenkins (75). This study is being reported here, not as another example of a successful program of student-to-student counseling, but as a vehicle for pointing out the likelihood of failure unless certain essential prerequisites for success have been carefully pro- vided for. The study was designed to adapt the successful tech- niques developed at Southwest Texas State College and apply them to a subgroup of college freshmen on a large university campus. A very high percentage of the freshman fraternity pledges at the University of Texas are forced to drop out of the pledge program each year because they are unable to meet the minimum grade-point average set by the Interfraternity Council for initiation. It was believed that a program of student-to-student academic adjustment counseling for fraternity pledges might alleviate this situation. Consequently, research was undertaken to determine if student counselors selected from the active membership of participating fraternities could provide effective academic adjustment counseling for their respective fraternity pledges.

During the spring semester of 1965, the experimental program designed to improve the grades of freshman pledges was explained to Interfraternity Council representatives. Each fraternity then discussed and voted on whether or not the fraternity wished to participate. The twenty fraternities who voted to participate nominated five persons as student counselor candidates from among their current active membership. Selected counselors were given an intensive thirty-hour training program the week before Rush Week in the fall. Appointed student counselors were subsequently paid $.90 per hour for each hour spent with their pledges.

The counseling program for the pledges was spread out over twelve weeks of the fall semester. Each pledge was exposed to four hours of orientation (large group) and four hours of counseling (small group) with regard to development of effective study habits and attitudes and discussion of specific academic difficulties the pledges were encountering. Instruments utilized during the counseling sessions included the Survey of Study Habits and Attitudes and the Effective Study Test. Since both were used extensively as counseling tools, they were considered to be part of the treatment variable and were thus judged inappropriate for use as a dependent or criterion variable in this study. Consequently, the first-semester grade-point average became the only criterion for evaluating the program's effectiveness.

Of the twenty fraternities originally agreeing to participate in the program, twelve actually did participate, but of these twelve, only six completed the entire twelve-week program. These six fraternities then comprised the experimental group (N=110). Two control groups were used: control group #1 consisted of the previous year's pledges for the six participating fraternities (N=150);

control group #2 consisted of pledges for the current year from the nonparticipating fraternities (N=186).

Results of the initial statistical analysis of grade-point averages for the counseled and control groups indicated that there was no significant increase in grade-point average for the experimental group over either control group. However, since experimental and control samples were not matched on measured scholastic aptitude or prior academic achievement, a predicted grade-point average formula was applied to all groups. This formula utilized high school rank and CEEB Scholastic Aptitude Test scores to predict a student's first-semester grade-point average at the University of Texas. Again the differences between the experimental and control groups were not significant, but the higher predicted grade-point averages for the control groups helped to explain the lack of significant differences in the first-semester grades of experimental and control samples.

The failure of this study to replicate the findings from other student-to-student counseling studies may be due to several factors. The quality of the counseling program may not have been as high as that employed in other studies due to lack of continued supervision of the student counselors throughout the twelve-week program. Pertinent to this point, it should be noted that only six of the fraternities actually completed the program, although twelve had initiated the student-to-student counseling for their pledges. Also, use of the fraternity as a context for the counseling program may have limited the program's effect. In fact, the pressures toward social participation in fraternity life may have been a competing goal that cancelled or negated the effect of the counseling program. Moreover, the counseling was accomplished at the fraternity house itself, rather than within the more formal office facilities of a counseling center. Also, the student counselors were fellow fraternity members and the continuing counselor-counselee interaction may have stressed social values over academic values. Finally, although the fraternity actives voted to participate in the program, the fall-semester pledges of the fraternity did not individually volunteer for the program, but were required to participate. Most certainly, this unsuccessful student-to-student counseling project was not a true replication of the program at Southwest Texas State College, in that the two approaches differed significantly in five important aspects—stated counseling objectives, available counseling facilities, effective counseling climate, routine counseling supervision, and systematic counseling follow-up.

The failure of this particular student-to-student counseling project offers striking proof that the student-to-student approach is likely to be successful only where realistic and systematic planning and supervision have accompanied program implementation. A successful program of student-to-student counseling cannot simply be "lifted" from one setting and installed intact at another location. Rather, the student-counseling-student approach must be carefully adapted to meet the student needs and local conditions prevailing on a specific college campus. Consequently, the following seven requirements are suggested as essential elements in a successful program of student-to-student counseling:

1. *Formulation of meaningful peer counseling goals.* The objectives for all student-counseling-student activities should be carefully spelled out in a manner that clearly recognizes student and institution needs, problems, and resources.

2. *Development of informed peer counseling support.* The student-counseling-student approach should be effectively sold in a manner that assures the appropriate support and involvement of administration, faculty, and students.

3. *Delineation of realistic peer counseling activities.* The counseling activities to be performed by student counselors should be carefully defined in order to make certain that selected procedures and materials are appropriate to stated counseling objectives and to the student-counseling-student approach.

4. *Provision of adequate peer counseling facilities.* The student-counseling-student effort should be provided with adequate office and classroom space, properly equipped and centrally located, in order to assure efficient program operation, effective program supervision, and manifest program recognition.

5. *Selection and training of peer counseling personnel.* All personnel, professional and student, directly involved in the student-to-student counseling program should be carefully selected and given appropriate training in order to assure their understanding of the duties and responsibilities assigned to the student counselors and the potentialities and limitations inherent in the student-counseling-student approach.

6. *Supervision of peer counseling activities.* The ongoing program of student-counseling-student activities should be continually supervised by professional personnel workers in order to assure efficient, realistic, and coordinated program operation.

7. *Evaluation and revision of peer counseling effort.* All aspects of the student-to-student counseling program should be evaluated systematically and the individual counseling activities should be eliminated, revised, or expanded, as appropriate, on the basis of their proven effectiveness.

As reported in an analysis presented elsewhere (24, 25), the program of student-to-student academic adjustment counseling possesses four characteristics essential to its adoption on other college campuses. First, it is economical in terms of both financial and personnel costs. Second, it is acceptable in terms of both student and faculty approval. Third, it is effective in terms of both study behavior and grade-average improvement. Finally, it is practical in terms of both necessary facilities and required supervision.

The two-year community college, with its emphasis upon open admissions, would appear to be a very appropriate setting for the successful implementation of the student-counseling-student approach. In fact, the program of student-to-student study skills counseling described in Chapter 3 has already been successfully adapted to at least two junior college campuses—Thomas Nelson Community College in Hampton, Virginia, and Laredo Junior College in Laredo, Texas. On both campuses, counseling on academic adjustment and study skills problems is being provided for all beginning freshmen by sophomore students employed for this purpose by the college counseling center. Training of the student counselors is accomplished during the summer through fifteen two-hour training sessions provided by the counseling center staff, with the trainees being selected from second-semester freshmen who are qualified to receive financial assistance through the college's work-study program. Counseling activities have been adapted to fit the community college situation, with the topics covered being similar to those listed in Table 12 under Survival Orientation, Test Interpretation, and Study Skills Counseling. These programs are not being described in greater detail because no research data are, as yet, available to evaluate their effectiveness.[2] However, preliminary reports received from professional counselors indicate that the student-counseling-student approach has been well received by the students and faculties at both colleges.

Several recently published reports indicate that the student-counseling-student approach has been successfully adapted to other areas of campus life. For example, Wharton, McKean, and Knights (126) report the successful use of student assistants for faculty advisors at Allegheny College, while Wolff (129) reports the effective use of undergraduates as campus mental health workers at the University of Rochester. Both investigations present research results that convincingly support the expanded use of student-to-student counseling under properly controlled conditions. Waits (124) reports an innovative peer counseling program introduced at Los Angeles City College in an effort to diagnose and deal with the special problems faced by ghetto students recruited into college from inner-city high schools where college preparatory instruction is not offered. In addition to counseling these students about their special adjustment problems, the student counselors also try to identify sources of student dissatisfaction with the college curriculum and operation. The student counselors then report on these potential problem areas to appropriate college administrators. Finally, a completely student-run and student-staffed Advising

---

[2] Detailed descriptions of the two community college peer counseling programs may be obtained by writing directly to Mrs. Ann Unger, counselor at Thomas Nelson Community College, Hampton, Virginia, and Mr. Warren L. Haslam, Director of Testing and Counseling, Laredo Junior College, Laredo, Texas.

Office was recently introduced by the School of Education at the University of Michigan (115). The stated purposes of this counseling service are to provide supplemental advising by experienced peers who have completed various program requirements, such as directed teaching, and to provide a place where students can talk informally about their aspirations and try to relate these to their selected program of studies.

Upcraft (121) reports a successful program involving the use of upperclass students to provide academic advisement for freshmen. In this program, the student counselor's role was the same as the typical faculty advisor in Justin Morrill College at Michigan State University. They had complete freedom to recommend courses and instructors. They helped students with the administrative complexities of enrollment and scheduling. They kept and used the academic files for freshmen. They advised students who were in academic difficulty or referred them to someone who could help them. They were available for informal personal counseling and as a source of general information about the college. They served as a vital communication link between the freshmen and the student relations office. Program evaluation made by both faculty and students indicates that the student counselors handled their assigned responsibilities in an efficient and effective manner.

Murry (95) likewise found upperclass student advisors to be competent in providing needed information about course requirements and university regulations so that freshman advisees could make appropriate choices regarding educational plans. Evaluation of the experimental student-advising-student program at Kansas State University led Murry to conclude that the advising outcomes obtained for student advisors appeared to be at least equal, and frequently superior, to those for faculty advisors. In this study, student advisors obtained significantly higher criterion scores than faculty advisors in all the "human interest" variables—friendliness, warmth, openness, and accessibility—assessed through a satisfaction scale completed by counselees.

Despite the potentialities inherent in student-to-student counseling, some college administrators and faculty members will undoubtedly be opposed or apathetic to the expanded use of student-counseling-student procedures. They will point out that the approach is potentially dangerous because student counselors receive only limited training and may not recognize the point at which a problem exceeds their capabilities. Although such concern is not without justification, the operational procedures reported in Chapter 3 were developed to minimize this danger. The careful delineation of the student counselor's duties, the systematic selection and training process, the continuous supervision by professional personnel workers, the open channels for communication and referral —all were designed to protect both the counselor and the counselee from peer counseling excesses.

Admittedly, all these measures still leave much to the judgment of the student counselor. Consequently, appropriate safeguards must be devised and made operational in order to protect the counselee, the counselor, and the counseling program. Some major factors to be considered in the utilization of upperclassmen as student counselors are as follows: (*a*) careful selection of would-be counselors, (*b*) effective in-service training for those who counsel, (*c*) continuous supervision of student counselors, (*d*) close communication between professional and student counselors, and (*e*) systematic channels for referral of problem cases. All these measures, however, still leave much to the judgment of the student counselors. Most of the opposition or apathy of some faculty members is probably based upon this inescapable fact. The trend, however, is toward increasing use of student-to-student counseling, for the inherent potentialities in the process are too great to be long ignored.

Where adequate counseling services are lacking, freshmen will naturally turn to upperclassmen to obtain needed advice and reassurance. More often than not, the assistance thus obtained is haphazardly given and erroneous, superficial, or biased in content. Such results are to be expected as long as the student-counseling-student process is unstructured and unsupervised. The use of student counselors, as described in Chapters 3, 4, and 5, substitutes selection, training, and supervision for indifference, misinformation, and chance.

In the final analysis, the student-counseling-student approach is best judged by the results that have been obtained. In a series of carefully controlled experiments, students receiving student-to-student counseling out-performed students not receiving such counseling by quite substantial margins. Comparison test-retest scores for counseled students showed significant improvement in measured study skills and academic attitudes. Grade-point averages for counseled students were significantly higher than those reported for uncounseled students. Counseled students testified overwhelmingly concerning the high value they placed on their peer counseling experience. The research results reported in Chapters 4 and 5 are thus consistent in suggesting that the use of carefully selected, trained, and supervised student counselors provides a meaningful and effective alternative to the largely unproductive college preparation and orientation programs now being offered by so many of our high schools, junior colleges, senior colleges, and universities.

Recent investigations into the college dropout problem (55, 94, 117) indicate that most colleges do need to do much more than they are now doing to maximize the likelihood of graduation by those whom they admit. Furthermore, unless effective action is taken, and taken quickly, the developing trend toward the relaxing of admissions requirements and the recruitment of disadvantaged students will undoubtedly result in a significant rise in the failure rate for entering freshmen.

Although operational economy and counseling effectiveness are important evaluation criteria, perhaps a more significant consideration is the personal commitment and involvement of the students who counsel. In this period when students are questioning the relevance of their learning experiences and are pressing for meaningful involvement in campus affairs, the student-counseling-student approach may offer an apprenticelike activity that provides a satisfying outlet for service motives while giving an added dimension to the student's preparation for future careers in teaching, social work, government service, or whatever.

Evidence as to the student counselor's sense of commitment and involvement is afforded by a follow-up of the student academic counselors employed by the Testing and Counseling Center at Southwest Texas State College during the 1959–60 through 1965–66 academic years. Of the seventy-four students employed as counselors during this seven-year period, twenty-nine, or 39.2 percent, decided to become professional counselors and have subsequently received their master's degree or counseling certificate. Only one of the twenty-nine had considered entering the counseling profession prior to their employment as student academic counselors. Furthermore, all but four of the remaining forty-five student academic counselors subsequently became elementary or secondary school teachers and all of them credited their employment as student academic counselors with providing training and experience that helped and inspired them to become more confident, effective, and dedicated teachers.

Further evidence as to the positive reaction of student counselors to their student-counseling-student experience is provided by Shafer (108). Following the successful implementation of a student-to-student counseling program at Madison College in Harrisonburg, Virginia, the nineteen student counselors employed for the project were interviewed to ascertain their reactions to the counseling experience. Four independent interviewers were selected from the faculty of the psychology department to meet with the student counselors individually and conduct taped interviews as a means of measuring results in terms of personal gains to the counselors. Each interviewer followed a structured outline in which the student counselors were asked questions to determine the extent of satisfaction, growth, and learning they had experienced through their participation in the program.

During these interviews, all of the nineteen student counselors stated that they themselves had resorted to some of the principles set forth in the *Effective Study Guide*. For example, the counselors were all carrying a full load of course work and they soon discovered that their commitment to the counseling program exerted a considerable amount of pressure for more efficient use of their own time. Consequently, they all stated that their involvement in the program had led them to learn how to organize and use their time better so that their own grades would not suffer.

All but three of the nineteen student counselors were preparing to become teachers, and they all viewed their experience in the program as valuable in their preparation for classroom teaching. The personal growth gained from their counseling experience may best be described by this excerpt from a report (108, pp. 39–40) on the interview results prepared by the project director:

These student counselors stated that they had used their counseling experience to apply some of the principles previously learned in their education courses as well as to seek new methods of teaching. They also found it necessary to develop different methods and techniques to meet the needs of different personalities. Through experience, the student counselors soon learned that the function of a teacher is to help students discover things for themselves, and that it is rarely possible to impart knowledge by "telling people what they need to know." Too, they learned that when they forced the counselees to do their own work, with help where it was needed, the results were significant.

An aspect of classroom teacher behavior most often referred to by the counselors was that of emotional control. The necessity for control of one's own emotions was stressed, and the counselors recognized a need to adjust their emotional state of mind to that of the counselee.

In relating to their counselees, one of the most difficult lessons for the student counselors to learn was that of accepting others as worthy individuals when their standards and their value systems differed to any great degree. When they learned that to try to solve problems of others, or to help them to solve their problems, on the basis of the counselor's terms resulted only in building an opposing force against which the counselee could struggle, they became more effective. Despite all of the coaching of the investigator, many of the student counselors had to learn through experience that each counselee was different and very much the product of her background culture. As understanding increased, some of the counselors discovered that counselees who exhibited indifference to academic achievement were in fact using such an attitude as a façade; this attitude lacked reality and was resorted to as a cover-up by the unsuccessful student. They detected several sources of underlying causes for the indifferent attitude. Students resorted to indifference when they were deeply hurt, frustrated, or confused. They also assumed an indifferent attitude when they felt the need for self-justification or when they needed an alibi for unpopular or unsuccessful social behavior.

As the student counselors increased in understanding of the counselees, they usually learned to understand themselves better. Through objective study of human behavior in themselves and others, they became aware of how their moods had affected others, what their weaknesses in relating to others were, what capacities and limitations they had, the necessity of being honest, and the necessity for self-control. Each student counselor stated that she had gained personally by participation in the program.

In view of these three factors—economy of operation, effectiveness of counseling, and involvement of students—the student-counseling-student approach should experience rapid acceptance as a routine counseling procedure. Just as group therapy was originally deemed a poor substitute for individual therapy but is now often the treatment of choice, so also may student-to-student counseling become, in many cases, the counseling procedure of choice. Whether or not this acceptance does develop will depend upon the proven productivity and the ready adaptability of the student-counseling-student approach.

Recent surveys of research findings (51, 55, 58, 73, 94, 106, 123) suggest that the factors influencing collegiate academic success are much more complex than most administrators had previously recognized. However, college administrators are coming to recognize that each entering freshman should be helped to make a satisfactory adjustment to the collegiate learning environment so that he can quickly begin to realize his full potentialities. On the basis of research completed to date, student-to-student counseling does promise to be an economical, practical, and effective means for providing this needed assistance for our entering freshmen.

In conclusion, it should be pointed out that all too few colleges and universities provide students an opportunity truly to identify with the academic program in a meaningful way. In his study of college influence upon student character, Eddy (62) concluded that the colleges that were most effective in reaching their students were those which afforded opportunity for involvement of students, participation of students, critical thinking of students, and commitment of students. The program of student-to-student academic adjustment counseling, as described in this book, does most definitely make provision for all four. Furthermore, this type of student involvement activity reflects positive, constructive behavior rather than the negative, destructive behavior that has characterized so much of the recent campus unrest accompanying student involvement efforts.

APPENDICES

A. Student Counselor Utilization Survey
B. Variables Obtained for Initial Factorial Investigation
C. Variables Obtained for Follow-Up Factorial Investigation
D. Student Counselor Evaluation Form
E. Survival Orientation Activity Sequence Check List
F. Test Interpretation Activity Sequence Check List
G. Test Interpretation Program Information Form
H. Transcription of Test Interpretation Session
I. Study Habits Evaluation Activity Sequence Check List
J. Scholastic Difficulty Analysis Form
K. Activity Sequence Outline: Note Taking Instruction
L. Personal Data Form
M. Occupational Analysis Form
N. Problem Summary
O. Test Results Report Form
P. Educational Analysis Form
Q. Counseling Evaluation Questionnaire
R. Distribution of Item Responses for Counseling Evaluation
S. Counseling Comprehension Test
T. Sentence Completion Survey
U. Rating Scale for Evaluating Student Reaction to the College Adjustment Seminar Study Habits Content
V. Rating Scale for Evaluating Student Reaction to the College Adjustment Seminar Study Motivation Content

APPENDIX A

Student Counselor Utilization Survey

DIRECTIONS: Please answer each question fully. Check all answers that apply. Use additional sheets if necessary. All answers will be treated with the strictest confidence.

A. Identifying Information
   1. Your name ....
   2. Your title ....
   3. Name of institution ....
   4. Institution address ....
   5. Approximate undergraduate enrollment ....
   6. Are undergraduate students utilized as student counselors to as-sist in the guidance of freshmen at your institution? ☐Yes ☐ No

> If your answer is "no," please return the questionnaire in the enclosed envelope without answering the remaining questions; if your answer is "yes," please answer the remaining questions before returning the questionnaire.

B. Utilization of Undergraduate Student Counselors
   1. Check where student counselors are systematically used on your campus:
      ☐ Freshman residence halls
      ☐ Instructional departments
      ☐ Study habits clinic
      ☐ Student social center (student union)
      ☐ Student religious center (chapel)
      ☐ Testing and guidance center (counseling office)
      ☐ Other ....

   2. Check if your student counselors routinely counsel with students individually or in groups:
      ☐ Individual students
      ☐ Small group of 2–6 students
      ☐ Intermediate group of 7–20 students
      ☐ Large group of 21 or more students

   3. Check types of counseling activities routinely performed by your student counselors:
      ☐ New student orientation
      ☐ Dormitory life supervision
      ☐ Study habits counseling
      ☐ Educational program planning
      ☐ Vocational guidance
      ☐ Religious counseling

☐ Psychological test   ☐ Personal-social problems
  interpretation   counseling
☐ Subject matter tutoring   ☐ Other ....

4. Check the types of counseling materials routinely used by your
   student counselors:

     Psychological Tests   Guidance Materials
☐ Scholastic ability test   ☐ College catalog
  scores
☐ Intelligence test scores   ☐ Freshman handbook
☐ Multifactor aptitude test   or guide
  scores   ☐ High school transcript
☐ Battery achievement test
  scores   ☐ College academic records
☐ Reading comprehension   ☐ College personnel records
  test scores
☐ English mechanics test   ☐ Biographical or personal
  scores   history data forms
☐ Study habits questionnaire   ☐ Occupational briefs
  scores
                                 ☐ Other ....
☐ Occupational interest   ....
  inventory scores
☐ Personality appraisal   ☐ Other ....
  questionnaire scores   ....

C. Selection and Training of Undergraduate Student Counselors
   1. Check the criteria employed in the selection of your student
      counselors:
☐ Scholastic ability test   ☐ Previous leadership
  scores   experience
☐ Study habits survey scores   ☐ Faculty members'
                                   evaluations
☐ Personality appraisal   ☐ Dormitory director's
  questionnaire scores   evaluation
☐ College grade average   ☐ Peer acceptance ratings
☐ College major and/or   ☐ Other ....
  minor   ☐ Other ....

   2. Check the amount of formal or on-the-job training given your
      student counselors:
                     Total Training Time
☐ No systematic training   ☐ 7–10 hours of training
☐ 1–3 hours of training   ☐ 11–20 hours of training
☐ 4–6 hours of training   ☐ More than 20 hours
                                   of training

3. Check the position title of all personnel directly involved in giving training to student counselors:

Training Personnel

☐ Academic dean

☐ Dean of students

☐ Dean of men and/or dean of women

☐ Director of testing and guidance

☐ Director of student union

☐ College chaplain

☐ Residence hall directors

☐ Education faculty members

☐ Psychology faculty members

☐ Professional counselors

☐ Student counselors

☐ Other . . . .

4. Check the instructional procedures and materials utilized in training your student counselors:

Procedure

☐ Reading assignments

☐ Lectures

☐ Demonstrations

☐ Group discussions

☐ Practice exercises

☐ "Buddy system" training

☐ Role playing

☐ Other . . . .

Materials

☐ Counselor's handbook or guide

☐ Workbook

☐ Check lists

☐ Movies and/or filmstrips

☐ Tape recorders

☐ One-way screen

☐ Rating forms

☐ Other . . . .

5. Indicate the pay given your student counselors:

☐ Unpaid

☐ Paid on hourly rate basis ($. . . . . . per hour)

☐ Paid through scholarship grant ($. . . per counselor)

☐ Paid on basis of counselee load ($. . . . per counselee)

☐ Other . . . .

☐ Other . . . .

D. Evaluation of Undergraduate Student Counselors

1. Do you feel that the student counselors make an effective and positive contribution to your institution's total guidance program?

☐ Yes   ☐ No   ☐ Uncertain or undecided

2. Do you plan to continue the use of student counselors at your institution?

☐ Yes   ☐ No   ☐ Uncertain or undecided

3. Do you feel that the guidance activities of your student counselors should be expanded beyond those they now perform?

☐ Yes   ☐ No   ☐ Uncertain or undecided

4. Do a significant number (5 percent or more) of your faculty members react negatively to the use of student counselors?
   ☐ Yes ☐ No ☐ Uncertain or undecided

5. Do you believe that the use of student counselors by colleges is likely to increase during the next ten years?
   ☐ Yes ☐ No ☐ Uncertain or undecided

Additional Comments

....
....
....
....
....
....
....
....
....
....
....
....
....
....
....
....

APPENDIX B

Variables Obtained for Initial Factorial Investigation

Number   Description of Variable

Academic Attitude Measures
01   Façade Detection Scale Score
02   Vocabulary Knowledge Differential Score
04   Inventory of Student Attitudes Score
05   Survey of Study Habits and Attitudes Score

Scholastic Ability Measures
03   Word Knowledge Test Score
07   ACE Psychological Examination Quantitative Score
08   ACE Psychological Examination Linguistic Score
09   Cooperative English Test: C2 Reading Comprehension Score
10   Use of Library and Study Materials Score

Life Style Orientation Measures
06   Student Biographical Inventory Score
11   Parental Educational Level Score
12   Parental Occupational Level Score
13   Parental Index of Social Status Score

Peer-Group Affiliation Measures
14   Study Companion Nominations Score
15   Study Companion Rejections Score
16   Study Companion Desirability Score
17   Social Companion Nominations Score
18   Social Companion Rejections Score
19   Social Companion Desirability Score
20   Hedonistic Orientation Score
21   Group Acceptance of Individual Score
22   Acquaintances' Valuation of Individual Score
23   Individual Acceptance of Group Score
24   Individual's Valuation of Acquaintances Score
25   Social Insight Score
26   Peer-Group Affiliation Score

College Achievement Criteria
27   High School Quarter Rank
28   High School Percentile Rank
29   First-Semester Point-Hour Ratio
30   Extracurricular Participation Rating
31   Index of Evaluated Participation Score

APPENDIX C

Variables Obtained for Follow-Up Factorial Investigation

Number   Description of Variable

Survey of Study Habits and Attitudes: Form E56
01   Student's Study Methods Score
02   Student's Educational Philosophy Score
03   Student's Teacher Valuation Score
04   Student's Achievement Drive Score
05   Student's Procrastination Avoidance Score
06   Student's Self-Confidence Score

Mooney Problem Check Lists: Form C
07   Health and Physical Development Score
08   Finances, Living Conditions, and Employment Score
09   Social and Recreational Activities Score
10   Social-Psychological Relations Score
11   Personal-Psychological Relations Score
12   Courtship, Sex, and Marriage Score
13   Home and Family Score
14   Morals and Religion Score
15   Adjustment to College Work Score
16   The Future: Vocational and Educational Score
17   Curriculum and Teaching Procedure Score

Cooperative School and College Ability Test: Form 1A
18   Verbal Ability Score
19   Quantitative Ability Score

Cooperative English Tests: Form X
20   Reading Comprehension Total Score
21   Mechanics of Expression Total Score

College Qualification Tests: Form B
22   Verbal Score
23   Numerical Score
24   Science Information Score
25   Social Studies Information Score

Parental Education and Occupation Questionnaire
26   Parents' Social Status Score

Peer Acceptance Inventory
27   Group Acceptance of Individual Score
28   Individual Acceptance of Group Score

Edwards Personal Preference Schedule
29   Achievement Need Score
30   Deference Need Score

31   Order Need Score
32   Exhibition Need Score
33   Autonomy Need Score
34   Affiliation Need Score
35   Intraception Need Score
36   Succorance Need Score
37   Dominance Need Score
38   Abasement Need Score
39   Nurturance Need Score
40   Change Need Score
41   Endurance Need Score
42   Heterosexuality Need Score
43   Aggression Need Score
Student Biographical Inventory: Form E56
44   Academic Orientation Score
45   Social Orientation Score
Companionship Nomination Blank
46   Study Companion Desirability Score
47   Social Companion Desirability Score
Attitudes Toward Personal and Family Living: Form CYSI
48   Orientation to Society Score
49   Authoritarian Discipline Score
50   Criticism of Education Score
51   Criticism of Youth Score
52   Family Problems Score
53   Self Inadequacy Score
Concerns and Problems in Personal and Family Living: Form CYSII
54   Family Tension Score
55   Personal Adjustment Score
56   Social Inadequacy Score
57   Resentment of Family Life Style Score
Academic Achievement Criteria
58   High School Percentile Rank
59   College First-Semester Grade-Point Ratio
Social Achievement Criterion
60   Extracurricular Participation Index Score

APPENDIX D
Student Counselor Evaluation Form

Name.................................... Sex.... Class...........
The above-named student is being considered for employment as a student
academic counselor with the Testing and Counseling Center. Please check
on the following five-point rating scale your appraisal of those traits which
most nearly characterize this student. In checking each item, you should
remember that about 20 percent of the student population would fall into
each of the five categories.

	Poor	Fair	Average	Good	Superior
Intellectual purpose: Academically ambitious; eager and inquiring attitudes.					
Maturity: Emotional development in relation to chronological age.					
Initiative: Develops own ideas; resourceful; creative and original; takes the lead.					
Reliability: Sense of responsibility; dependable; conscientious; prompt to meet obligations.					
Personality: Makes a good impression; self-confident; poised; courteous and well mannered.					

Do you know of anything about this student that would significantly limit
his or her effectiveness as a student academic counselor?

....
....
....
....

Do you know of anything about this student that would probably enhance
his or her effectiveness as a student academic counselor?

....
....
....

....
        Date   Signature

APPENDIX E

Survival Orientation Activity Sequence Check List

A. Establish Group Rapport
 1. Introduce Student Academic Counselors
  a. State personal data (hometown, college major, etc.)
  b. State employment data (employer, job duties, etc.)
 2. Set Atmosphere for Session
  Material: Summary Report Form (Appendix A-2)
  a. Explain necessity for attendance report
  b. Circulate Summary Report Form
  c. Review your own freshman daze
  d. Encourage asking of questions
  e. Stress informality of session
 3. Explain Survival Orientation Objectives
  a. To discuss common college adjustment problems
  b. To answer questions about college life
  c. To advise on available sources of assistance
B. Report College Survival Facts
 1. Review College Enrollment Situation
  a. Compare 1962 and 1967 enrollment figures
   * 3,600,000 students enrolled in fall, 1962
   * 1,560,000 or 40% were freshmen
   * 4 of 10 freshmen or 624,000 did not continue beyond the first year
   * Anticipated 60% freshman increase by 1967 due to postwar birth rate
   * Construction rate provided for only 25% increase
  b. Report consequences of supply-demand imbalance
   * Selective admission program now required at all 4-year colleges (SWT=ACT)
   * Instructors have raised standards for each letter grade
   * Scholastic probation and dismissal program rigidly enforced
   * Increasingly difficult to get in and to stay in college
 2. Review College Graduation Requirements
  a. Explain process for evaluating college credits
   * Semester hour is usual college credit unit

NOTE: Appendix numbers cited in this check list are for the appendices in the *Student Counselor's Handbook*.

* 3-hour course: three 1-hour class periods weekly for 18-week semester with 2-hour homework assignment for each class hour
* 4-hour course has additional 4-hour laboratory period
* 1-hour course has no homework assignment for each class hour
* 128 semester hours with "C" average required for BA or BS degree
* Course Numbering System: four-number code used—1st is classification number, 2nd is credit hours value, 3rd and 4th are course numbers
* Normal semester load is 16 or 17 hours
* 56 hours of required courses
* Major=24–52 hours; minor=18–24 hours

  b. Explain process for determining scholastic standing
* 9 quality points and 9 semester hours to stay off scholastic probation
* Need to pass at least 6 hrs. to avoid scholastic suspension
* Quality Point System: "A"=3 points, "B"=2 points, "C"=1 point, and "D" or "F"=0 points

C. Report Typical Freshman's Adjustment Problems
  1. Examine Typical Freshman Schedule
    Material: *Effective Study Guide* (pp. 9–11)
    a. Explain time requirement for classes and labs
    b. Add time requirement for outside preparation
  2. Review Major Academic Adjustment Areas
    Material: *Effective Study Guide* (Chapters II, III, and IV)
    a. Survey organization for effective study
* Budgeting your time
* Organizing your study environment
    b. Survey techniques for effective study
* Reading your textbook assignments
* Taking your lecture notes
* Passing your exams
* Writing your themes and reports
    c. Survey motivation for effective study
* Motivating your studying
* Accepting your responsibilities

D. Interpret Effective Study Test Scores
  Material: EST Individual Report Form (Appendix A-3)
  1. Explain Percentiles and Norms Used
    a. Illustrate meaning of percentiles
    b. Identify normative population used

2. Explain Meaning of Basic Scales
   a. Illustrate how "higher" and "lower" blanks are filled in
   b. Restate subscale definitions in own words
3. Demonstrate Use of Profile
   a. Explain how profile of test results is drawn
   b. Illustrate how strengths and weaknesses may be identified
   c. Have students summarize needed corrective measures

E. Analyze Time Budgeting Problems
   1. Present Problem Overview
      a. Discuss necessity for time budgeting
         * Contrast between high school and college
         —Amount of outside study required
         —Time duration of assignments
         —Absence of prodding by parents and teachers
         —"Average" high school student is in 4th quarter of college class
         * Contrast between different students
         —Different ability levels
         —Different achievement backgrounds
         —Different college majors
      b. Report advantages of time budgeting
         * Makes time for other activities
         —60% to 80% of "open" time is usually wasted
         —Studying during "open" time frees evening time
         * More efficient use of study time
         —Minimizes procrastination and vacillation
         —Organizes study time according to need
         —Assures studying right subject at right time
   2. Discuss Time Budgeting Principles
      Material: Fred Fish's Daily Activity Schedule (Appendix A-4), Frank Frosh's Daily Activity Schedule (p. 14 in *Effective Study Guide*), and Time Schedule Comparison Key (Appendix A-5)
      a. Compare schedules to explain reviewing for lecture and participation courses
         * Prime study time is "open" time between classes
         * Use free time between classes for concentrated reviewing
         * Review just before participation classes (math, foreign languages, speech, etc.)
         * Review just after lecture classes (history, science, etc.)
      b. Compare schedules to explain organization and duration of preparation periods
         * Establish habits of regularity in studying (same study activity at same time)

* Don't schedule studying during normal recreation period (4–7 P.M. daily, Saturday afternoon)

* Schedule 1–2-hour study periods for a given subject (efficiency versus fatigue)

* Allow 5–10-minute break for each hour of study (something different to break monotony)

* Assure proper balance between rest, play, and study (8 hours sleep, 8 hours study, 8 hours recreation)

* Allow 20–30 minutes between study and bedtime (relieve tension by bathing, pleasure reading, etc.)

* Leave Saturday afternoon and evening and Sunday morning and afternoon free for social activities

* Schedule a catch-up study period for Sunday evening (favorite time for pop quiz is Monday morning)

* Strive to eliminate wasted time suitable for study (time between classes, waiting time, etc.)

* Be flexible in following your time budget (use common sense in changing activities to meet demands)

* Follow cliche: Plan your work and then work your plan!

c. Review hints on time planning

Material: Daily Activity Schedule (Appendix A-6)

* Build schedule around fixed time commitments

* Allow for known strengths and weaknesses

* Establish habits of regularity

* Use free periods between classes for reviewing

* Allow for flexibility in preparation periods

d. Discuss use of Daily Activity Schedule

* Use as blueprint for organizing time

* Use until time budgeting is habitual

* Use as freshman, not as upperclassman

* Use as a flexible tool, not as a rigid rule

F. Analyze Note Taking Problems

Material: Sample Lecture Notes on Taking Lecture Notes (Appendix A-7)

1. Present Problem Overview

a. Report variations in lecture use

* Contrast between high school and college

* Contrast between different academic departments

* Contrast between different professors

b. State reasons for taking good lecture notes

* To aid you in studying for examinations (supplement and clarify textbook; exams are 40–50% from notes)

* To aid you in understanding the professor (his emphasis and evaluation of materials)
2. Discuss Listening Process
   a. Explain Rule #1: Be Prepared
      * Read textbook assignments beforehand
      * Review previous lecture notes beforehand
   b. Explain Rule #2: Learn Your Professor
      * Organization of lectures
      * Cues to major points
   c. Explain Rule #3: Listen-Think-Write
      * Be attentive to what is said
      * Critically evaluate what is said (importance and relationship of material)
      * Restate what is said (be selective and use your own words)
   d. Explain Rule #4: Use Proven Procedures
      * Separate notes from different courses
      * Date notes and number pages
      * Use only abbreviations that you can understand
      * Use underlining and other emphasis marks
3. Discuss Formats for Taking Notes
   a. Explain sentence form
      * Unorganized series of simple statements
      * Likely to copy professor's statements word-for-word
      * Best for following unorganized lecturer
      * Difficult to study, as major and minor points are not differentiated
   b. Explain standard outline form
      * Uses roman numerals, capital letters, arabic figures
      * Uses indention to different depths
      * Easy to study; major and minor points clearly differentiated
      * Requires thinking and organization to highest degree
      * Almost impossible to copy professor's lecture word-for-word
4. Discuss Immediate Reviewing
   Material: Student-to-Student Tips—About Taking Class Notes
   a. Explain Rule #1: Review Lecture Notes Immediately After Class
      * Do clarify and expand your notes
      * Don't waste time recopying your notes
   b. Explain Rule #2: Correlate Lecture Notes with Reading Assignments
      * Use cross-reference process
      * Reveals instructor's bias and emphasis

    c. Explain Rule #3: Recite Major Points Covered in Lecture
* Process will reinforce learning
* Process will identify unlearned materials

G. Analyze Scholastic Motivation Problems
  1. Examine Reasons Why Students Go to College
    a. Because everybody else goes
    b. Because parents make them go
    c. To avoid being drafted
    d. To keep from going to work
    e. To prepare for higher paying jobs
    f. To gain knowledge for knowledge's sake
  2. Read Benchley's Essay on College Life
    Material: Studying Can Be Fun When Properly Done (Appendix A-8)
    a. Question author's study methods
    b. Question author's study motivation
  3. Discuss Essential Steps to Improve Scholastic Motivation
    a. Make a realistic evaluation of your own strengths and weaknesses
    b. Ask yourself why are you going to college and what you want from college
    c. Develop meaningful vocational objectives for yourself
    d. Plan an appropriate educational program for yourself
    e. Recognize that maturity requires self-discipline and responsibility
    f. Recognize that you will get out of college what you put into it

H. Invite Questions about College Life
  1. Answer Student's Questions
    a. Questions about academic regulations
     * Excused absences and "cuts"
     * Grace period and dropping courses
    b. Questions about organized extracurricular programs
     * Student Union Building activities
     * Departmental clubs

I. Inventory the Rewards of College
  1. Analyze the Rewards of Job Preparation
    Material: Educational Level and Job Type (Appendix A-10)
    a. Report the financial rewards of college training
     * $465,000–$230,000=$235,000 difference between lifetime earnings of high school and college graduates
     * Averages out to about $320 for each day attending classes

  b. Report the prestige status of college graduates
  * Creative nature of jobs held by college graduates
  * Managerial function of jobs held by college graduates
2. Analyze the Rewards of Gaining Knowledge
  a. Discuss abilities developed during college
  * Ability to *locate* information
  * Ability to *interpret* information
  * Ability to *evaluate* information
  * Ability to *organize* information
  * Ability to *communicate* information
  b. Discuss opportunity for intellectual stimulation
  * Fun of finding out *why*
  * Fun of finding out *how*
3. Analyze the Rewards of Learning to Live
  Material: Shall I Join? (Appendix A-11)
  a. Discuss opportunity to demonstrate maturity
  * More independence and self-reliance
  * More responsibility and self-discipline
  b. Discuss opportunity for social interaction
  * Exposure to new and/or different ideas
  * Chance to form new friendships
  c. Discuss opportunity to improve evaluative and communicative skills
  * Preparation for democratic citizenship
  * Preparation for expressing individuality

J. Survey Sources of Student Assistance
1. Describe Help Available from Course Instructors
  Material: *Student-to-Student Tips*—About Student-Teacher Relationships
  a. Discuss responsibility for seeking assistance
  * Instructors are always willing to help
  * Office hours are posted on door
  * Student is responsible for seeking out instructor
  b. Discuss proper approach to instructor
  * Positive desire to learn is right approach
  * Excuse-making, apple-polishing, or critical negativism are wrong approaches
  c. Discuss type of help to request
  * Do request specific clarification of requirements for future assignments
  * Don't request help with carelessly planned or vaguely conceived reports or projects

        * Do request explanation of corrections noted on returned
          assignments or tests
        * Don't challenge grading of returned assignments or tests
2. Describe Personnel Services Available to Freshmen
   Material: Sources of Student Assistance (Appendix A-12)
   a. Discuss Student Employment Office
      * College work-study program
      * On-campus part-time employment other than work-study
      * Full-time and part-time off-campus employment
   b. Discuss Student Loan Office
      * Short-term loans for emergencies
      * Long-term loans to finance education
        —Texas Opportunity Plan
        —NDEA Loan Program
        —Loans from private foundations
   c. Discuss Testing and Counseling Center
      * Vocational Counseling Laboratory
        —Counseling provided by professional staff
        —Testing of aptitudes and interests
        —Counseling on educational and vocational plans
        —Use of Occupational Information Library
      * Reading Improvement Clinic
        —Self-service operation supervised by trained upperclass-
          men
        —Improvement of reading comprehension emphasized
        —Improvement of reading speed secondary
      * Study Skills Clinic
        —Guidance provided by student academic counselors
        —Individualized counseling covers six study skills areas
        —Not a substitute for tutoring in a specific course
3. Offer Additional Guidance
   Material: Counseling Request: Test Interpretation
   a. Describe Test Interpretation Program
      * Counseling given on student-to-student level
      * Designed to help average or below-average student
      * Report results of freshman tests (ACT and SSHA)
      * Review proven techniques for effective study
      * Offered for first four weeks of semester
      * Participation limited to 400 freshmen
      * Session lasts for one two-hour period
   b. Advise on how to obtain additional counseling
      * Sign up for all laboratories at Testing and Counseling Cen-
        ter (Ed. Bldg. 213)
      * Sign up for Test Interpretation Program right now

APPENDIX F

Test Interpretation Activity Sequence Check List

A. Establish Group Rapport
   1. Make Appropriate Introductions
      a. Ask counselees to identify themselves
      b. Identify yourself to counselees
   2. Set Atmosphere for Session
      a. Encourage asking of questions
      b. Stress informality of session
   3. Explain Test Interpretation Objectives
      a. To report the results of freshman tests
      b. To review proven techniques for effective study

B. Explain College Success Factors
   Material: 4-A Approach to Forecasting Scholastic Success (Appendix B-3)
   1. Explain Role of Academic Ability
      a. *Your learning potential*: Your intellectual capacity for learning the materials presented in college courses
      b. Verbal Aptitude (operations involving use of words) and Numerical Aptitude (operations involving use of numbers)
   2. Explain Role of Academic Achievement
      a. *Your learning background*: The foundation of knowledges and skills you have already acquired through schooling
      b. Reading Skills (speed and comprehension) and Writing Skills (mechanics and effectiveness)
   3. Explain Role of Academic Adjustment
      a. *Your learning behavior*: Your mastery of basic study skills and your efficiency in doing academic assignments
      b. Study Organization (time and place) and Study Techniques (reading, writing, and examination behavior)
   4. Explain Role of Academic Attitudes
      a. *Your learning motivation*: How do you feel about college and teachers and your desire for academic learning
      b. Study Attitudes (feelings and beliefs) and Study Expectations (goals and aspirations)

NOTE: Appendix numbers cited in this check list are for the appendices in the *Student Counselor's Handbook*.

C. Interpret American College Test Scores
   Material: Test Results Report Form (Appendix B-4)
   1. Explain Meaning of Scores
      a. Illustrate meaning of percentiles
      b. Identify normative population used
      c. Restate score definitions in own words
      d. Illustrate profiling of test results
   2. Stress Limitations of Test Results
      a. General rather than specific indicators
      b. Influenced by many external factors
      c. Interpret in context of past performance and present motivation

D. Interpret Survey of Study Habits and Attitudes Results
   Material: SSHA Diagnostic Profile (Appendix B-4), Test Booklet, Answer Sheet, and Subscale Illustrator
   1. Explain Centiles and Norms Used
      a. Illustrate meaning of centiles
      b. Identify normative populations used
   2. Explain Four Basic SSHA Scales and Derived Scores
      a. Illustrate how "higher" and "lower" blanks are to be filled in
      b. Restate subscale definitions in own words
      c. Use appropriate illustration to explain each subscale
   3. Explain Use of Diagnostic Profile
      a. Explain how profile of test results is to be drawn
      b. Illustrate how to identify strengths and weaknesses
      c. Have students summarize needed corrective measures
   4. Discuss Individual SSHA Items
      a. Discuss deficient study habits
         (items in the two columns on left half of answer sheet)
      b. Discuss deficient study attitudes
         (items in the two columns on right half of answer sheet)

E. Analyze Textbook Reading Problems
   1. Present Problem Overview
      a. Explain contrast between high school and college
         * Size of reading assignments
         * Ownership of textbooks
         * Difficulty level of textbooks
      b. Give reasons for developing efficient reading skills
         * Improves preparation for exams
           (organized basis for systematic review)
         * Conserves time for other activities
           (increased comprehension improves remembering)

2. Explain SQ3R Reading Formula
   (System produces an 80% improvement in remembering for same amount of study time)
   a. Explain Step #1: Survey—Orient you to what the assignment is about
      * Read introductory and summary paragraphs
      * Inspect illustrations and tables
      * Examine headings and subheadings
   b. Explain Step #2: Question—Arouse your curiosity about the material
      * Who, what, where, when, why?
      * Relationship to previous material?
   c. Explain Step #3: Read—Participate actively to increase comprehension
      * Emphasize active participation and understanding
      * De-emphasize speed and passive enjoyment
   d. Explain Step #4: Recite—Immediate recitation reveals what you have learned
      * Restate material in your own words
      * Identify potential test questions
   e. Explain Step #5: Review—Frequent, short reviews retard forgetting
      * Negatively accelerated curve of forgetting
      * Role of retroactive inhibition

3. Demonstrate Textbook Outlining
   Material: Reading and Remembering Guide
   a. Have students read "unmarked" and "marked" material
      * Note comparative reading time
        (reduced to about 1/3 time)
      * Note comparative reading comprehension
        (increased by about 80%)
      * Extend comparison to exam over 300 pages within 48 hours
   b. Summarize value of textbook outlining
      * Application of "Active Reading" principle
      * Organizes ideas into logical sequence
      * Differentiates major and minor points
   c. Discuss how to begin textbook outlining
      * Survey the entire chapter for total organization
      * Skim the initial chapter unit for concept coverage and organization
      * Read the initial chapter unit actively—underlining as appropriate

       * Use the standard outline form to organize the concepts presented in the initial chapter unit
       * Repeat the skimming-reading-outlining process for subsequent units in the chapter

F. Analyze Theme and Report Writing Problems

  1. Present Problem Overview

    a. Explain contrast between high school and college
       * More courses utilizing written reports and themes
       (science, social science, English—25% to 50% of course grade)
       * Purpose of written reports and themes
       (encourage student to learn nature and sources of information in specific field)
       * Importance of written reports and themes
       (main opportunity to demonstrate capacity to locate, interpret, evaluate, organize, and communicate)

    b. Survey types of written assignments
       * Themes and essays written in class
       (brief theme or essay—no references, personal experience, or subjective reaction)
       * Laboratory reports
       (chemistry, physics, biology report on lab experiment)
       * Themes or reports written out of class
       (topic theme or outside reading report—use and citation of references usually required)
       * Semester research report or term paper
       (report based upon intensive library research and backed up by extensively cited bibliography)

    c. Discuss basis for grading written assignments
       * Neatness and organization
       (appearance, legibility, coherence)
       * Originality and self-expression
       (effectiveness in presenting own ideas)
       * Variety of information sources
       (types and number of references)
       * English mechanics
       (grammar, spelling, punctuation, capitalization)

  2. Analyze Successful Theme and Report Writing
    a. Discuss steps for effective theme writing in class

    Material: Student-to-Student Tips—About Writing Themes in Class

* Select a subject with which you are familiar
  (you cannot write intelligently about unfamiliar things)
* Make your subject suitable for a short time
  (select a narrow, definite, essential, interesting phase of
  the broad subject)
* Think about the subject and list ideas to be presented
  (list both major topics and supporting concepts)
* Organize your ideas into a brief, logical outline
  (use cue words or phrases instead of complete sentences)
* Write your theme systematically
  (pay attention to coherence, to transition, to emphasis)
* Review and polish your theme
  (check for grammar, spelling, and punctuation errors)
* Give special attention to neatness
  (write legibly and make all corrections neatly)
* Never repeat an English mechanics error corrected earlier
  (English instructors tend to assess double penalty for re-
  peated errors)
b. Discuss steps for effective report writing
  * Select an interesting and challenging topic
    (topic of interest to *you* and to *instructor*)
  * Gather comprehensive information on topic
    (use indexes, abstracts, encyclopedias, card catalog, etc.)
  * Organize your information logically and systematically
    (use 3 x 5 cards for reading notes and "idea page" for own
    ideas)
  * Prepare a detailed outline of your report
    (use cue words and phrases instead of complete sentences)
  * Dash off initial draft of your report
    (get your ideas down on paper—emphasis on content)
  * Polish rough draft of your report
    (check for English mechanics and effectiveness of expres-
    sion)
  * Follow the prescribed format for report
    (title page, table of contents, footnotes, quotations, bibli-
    ography, etc.)
  * Know and use basic rules of English mechanics
    (grammar, spelling, punctuation, capitalization)
  * Criticize, evaluate, illustrate, attack, defend as appropriate
    (show you have been thinking instead of copying)
  * Submit report in attractive form
    (type and put in binder)

* Show that you have pride in your effort
(evidence: promptness, variety of sources, comprehensive
coverage)

G. Analyze Examination Taking Problems
   1. Present Problem Overview
      a. Explain contrast between high school and college
         * Spacing of examinations
         (fewer exams given; mid-term and final may be all)
         * Weighting of examinations
         (primary basis for assigning grades; cannot use outside
         written work to compensate for low test scores)
         * Coverage of examinations
         (covers larger units of material, longer time periods, and
         greater depth of knowledge)
         * Nature of examinations
         (increased use of power-type essay examinations and pro-
         ficiency tests)
         * Teacher guidance of studying
         (study questions and practice exercises rarely used; no
         teacher pressure to motivate keeping-up)
      b. Discuss importance of learning instructor's test technique
         * Find out what type test he usually gives
         * Find out usual or favorite source for test questions
         (lecture content, textbook assignments, outside readings)
         * Study lecturing to determine procedure for emphasizing
         points
      c. Discuss timing of reviewing
         * *First review* immediately following initial learning
         * *Periodic reviews* to counteract forgetting process
         * *Intensive final review* or cramming prior to examination
         * Begin studying for final on first day of semester instead of
         last day before final
      d. Discuss methods of reviewing
         * Cross-reference lecture notes and textbook underlining
         * Predict likely questions and formulate answers in your
         own words
         * Organize small-group (3–4) study sessions
         (advantages: motivation to prepare, verbalization of mate-
         rial, and hearing different viewpoints)
         (disadvantages: unprepared member and bull-session tend-
         ency)
         * Prepare systematic condensation of material

2. Analyze Procedures for Effective Test Taking
   Material: Student-to-Student Tips—About Preparing for Tests
   and about Taking Tests
   a. Give specific suggestions for taking essay examinations
      * Divide available time according to number and weighting
        of questions
      * Read all questions before answering any
        (will minimize overlapping and/or repetition answering)
      * Answer the easiest question first
        (will build self-confidence at beginning of test)
      * Outline your answer before you start writing
        (assures all pertinent points are included and effectively
        organized)
      * Know what kind of answer the questions require
        (key is action verbs such as illustrate, trace, discuss, list,
        compare, etc.)
      * Write legibly and make corrections neatly
      * Recheck answers for content accuracy
      * Recheck answers for errors in grammar, spelling, and
        punctuation
   b. Give specific suggestions for taking objective examinations
      * Read directions twice and underline key words
        (true-false versus mostly true or false)
      * Answer questions in order without skipping or jumping
        around
        (many students omit and fail to return)
      * Identify doubtful answers by mark in margin
        (recheck if time permits; change only if reasonably sure)
      * Don't dwell too long on one question
        (make best guess and return later if time permits)
      * Read a true-false question twice and look for:
        —Qualifying words, such as "never," "sometimes," "usual-
        ly," "always"
        —Modifying words, such as "all," "most," "some," "none"
        —Limiting phrases, such as inserted dates or locations
        —Negative wording, especially use of double negatives
        —Multiple ideas or statements
        —Incomplete or textbookish sentences
        —Ambiguous or nonspecific terms
      * Read a multiple-choice question as a series of true-false
        questions and look for:
        —Grammatical inconsistency between stem and responses
        —Differences in length or organization of responses

H. Offer Additional Counseling
  1. Describe Operation of Testing and Counseling Center
     a. Service is free to all students
     b. Student-to-student counseling used where possible
     c. Voluntary participation by counselees
  2. Review Systematic Guidance Programs
     a. Study Skills Clinic
        * Taking your lecture notes
        * Managing your time
        * Reading your textbook assignments
        * Improving your memory
        * Writing your themes and reports
        * Passing your examinations
     b. Reading Improvement Clinic
        * Improving your reading comprehension
        * Improving your reading speed
     c. Vocational Guidance Clinic
        * Selecting your college major and/or minor
        * Determining your best occupational fields
  3. Provide Opportunity to Request Further Counseling
     Material: Counseling Request Cards for all programs
     a. Identify and discuss specific student needs as appropriate
     b. Emphasize importance of responsibility about attendance
     c. Distribute and collect counseling request cards
I. Evaluate Comprehension of Counseling Content
  Material: Counseling Comprehension Test Booklet (Appendix B-6)
     and Answer Sheet (Appendix B-7)
  1. Administer Counseling Comprehension Test
  2. Mark Incorrect Responses on Answer Sheet
  3. Determine Reason for Answering Incorrectly

APPENDIX G

Test Interpretation Program Information Form

Name......................... Sex.... Age.... SS#.........
Have you taken the ACT? Yes.... No....; If yes, when ....
Marital Status........... Major........... Date.............

College
Address................................. Phone.............
High School....................... Date Graduated...........
Scholastic Quarter: 1 2 3 4   High School Size: B A AA AAA AAAA

Most Liked High School Subjects	Least Liked High School Subjects
1.	1. ....
2.	2. ....
3.	3. ....

Scholastic, Social, or Athletic Awards and Honors

1. ....   4. ....
2. ....   5. ....
3. ....   6. ....
Present Employment..................... Hours per Week......

Previous Employment Data

Job Description	Duration	Attitude
1...	....	L ? D
2...	....	L ? D
3...	....	L ? D

American College Test		Survey of Study Habits and Attitudes		Effective Study Test	
Score	*Centile*	*Score*	*Centile*	*Score*	*Centile*
Eng.		DA			
Math.		WM		RO	
Soc. S.		SH		SO	
N. Sci.				WB	
		TA		RB	
Comp.		EA		EB	
		SA		TSE.....	
TIP		SSL	VGL	RIL	OTHER

Counselor: ....

APPENDIX H

Transcription of Test Interpretation Session

Counselor. Hello! Let's start the counseling session off by getting acquainted. Why don't we go around the table and each one of you introduce yourselves so we can get to know each other?

Nancy. I'm Nancy Rogers from Corpus Christi.

Judy. I'm Judy Walker from Del Rio.

Agnes. I'm Agnes Hester from Weslaco.

Karen. I'm Karen McCallum from Houston.

Counselor. I'm Veleda Deschner, your counselor. As you know, you have all volunteered to come to this counseling session. Let's review what we hope to accomplish during the next two hours. First of all, we are going to give you the results of the tests that you took during Freshman Orientation Week. Then we are to look at your study habits and attitudes, and, if you have any that are deficient, we are going to try to help you remedy your mistakes. Next, we are going to discuss the Center's vocational and educational guidance programs and give you an opportunity to sign up for this additional help. Finally, we are going to have a quiz over this session's activities in order to see if I have left some points uncovered or if you have misunderstood some of the information given. Let's begin by discussing some of the factors that influence your scholastic success in college. [*Illustrates on chart.*] As you can see from this chart, your success in college depends primarily upon four things: your academic ability, your academic adjustment, your academic achievement, and your academic attitude. Academic ability means how much potential you have for learning, and this is something you cannot do very much to change. Academic achievement means the background of schooling that you have had up until now—grammar school, high school, everything you have retained from your learning experiences. Academic attitude means how you feel about college, your goals in college, what you hope to accomplish. Academic adjustment means how you react to things that you encounter in college, how you apply yourself in your studying, your learning behavior, in other words. These four things—ability, achievement, attitude, and adjustment—interact to determine how well you will do in college. Whereas your ability and achievement are relatively stable, there is something that you can do to change your attitudes and your adjustment. For instance, a good academic attitude on the student's part can often compensate for below-average scholastic ability. Or, if your high school background is not as good as it should be, you can study harder and thereby bring up your grades. So you can do something about relatively low ability or poor learning background by compensating with good study habits and attitudes. Do you understand what I mean by compensating?

Girls. Yes, we understand!

Counselor. Okay. Now, let's look at your Test Results Report Forms and see how you scored on the freshman tests. [*Distributes forms to counselees.*] You'll see that the scores are broken down into three categories: first, the results of your ability test; then, the results on your reading achievement test; and, last, the results on your attitude test. As you can see, the ability and achievement areas each contain several scores, and a definition for each score is printed on the form. Let's go around the table and each of you, in turn, read one of the score definitions. After you have read it aloud, restate the definition in your own words and tell us what the score means to you. Also, you will see the words "score" and "centile" above the column of numbers written on the left. Are these terms still familiar to you?

Agnes. I've forgotten what centile means.

Counselor. Could any of the rest of you help her out on this?

Nancy. The centile is, well, it's like if you scored at the 70th centile it means that, of one hundred freshmen, seventy are below you and thirty are above you.

Counselor. Okay. And the raw score is just the number of questions that you got right. Remember, also, that you are only being compared with the other freshmen at this college, not with those at colleges all over the nation. It's strictly a local comparison.

Judy. Does that mean only the freshmen here?

Counselor. Yes. Both boys and girls. So when you see your centile rating you should remember that you are being compared with freshmen at this college, and only with the freshmen at this college. Now would you please start, Nancy, and read the definition for the English Usage score on the American College Test?

Nancy. Your English Usage score indicates your mastery of the basic elements of correct and effective writing: punctuation, capitalization, diction, phraseology, and organization of ideas. Do you want me to read the rest of it?

Counselor. No, that's enough. Could you restate that definition in your own words?

Nancy. Well, I believe it means that this score tells whether or not you use good English to express your ideas. How clearly and correctly you can write something.

Counselor. Yes, Nancy, that's right. Now all of you should fill in the blanks for how many out of one hundred students are lower than you are, and for how many out of one hundred are higher than you are.

Karen. My centile is 50! Is that terrible or good or what?

Counselor. Between the 90th and the 99th centile means high to superior, from the 75th to the 90th is above average, between the 25th and 75th is the average area, between the 10th and the 25th is below average, and everything below the 10th centile is considered low or very low. So you can place yourself according to those labels if you want to. Okay, let's go on to the Mathematics Usage score. Judy, will you read that one?

Judy. Your Mathematics Usage score indicates your mastery of the mathematical principles used in the solution of quantitative problems and in the interpretation of graphs and charts. This just measures how good you are at solving math problems, doesn't it?

Counselor. Yes, it measures your math ability. Now, let's fill in the blanks. Okay, Agnes, let's go on to the Social Studies Reading score.

Agnes. Your Social Studies Reading score indicates your ability to read, evaluate, and draw significant conclusions from social studies reading materials as well as your general understanding of basic social concepts and terminology. Well, isn't that just another way of saying it measures how well you read and understand social studies materials?

Counselor. That's right. Of course, it also measures how well you understand the basic ideas and terms commonly found in social studies reading materials. Karen, will you take the next definition?

Karen. Your Natural Science Reading score indicates your ability to read, evaluate, and draw significant conclusions from natural science reading materials as well as your general understanding of basic scientific principles and terminology. Well, isn't that the same thing as before except it's for natural science instead of social studies? This one simply measures how well you can read and understand natural science reading materials.

Counselor. That's it. Now, Judy, can you tell me what the composite score is?

Judy. Well, it's the combined average of the four scores we've just been talking about.

Counselor. Okay. Agnes, can you add anything else to that?

Agnes. It says here that the composite score provides *one* basis for an overall estimate of your general ability to succeed in college.

Counselor. Yes! And, remember, there are other factors like academic attitude that are very important too. Okay, fill in the blanks on your form, and then we'll move on to the Davis Reading Test. Karen, would you read the first one?

Karen. Your Reading Speed score indicates the rapidity and accuracy with which you read the kinds of material that college students are ordinarily required to read. This is just how fast you read with understanding.

Counselor. Yes, this score refers to how rapidly and accurately you read college-level materials. Let's go on to the Reading Level score, Nancy.

Nancy. Your Reading Level score indicates the depth of understanding that you achieve while reading the kinds of material that college students are ordinarily required to read. Well, this is how well you can understand the material that a college student has to read.

Counselor. What is the importance of this as compared with how rapidly you can read?

Nancy. If you can read fast, but you don't comprehend or understand, it doesn't do much good.

Counselor. That's it! Now if you will turn your forms over, you'll see a profile for your test scores. The profile is designed to help you see, in graphic form, how you scored on these various tests. A graph helps you to see more easily where you are low and where you are high, where your weaknesses are and where your strengths are. If you have a weakness, it is likely to show up in your college work. Thus it's good to be forewarned about your weak points. Remember, if you recognize that you are weak in an important area, such as math ability, you can compensate by working harder and giving it more of your study time. Now, let's draw your graph. You already have your centiles recorded in the boxes above each score name. Simply plot a graph of the centiles to see how you rank on the various scores.

Karen. Mark the centiles on these lines?

Counselor. That's right. Mark the obtained centile value on each line and connect the marks to draw your graph. [*Counselees plot their profiles.*] Okay. Now, let's go around the table and summarize your strong points and your weak points, especially noting those points that may give you trouble in college. Also, let's discuss some way of overcoming your weaknesses, or compensating for your low scores. Nancy, would you start—what did you learn from your graph?

Nancy. My lowest point is my Mathematics Usage, which I had expected, and my highest point is English Usage. The rest of my scores are about average.

Counselor. Then your other scores fall between the 25th and 75th centiles? Okay. Have you run into any trouble with math yet?

Nancy. Well, I don't particularly like math. I make B's and C's, but I don't particularly like it.

Counselor. Do you find that you have to study harder in this area?

Nancy. Yes, I do.

Counselor. Well, you will probably have to continue to apply yourself more in math and math-related subjects. And English Usage is your strong point. Do you have any questions about this?

Nancy. No, I've always done better in English than in Math.

Counselor. Yes, this shows that you will probably continue to be strongest in your English courses. Okay, Judy, what have you discovered about yourself?

Judy. Did you say that twenty-five or below is below average?

Counselor. Yes, below the 25th centile is regarded as below average.

Judy. Then I guess that I am below average in my Reading Speed and Reading Level. And my highest, or above-average areas, are my English Usage and Mathematics Usage scores. Everything else is about average.

Counselor. Yes, your profile shows that you are fairly high in everything but the reading skills. There you fell down quite a bit.

Judy. I just can't read!

Counselor. Did you have trouble with this in high school?

Judy. Yes.

Counselor. Judy, if you are interested, you can take advantage of a special reading improvement course offered by the college. It's a non-credit course taught in the reading clinic. In the course, you don't have homework; you simply work to improve your reading skills through exercises during class. The purpose of the course is to speed up your reading rate and to improve your understanding of what you read. You also learn how to outline reading assignments and how to improve your vocabulary. You can register for this course any time that you like. Do you think that you would be interested in the course?

Judy. Yes. I think that I'll try it next spring.

Counselor. If you do it should help you to improve your reading. Now, Agnes, what did you find out about yourself?

Agnes. Well, I have two low points. The lowest one is my English Usage and the next lowest is Mathematics Usage. The rest of them are average, except Reading Level, which is just barely in the above-average area.

Counselor. Agnes, have you heard about the English labs?

Agnes. No, I don't believe I have.

Counselor. Well, these English labs are provided by the English Department for students having trouble writing themes or with their grammar, or punctuation, or spelling. The lab meets at 4 o'clock on Tuesdays and Thursdays, and they have assistants who go around and help you learn to write themes and such as this. If you are interested, you can go and get help in these areas.

Agnes. Does it matter who your teacher is?

Counselor. No, it doesn't matter at all. Anyone can go and ask for help. Are you taking math this semester, Agnes?

Agnes. No, I'm not. I don't have to have but two math courses because I'm in elementary education.

Counselor. Well, I know you realize that you'll just have to work a little harder when you do take math to compensate for that low score. Karen, what did you find?

Karen. Well, my Mathematics Usage and English Usage are the only things that are above average. My Reading Speed is low and so is my Reading Level. When you sign up for that reading course, do you just sign up during registration?

Counselor. No, you come here to the Testing and Counseling Center and sign up. You can sign up any time you want to and we start new classes every week or so.

Karen. Everything else is about average, but these low reading scores really have me worried.

Counselor. So, your main problem is the same as Judy's—improving your reading skills.

Judy. How often does the reading class meet?

Counselor. It meets for fifty minutes, three times a week. Reading is a very essential skill for college students, Judy. I don't need to tell you this because you've probably already found it out. The reading assignments are so extensive that, if you can't read fast and comprehend accurately, you're quickly going to be in trouble. The sooner that you improve your reading skills, the sooner your grades will start to show improvement. Are there any more questions about these test results? If not, we are going to go on to another form—the one for your study habits and attitudes. [*Collects Test Results Report Forms and passes out Diagnostic Profiles.*] Let's handle this form the same way we did the last one. First, we'll go around the table and find out what each score means and how you ranked among the freshmen at this college. Now, this form reports both your study habits and your study attitudes. Your study habits are the way you apply yourself and the way you work; and your study attitudes are the way that you feel about your work and other things at college. Nancy, would you start off with the Delay Avoidance Scale?

Nancy. Delay Avoidance Scale measures your promptness in completing academic assignments, your lack of procrastination, your freedom from wasteful delay and distraction. Well, this just says how fast you get your work done, whether you wait until the last minute to do it, or whether you do it when it is first assigned.

Counselor. Yes. Now, remember that this measures your promptness in completing study assignments. For instance, if you have a high score, what do you think it means? That you tend to put things off or that you are good about getting your assignments done on time?

Nancy. It would mean that you are good about getting them done on time.

Counselor. Right. Now let's see how each of you ranked, then, by filling in the blanks on your form. Let's go on to the Work Methods Scale, Judy.

Judy. Work Methods Scale measures your use of effective study procedures, your efficiency in doing academic assignments, your how-to-study skill. I guess the Work Methods Scale just measures your know-how for studying.

Counselor. One thing needs to be made clear here—the Work Methods Scale starts measuring your study behavior after you sit down to study. That is, it measures the way that you study and the procedures that you use when you are studying, whereas the first scale, the Delay Avoidance Scale, measures how much time you tend to waste before you actually go to work.

Judy. What is procrastination?

Counselor. It's your tendency to put things off. Do you see the difference between Delay Avoidance and Work Methods—what each one measures?

Judy. Yes, I understand what they measure.

Counselor. Okay, fill in the blanks and let's move on to the Study Habits score. Agnes, you're next.

Agnes. Study Habits score combines the two preceding scores to provide an overall measure of your scholastic behavior. It just combines all of your habits that came under Delay Avoidance and Work Methods.

Counselor. Okay, let's check how your study habits compare with those of the other freshmen here. Now, let's move on to your attitude scores. Karen, you take the Teacher Approval Scale.

Karen. Teacher Approval Scale measures your opinion of teachers and their classroom behavior and methods. This is how you feel about the people who teach you.

Counselor. Yes, let's not get this one mixed up. Sometimes students think that this scale measures how teachers feel about them, but it is the other way around. Nancy, take the next one, Education Acceptance.

Nancy. Education Acceptance Scale measures your approval of educational objectives, practices, and requirements. This just states what you think of education and what your objectives are in going to college.

Counselor. Whose educational objectives are you approving?

Nancy. The ones that are set forth by your instructors, and also the demands that are made on you by the college.

Counselor. That's it. Okay, let's move to the Study Attitudes score.

Judy. Study Attitudes score combines the two preceding scores to provide an overall measure of your academic beliefs. This just combines your Teacher Approval Scale and your Education Acceptance Scale.

Counselor. And this gives you an overall picture of your academic attitudes. Now, Agnes, what's Study Orientation?

Agnes. Study Orientation score combines your scores on all four scales to provide a single measure of your study habits and attitudes. Well, it combines Delay Avoidance, Work Methods, Education Acceptance, and Teacher Approval.

Counselor. Yes, it's simply your total score and provides an overall picture of how you feel toward the academic environment and the role of the student. Now, turn your profile over and draw the graph so that you can better see exactly how you stand on each scale. Make a separate graph for your habits and for your attitudes so that it will be easier for you to compare these two areas. The last one, Study Orientation, you are to color in like on a thermometer. [*Counselees plot their profiles.*] Now that you have drawn your graph, look at it carefully to see if you have a special weakness, either in your study habits or in your study attitudes.

Judy. My Work Methods are bad; they are not below average, but they are not as good as my other habits and attitudes.

Counselor. Were you conscious of this before?

Judy. No, I didn't really realize it.

Counselor. You haven't been in college long enough for mid-terms. You will probably run into difficulty then if you have poor work habits. Do you organize your studying?

Judy. I thought I did, but I guess not enough.

Counselor. When you sit down to study, do you get everything together that you will need for each subject before you begin?

Judy. Yes, usually I do, but sometimes I never know until I sit down what I am going to study.

Counselor. I see. Well, this helps explain why your Work Methods score was low. If you plan your studying beforehand, you can be sure of having everything you need at hand. This will eliminate having to get up to get things, which always spoils your concentration. Planning ahead of time also pays off because it makes your studying go a lot faster. Nancy, did you find anything particularly low?

Nancy. My lowest one was Delay Avoidance.

Counselor. Well, do you find that you do tend to put things off?

Nancy. Yes, I do. I wait until just about the last minute.

Counselor. Have you tried to overcome this habit?

Nancy. Well, for themes, I try to start just as soon as the teacher makes the assignment, instead of waiting until the night before they're due.

Counselor. One thing about themes and reports, you usually have to do some library research on the topic you're writing about, and if you wait until the last minute, you may find that somebody else has checked out the books you need. If you start early, you'll probably have all the books available to use and you won't have to worry about them being checked out when you need them. Anything else?

Nancy. That was the lowest one. The rest are about average.

Counselor. Karen, what about your scores?

Karen. My habits are all pretty high, but my attitudes are terrible, especially my Teacher Approval. I had no idea, really, that it was going to measure this low.

Counselor. Let's look at that for a minute. What did you base your Teacher Approval on? When you answered the questions, what were you thinking about?

Karen. Well, I've got this aunt who is a school teacher, and everything about her is absolutely terrible. I guess maybe I was thinking about her when I answered the questions because, every question that I came to about teachers, I would think about her.

Counselor. Perhaps having her in mind colored your attitudes toward all teachers, and when you were answering the questions, you didn't think of teachers as a group. Instead, you based all your responses on this one terrible teacher, thus lowering your Teacher Approval score unduly. Did anyone else do this—find yourself thinking back to a particularly good or bad teacher and answering all the questions according to her? Basing your opinion on a specific person or action will always color your viewpoint. However, unless you recognize this, the colored viewpoint is still the one that influences your behavior. Karen, what else was low?

Karen. Education Acceptance. I really don't feel like I have that bad an attitude; at least, I don't now. I might have misunderstood some of the questions.

Counselor. Well, what are your reasons for coming to college?

Karen. I know what I want out of college—I'm going to major in business education, and I just want to get through. And I don't feel like I have a real bad attitude toward it. I expect that it could be improved, of course. My study habits are good, and my grades have always been good.

Counselor. Your goal is to get through and major in business education? What about the routine demands of college, all the studying that you have to do?

Karen. Well, I found that it was hard at first, but the longer that I stay here the easier it gets to get into the habit of studying at certain times.

Counselor. It's good that your attitudes have improved since you took the test. Okay, Agnes, what did you find?

Agnes. My lowest is Teacher Approval, also, and the next lowest is Education Acceptance. I don't know why, but Teacher Approval, although not real low, was the lowest.

Counselor. Attitudes toward college are very important because your attitudes influence the way you react to various academic demands, such as outside assignments and having to study when you would prefer doing something else. So, if you find that you have a bad attitude toward something, if you can get at the basis of it, maybe you will see how ridiculous it is or at least understand why you feel as you do.

Karen. I've noticed here at college that students are always going to see their teachers, which is something that I never think about doing.

Counselor. What about the rest of you? Have you ever done this?

Agnes. I was always afraid that someone would accuse me of buttering up the teacher.

Judy. My math teacher here at college has helped me a whole lot. If I have a problem, he's always glad to help me.

Counselor. Nancy, do you find that to be true?

Nancy. I've been like Agnes. I don't go to see them because I thought that they would think you were trying to get ahead of somebody or something.

Counselor. Maybe if you didn't have anything important to discuss, then they might resent your taking up their time. But if you have some definite questions to ask, or really have something important to discuss, I don't think then that they would mind helping you. The teachers are there to do a job, and they usually are real cooperative.

Nancy. I see what you mean—helping students is part of their job.

Counselor. Now that we have discussed your scores, you are to write a short summary of your strong points and weak points in this space below your graph. Also, write down what steps you can take to improve your weak areas. [*Counselees write summary.*] Perhaps you have forgotten the test used to measure your study habits and attitudes. To help you better understand your weaknesses, I am going to hand out the test again, together with your answer sheet. We'll look over how you answered the questions and see, perhaps, why you scored low in some areas. For instance, Karen said she didn't understand why she made such a low score on Education Acceptance. Let's see what some of the reasons were. On your answer sheet, some of your answers have been circled. The ones circled in red represent poor attitudes, and the ones in blue represent poor habits. These are the ones that were answered contrary to the way good students generally answer them.

Agnes. These aren't wrong answers that are circled?

Counselor. We won't say that they are necessarily wrong, but they are answered contrary to the way good students generally answer.

Agnes. I see.

Counselor. Let's look at the circled answers. Read them over to yourself, and, if you find one that you would like to talk about or that you don't understand or don't agree with, let's read it aloud and talk about it.

Karen. What about number 4?

Counselor. What is it—an attitude or a habit?

Karen. It's an attitude.

Counselor. Okay, let's take the attitudes first.

Nancy. I got that one wrong, too, number 4.

Counselor. Okay, Karen, would you read it?

Karen. I feel that I would study harder if I were given more freedom to choose courses that I like. Well, it seems to me that's just logical —if you're studying something that you are interested in, you just naturally study it harder.

Nancy. I agree. Something that you like, you will put out more effort on because you enjoy it more. The subject that you don't like, you won't study as hard for, although you should.

Counselor. Judy, do you agree with this?

Judy. I don't know. If you only took courses that you liked, you wouldn't get a very broad education. There are courses that you don't necessarily like, but that you ought to take anyway. Basic courses.

Agnes. Wouldn't you say that when you like things it's usually because you are good in them? If you don't like them, then you need to work harder.

Counselor. Agnes has a point there. For instance, if you are low in math, in order to make a good grade you'll have to study harder than you would if you liked this subject and were good at it. Why do you think that there are certain courses that everyone is required to take, especially when you are a freshman? Courses that you must take even though they are not in the field that you intend to major or minor in.

Nancy. Because there are some required courses for everyone.

Counselor. Why do you think that this is done? Is there a purpose for having required courses?

Karen. If you only took courses that you liked, they would all be in one field, and your knowledge would be all in one field.

Counselor. Also, every field is related in some way to other fields. Knowledge in only one field is going to limit you severely later on, because you are always going to be associated with people who are interested in things other than your own particular field of interest. Also, you must know something about the world outside your own field of specialization if you are to properly exercise your responsibilities as a free citizen. So, you get your broad education while you are a freshman and sophomore, then you can specialize later on. Also, you will be more well rounded and you will better know what you are really interested in, because you have been exposed to more fields. Are there any more questions about attitudes questions?

Karen. Yes, number 11. I believe that the easiest way to get good grades is to agree with everything your teacher says.

Counselor. What about this? Do you actually think this is true? How did you answer it?

Karen. I answered it almost always.

Agnes. Was that because of your aunt?

Karen. It surely was. That's the way she grades. I'm around her all the time, and she's always talking about the kids in her class that she likes. They always agree with her and are pleasant, so she gives them A's.

Counselor. Well, now, do you feel that, generally speaking, teachers tend to discourage differences of opinion with themselves?

Nancy. I think that it depends on the teacher, but most of them want you to give your own opinion.

Agnes. It does make the class more interesting. But there is a right way to do it—maybe that's what Nancy had in mind. If you just argue for the sake of arguing, they usually resent it, but if you have something to back up your opinion, very few teachers will resent your speaking up.

Counselor. That's a very good analysis. Now, does anyone else have an attitude item she wants to discuss?

Judy. What about question number 20? I think that teachers expect students to do too much studying outside of class.

Karen. I missed it too. You do spend six hours a day in class, and then they want you to go home and do a lot of homework. Of course, it's a little different in college.

Counselor. Considering college, do you still agree with the statement?

Judy. I know that since I've come to college I've had to study a lot more than I did in high school.

Counselor. Do you think that this is expecting too much of the student? Agnes, how do you feel about this?

Agnes. It goes back to what I said a little while ago—if you are good in a subject, you'll do better in it because you like it better. So you'll probably spend less time studying. During the first two years, when we are taking the required courses, we're bound not to like some of them because they are not in our field, so we'll probably have to work harder, until we get into our major field. Then we probably won't have to spend quite as much time studying.

Counselor. That's fine, but what do you think is the purpose of all this homework? Is there too much outside work?

Agnes. Well, I didn't have to study much in high school. I made A's and B's and a couple of C's. I imagine that the teachers know that most of us didn't study much in high school, and they just kinda want to hit us hard right at first to get us used to it.

Judy. I have so much studying to do that I just stay up late every night. I really don't have the time to do the things that I really want to do.

Counselor. Do you have a special time to study? Do you have a specific time for studying certain subjects or do you just study whatever you happen to need for the next day?

Judy. I just study whenever I get a chance.

Counselor. Do you plan your day in any way?

Judy. No, I don't follow much of a plan. Just the regular routine of going to classes and eating.

Counselor. Since you do have more demands on your time in college than you had in high school, it is even more a necessity that you learn to budget your time and schedule what you have to do at the best time possible. It's something that you have to get into the habit of doing. Later on, I'll show you how to schedule your time so that you will actually have more time for doing other things than studying all the time. Are there any other attitude items to be discussed?

Judy. I also missed 31: Daydreaming about dates, future plans, etc., distracts my attention from my lessons while I am studying.

Counselor. Where do you study?

Judy. Usually on my bed. Sometimes I study at my desk if I have to write something.

Counselor. Whose picture do you keep on your desk?

Judy. I have a picture of my boyfriend. When I get tired of studying, I like to sit there and look at his picture.

Counselor. Maybe this is why you have the problem—your study environment is actually helping to distract you. There are just too many things there to daydream about. Do any of you ever go to the library to study?

Karen. Sometimes I've gone there at night.

Counselor. Do you find that you can concentrate better at the library?

Karen. Yes.

Counselor. Why?

Karen. Because you are freed from telephone calls for one thing.

Nancy. And somebody is always coming in my room when I try to study.

Agnes. If your boyfriend wants to visit, you can always go to the library and study together. That way you kill two birds with one stone.

Counselor. If you do go with your boyfriend, you will probably get more studying done if you sit facing the wall. One thing about the library, it eliminates the bull sessions, and background noise is greatly reduced. Are there any other attitude items to be discussed? If not, let's go on to the study habits questions.

Agnes. How about number 93? I lose points on the true-and-false and multiple-choice examinations because I change my original answer only to discover later that I was right the first time.

Counselor. If you are more or less making an educated guess, it is a generally accepted truth that your first answer on a true-false or multiple-choice test is most likely to be correct. Unless you are absolutely positive that your first answer is incorrect—unless you definitely remember some fact that would change your answer—your first answer is more likely to be correct than a second-guessed answer. This is because your first answer is rarely a pure guess, but more often than not is based upon partial knowledge—an educated guess.

Karen. What about number 66? Prolonged reading and study gives me a headache.

Counselor. Have you had your glasses checked recently?

Karen. Not recently.

Counselor. Well, it could be that or it could be eyestrain.

Karen. The lamp on my desk almost blinds me sometimes.

Counselor. Then your light is probably not evenly distributed and the resulting glare strains your eyes. You should have a lamp that distributes the light evenly over your desk, not a gooseneck lamp that concentrates the light on your book.

Judy. I missed number 50. Telephone calls, people coming in and out of my room, bull sessions with my friends, etc., interfere with my studying. They do!

Counselor. What could you do about it?

Judy. I guess that studying in the library would be the best thing.

Counselor. Can anyone suggest another solution?

Agnes. It's awfully quiet at 5 o'clock in the morning.

Counselor. Yes. Judy, there are various ways that you can remedy this —studying in the library, getting up early to study, etc.

Karen. What about number 80? I like to have a radio or phonograph playing while I'm studying.

Counselor. That one always comes up. Some students argue that music helps them study. Maybe, for some people, it does, but it can also be a real distraction. If it's low-level background music, maybe that won't bother you. Music is generally listened to for enjoyment rather than for background, however, so it can be distracting while you are studying. You'll just have to check this out for yourself.

Agnes. I can't study with the radio turned on because there is talking after each record.

Counselor. Agnes has a point; the commercials breaking in all the time can really be distracting. Okay, are there any more questions that you want to discuss? No? Now, we have been discussing all along about the arrangement of your room. Let's look at these illustrations and see which of them looks most like your room—the picture on the left or the picture on the right. [*Displays Study Site Illustration: This or This?*]

Karen. My room isn't that dirty or messy—and it isn't that well organized either—kinda in between the two.

Judy. I have been in some rooms just about like the one on the left.

Counselor. Let's look at the two and compare points that are good and bad.

Nancy. In this one, the desk is in front of the window. He'd probably be looking out the window most of the time.

Counselor. What should be done about that?

Nancy. You should put your desk flush against a solid wall so that you can't look out a window or door.

Judy. No pictures on the wall, either.

Agnes. And the gooseneck lamp—we just talked about it. He would have a glare from that.

Karen. The one on the left has everything so neatly arranged. The one on the right couldn't know where anything is.

Judy. Look how he is sitting.

Nancy. We mentioned it before—the distractions: radio, picture, food, etc.

Judy. The radio is probably turned on, too.

Counselor. Almost everything about the room on the right is disturbing to concentration. I think that you have seen from these two illustrations the correct way to arrange your room so as to have a good study environment. One effective way to keep people from barging into your room right in the middle of studying is to hang a "do not disturb" sign on your door. Here are some signs that you may take with you to use in the dorm. [*Distributes Do Not Disturb Signs.*]

Nancy. Say, these are real cute.

Counselor. Another thing that you can do, if you and your roommate can cooperate, is to set a study time and observe quiet hours in either the afternoon or the evening. This brings up another thing that we have been hitting at—the necessity for budgeting your time. As Judy says, she doesn't have time to do anything else but study. She doesn't have time to do the other things that she really wants to do. Here are two different time budgets. [*Displays Daily Activity Schedules for Fred Fish and Frank Frosh.*] This one is for Fred Fish and this one is for Frank Frosh. Let's look at them and compare their schedules. Do you see anything that is better about Frank Frosh's schedule as compared with Fred Fish's?

Nancy. Fred Fish doesn't say what he is going to study during his study periods. It just says study. He has blocked off study time, but his schedule doesn't say what he will be studying.

Karen. It seems to me that, if he had longer blocks of study time, he could settle down and study better.

Counselor. Longer blocks might be okay if you break them up some. You can concentrate better if you study for about an hour, then take a short break. What I think Nancy is referring to here is the fact that he has not listed specific things to study. He just has study written down for three straight hours.

Nancy. Also, he has recreation after English and before math. Shouldn't he be studying then?

Counselor. Yes. He could use that hour between classes effectively for reviewing English lecture notes or checking over his math homework.

Judy. Also, he has study scheduled from 7 till 11 on Saturday morning. I don't believe he'll do that. He'll probably sleep late instead.

Counselor. Judy has brought up an important point here. A time schedule must be practical if you are really going to follow it. Certainly, nobody is likely to get up at 7 o'clock on Saturday morning to study for four hours. If you do make such a schedule, you are just going to throw it out and say that time budgeting doesn't work. Your schedule must be realistic and must be practical. Do you see anything else wrong with his schedule?

Karen. What about catch-up studying on Sunday night?

Counselor. Yes. It's a good idea to have a catch-up study period after the weekend.

Agnes. When would he do his weekend homework? I guess on Friday night, but that is certainly a long time until Monday morning.

Nancy. Is he really going to start studying every evening at 6 o'clock, right after dinner when everybody else is still moving around?

Karen. That isn't very realistic. That's usually bull-session time.

Judy. Everybody is really noisy then.

Agnes. His schedule is especially bad on Tuesdays and Thursdays. He's going to study all morning, have lunch, P.E., chemistry lab, work, and dinner. Then he's going to study again for four hours right after dinner. He doesn't have any recreation time scheduled at all.

Counselor. That is another important point. He has overloaded his classes on M-W-F; then he is overloading his studying on Tuesday-Thursday. He doesn't have a balanced schedule. Do you find any other defects? What about his studying before history and after math? After history, Frank Frosh has a review period scheduled, but Fred Fish has math after his history class. It's a good idea to have a review period after a lecture class so that you can check your notes and make them readable. That's an important point to remember during registration so that you will schedule your classes more reasonably. Provide for review time after your lecture classes and before your participation classes so that you can check things over right after or just before these classes.

Agnes. Even if he has to schedule the two classes together, he could still review here between 10 and 11, which would be better than waiting till that night or the next day, or waiting for three or four weeks until he has to study for a quiz.

Counselor. Yes. Okay, we have pretty well covered the main problems illustrated by these two schedules. Would you be interested in making a schedule of your own? [*Distributes Daily Activity Schedules.*]

Judy. It ought to help me.

Nancy. I think that it would help me get things done on time.

Counselor. Have you ever thought of going to college as, in effect, being like working on a job? In some ways it really is a more demanding job than if you actually were out working. At least you have to spend more hours per week on it. You can't just work eight hours and then go home and forget it till the next day. If you have a test or homework due the next day, you'll just have to sit down and start studying.

Karen. Why are there two blank schedules?

Counselor. The first one is for this semester, Karen, and the second one is for next semester. Before we can begin working on this semester's schedule, though, there are some general rules we should look at. Let's look at the directions. Nancy, what is the first step?

Nancy. Record inflexible time commitments. Write in all your regularly scheduled activities, such as classes, labs, church services, employment, band practice, club meetings, etc.

Counselor. Let's do that now. Write down your fixed activities in red pencil. This includes not only your classes, but other commitments that you have to meet, such as church services, work, etc. [*Counselees begin filling out schedule.*] Freshmen often make the mistake of scheduling for straight classes—one right after another. This doesn't give them any time for reviewing between classes. If you made this mistake, it is one thing that you can correct when you register for next semester. Do any of you work? No? Okay, Judy, would you read the next step?

Judy. Schedule activities essential to daily living. Set aside ample, but not excessive, time for eating, sleeping, dressing, laundry, etc.

Counselor. These are your routine daily living activities. Let's do this in plain pencil. [*Counselees continue filling out schedule.*]

Agnes. Should we schedule the weekend too?

Counselor. It's a good idea, unless you go home over the weekend and never do any studying then.

Agnes. I never go home on weekends.

Counselor. Be sure and put down everything that takes up a lot of time. Okay, Agnes, let's go on to step three.

Agnes. Schedule review times. Reserve time for reviewing either before or after each class, as appropriate. For a lecture course—history, English, etc.—the time immediately following the class period should be kept free for revising and expanding your notes; for a participation course—speech, foreign language, etc.—the time just prior to class should be reserved for studying the day's assignment.

Counselor. Okay, these are your review periods. They are very important, especially those after lecture classes.

Agnes. What color should we use?

Counselor. These should be in blue. Have any of you formed the habit of revising your lecture notes after class?

Karen. All my classes follow each other and I don't have any time until afternoon.

Counselor. Well, you should do it as soon as possible even if it isn't right after class.

Agnes. I have a free hour right before lunch. Should I review chemistry then?

Counselor. It would be a good idea.

Nancy. Is it better to study before an English class or after?

Counselor. It depends on what type of class it is. If you have to prepare something, save time beforehand. If it is mostly a lecture class, schedule time afterward.

Judy. Should you get your math homework the day that it is assigned or the night before it is due?

Counselor. It probably would be easier to do it as soon as possible because it is very easy to forget how to work problems. Then you could also schedule a short review before class.

Agnes. You would also have time to get help if you needed it.

Karen. I have my speech class at 8 o'clock. I guess I could get up earlier and review before class.

Counselor. Okay, Karen, would you read the next step?

Karen. Block off recreation time. Set aside regular time for such recreational activities as dating, bull sessions, TV viewing, etc. Schedule these activities in moderation, however, as all play and no work will only lead to academic failure.

Counselor. Okay. Schedule your time for recreation. Try to pick times that won't interfere with your studies, however.

Agnes. Does this include weekend stuff?

Counselor. Yes, you can include your weekends. Nancy, don't you usually have recreation right after dinner?

Nancy. It's a good time for bull sessions.

Counselor. Okay, let's move on to the preparation periods. We'll put this in blue pencil. Nancy, would you read step 5?

Nancy. Schedule preparation periods. For each course, schedule sufficient time for preparing outside assignments. The amount of time to be scheduled for each course will depend upon the difficulty level of the material, your ability to master the material, and the efficiency of your study methods. Preparation periods should be scheduled at times when interference is at a minimum and should be long enough to permit the accomplishment of a significant amount of work.

Counselor. Okay. Now schedule appropriate preparation periods for your classes.

Agnes. It's not all right to just mark off a big block of time as study time?

Counselor. No, it is better to indicate a specific subject for each study period.

Karen. Should you prepare your homework on the same day that you have a class, or on the next day?

Counselor. This depends on the class itself, of course, but usually the assignment is fresher on your mind if you do the homework immediately. Also, in making out your schedule, remember which subjects are more difficult for you. If you know that you usually need to spend more time on a certain subject, be sure to allow for this extra time. Okay, has everyone finished? Do you think that this time schedule is practical enough to be of real use to you?

Nancy. I think mine will be.

Judy. Mine too! I think that I'll get my studying done better.

Nancy. I didn't realize that I have so much free time until I started putting everything down.

Karen. Neither did I.

Agnes. I don't know if it will work or not, but I'll try it.

Counselor. Well, that's all we can ask of you. [*Distributes "Reading and Remembering Guide."*] We were discussing reading a little earlier, and some of you were concerned about your reading scores and the fact that you couldn't read as rapidly or comprehend as well as other freshmen. This *Reading and Remembering Guide* will give you some specific suggestions about how to read textbook assignments. It's essential that you recognize that you cannot read a history assignment the same way you read a novel. In a novel you can just breeze through because you don't have to remember facts. In reading your textbooks, however, it's important that you remember facts and that you be able to connect together the ideas presented in the book. The Survey-Q3R method was devised to help you to read actively, instead of passively. By this, we mean that you should underline important ideas and make notes in the margin as you read. Do something to make it active reading, instead of passive reading. Let's look at the reading guide. First, it says to survey the material. In other words, go over the assignment, read the introductory and summary paragraphs, and look at the illustrations, tables, headings, and subheadings. This will give you some idea of what is covered in the assignment. Then ask yourself questions about the material to be read. What is it all about? What major ideas are to be presented? Then read the assignment carefully for meaning. While you are reading, be sure to underline important points. In college, underlining is not a penalty when you resell your books. Be sure to underline only the key words and phrases, though. Too much underlining can be as confusing as none when you start reviewing. Fourth, recite from memory the main points that are presented in the assignment. Finally, review the assignment after reading it, and again in a few days. If you will do this, it should help you remember what you have read. As you can see, the guide is marked up the same way that you should underline your own reading assignments. Are there any questions?

Judy. This looks like a very good way to study.

Counselor. Yes, and it does save a lot of time when you get ready to review for an exam. Are there any questions about this method? Would it take up too much time?

Nancy. It won't take as much time as I have been spending.

Judy. It will probably help us make better grades, too.

Agnes. Studying for exams would be a cinch if your textbook was marked up like this.

Counselor. Yes. Okay, did you read your *Effective Study Guide* before coming today?

Agnes. Yes, but I forgot to bring mine.

Counselor. I have an extra copy. Look through the booklet and see if you have any questions about anything in it.

Judy. Here it says not to sit on an easy chair, lie on the bed, or study while wearing your pajamas. I thought that you could study better if you were comfortable.

Counselor. There is a difference between being comfortable and being so relaxed that you just about go to sleep. If you sit up in a business-like way, you can concentrate better and are less likely to fall asleep or have your mind wander from the book. This is what they mean by that. Do any of you study in your pajamas?

Judy. I usually do.

Counselor. Do you often find yourself getting sleepy after studying for a while?

Judy. Yes.

Nancy. Studying on my bed makes me sleepy, too.

Karen. How about taking notes—how do you know what to take down?

Counselor. You have to train yourself to listen for the teacher's outline. Most teachers do lecture from an outline, you know. Look for lead sentences. They will be your clues.

Agnes. If you read your assignment ahead of time, you'd know better what to expect—you'd know more or less what the main points are going to be.

Counselor. Yes. It surely helps to know something about the subject beforehand. The pamphlet also stresses the importance of your scholastic motivation. Agnes, can you tell us why?

Agnes. Well, let's see. You can say a lot for ability and a lot for achievement, but if you don't have the motivation to go to college and do something positive while in college, why you probably won't be a very good student. In fact, it might even lead to failure.

Counselor. Yes, that's it. It is a good idea to examine your reasons for going to college and try to decide what your college goals are. After all, college does offer more than just social life and job training. [*Distributes Counseling Appointment Request Forms.*] The Testing and Counseling Center provides additional counseling services for freshmen. If you are undecided about a major and feel that you want to start thinking about it seriously, then you might be interested in signing up for vocational guidance. It doesn't cost anything and is given by one of the Center's vocational counselors. It is for anyone who definitely needs help in choosing a major. Educational guidance is provided for anyone wishing help in planning his study program and is given by one of the faculty advisors. Special faculty advisors are provided for nonmajors, and majors go to the faculty advisor for their major department. Are there any questions?

Agnes. Could you get educational guidance even though you haven't decided on a major?

Counselor. Yes. Although vocational guidance might help you decide on a major first. If you are interested in obtaining either type of additional counseling, please fill out this form and indicate the times you cannot come.

Nancy. I think that I know what my major is, but I'm not sure. May I request vocational guidance later if I want it?

Counselor. Yes.

Agnes. Does vocational guidance just show your abilities? Or your interests, too?

Counselor. Both. The purpose is to help you decide upon a satisfying vocation for yourself. But this is not guaranteed. You also get information about job opportunities and working conditions for different careers. It usually takes from six to eight hours time.

Judy. Does it cost anything?

Counselor. No. It's a free service.

Karen. What if we just want to see a faculty advisor?

Counselor. Then just check the educational guidance box and write in your major on the bottom. The card will be sent to the faculty advisor for your major and he will contact you in a week or so.

Judy. I don't have a major, but I plan to get married before I finish college. Should I go ahead and request vocational guidance?

Counselor. That's up to you, Judy. But if you don't get married for awhile, you will need a major later on.

Judy. Yes, and I might go back to college after I marry.

Counselor. That's right. But don't sign up for vocational guidance unless you really feel that you are ready to make some decisions.

Judy. Maybe I had just better wait a while.

Counselor. Okay, you have one more thing to do. [*Distributes Counseling Comprehension Test.*] I would like to find out what you have misunderstood during this session, or if I have forgotten to cover something. Read the directions to this test and then answer the twenty-five true-false questions. After you finish, I will score your answer sheet, and then we'll go over the ones that you missed. [*Counselees answer questions and pass answer sheets to counselor for scoring.*]

Counselor. Now that I have scored your answer sheets, you can see which questions you missed. Agnes, did you miss any?

Agnes. I missed the first one. Ranking at the 78th centile means that you answered 78 percent of the questions correctly. It sounded like what it should be.

Counselor. Judy, do you know what centile refers to?

Judy. If you are at the 78th centile, that means that 78 of 100 students were below you and 22 were above you.

Agnes. Oh, that's right! It refers to students, not to questions. I missed number 11, too. Study Habits that are effective for girls are not likely to be effective for boys. I said that it was true, but I guess it's not.

Counselor. Generally speaking, the study methods that are effective for girls are equally effective for boys. The dorms may be a little different, but effective study behavior is about the same.

Judy. I missed number 9. Your Delay Avoidance score measures your promptness in accomplishing academic activities. I put false.

Counselor. Agnes, what do you think about this?

Agnes. It is the promptness with which you get homework and other assignments done.

Counselor. Yes. Delay Avoidance refers to how fast you actually get down to work.

Nancy. I missed number 6. Ranking at the 50th centile means that you are below average. I put that it was true.

Counselor. What is the range for average?

Karen. 25th to 75th centiles.

Nancy. Then this is just right in the middle.

Counselor. Yes. Are there any more?

Agnes. I missed the last one. The centile values used in reporting your test scores indicate how you compare with college freshmen nationally. I put that it was true.

Karen. Remember that she said that it was just the freshmen here?

Agnes. Oh, yes.

Counselor. Yes, we use local norms to report all test results. Are there any more questions?

Karen. I wasn't too sure about number 15. The average freshman should spend two hours on outside preparation for each hour spent in class. I didn't have any idea how much time to spend.

Counselor. It varies, of course, but two hours is about average. This point is covered in your *Effective Study Guide.* Are there any other questions? No? Well, that's all. Thank you for coming.

Judy. I'm glad I came. Thank you.

Nancy. Me, too.

Karen. Thank you.

Agnes. Same here.

APPENDIX I

Study Habits Evaluation Activity Sequence Check List

A. Examine Residual Study Problems
   Material: Study Skills Surveys
   1. Review Study Organization Survey
      a. Discuss *all* questions answered "yes"
         * Analyze probable cause of each problem
         * Survey possible cures for each problem
      b. Check use of Daily Activity Schedule
         * Has student developed habits of regularity?
         * Has student maintained proper balance between work and play?
         * Has student procrastinated in preparing assignments?
         * Has student wasted prime study time?
   2. Review Study Techniques Survey
      a. Discuss *all* questions answered "yes"
         * Analyze probable cause of each problem
         * Survey possible cures for each problem
      b. Check use of suggested study techniques
         * Techniques for taking lecture notes
         * Techniques for reading textbooks
         * Techniques for theme and report writing
         * Techniques for preparing for and taking tests
   3. Review Study Motivation Survey
      a. Discuss *all* questions answered "yes"
         * Analyze probable cause of each problem
         * Survey possible cures for each problem
      b. Examine student's expectations about college
         * Why did student come to college?
         * What does student want from college?
         * What are student's present educational plans?
         * What are student's future occupational plans?
B. Examine Student-Teacher Relations
   Material: *Student-to-Student Tips*
   1. Discuss Responsibility for Seeking Assistance
      a. Office hours are posted on door

NOTE: Appendix numbers cited in this check list are for the appendices in the *Student Counselor's Handbook.*

    b. Student is responsible for seeking out instructor
2. Discuss Proper Approach to Instructor
    a. Positive desire to learn is right approach
    b. Excuse-making, apple-polishing, or complaint-making are wrong approaches
3. Discuss Do's and Don'ts about Requesting Help
    a. Do request specific clarification of requirements for assignments
    b. Don't request help with carelessly planned or vaguely conceived assignments
    c. Do request explanation of mistakes noted on returned assignments or tests
    d. Don't challenge grading of returned assignments or tests
4. Offer Some Tips on Teacher Relations
    a. Explain all absences to your instructor and arrange to catch up as quickly as possible
    b. Stay alert and attentive in class at all times
    c. Ask your instructor where you can obtain needed help if your background is deficient
    d. Be courteous to your instructor both inside and outside of class

C. Check Student's "Reality Orientation" about Courses
   1. Survey Probable Mid-Semester Grades
    a. Have student list all courses and anticipated grades
    b. Have student explain basis for anticipated grade in each course
   2. Survey Professional Basis for Awarding Grades
    a. Have student list graded material for each course (tests, themes, reports, homework, etc.)
    b. Have student assess professor's basis for assigning course grade (weighting of tests, homework, reports, classroom participation, etc)

D. Discuss Probable Reasons for Unsatisfactory Grades
   1. Report Unsatisfactory Grades to Student
   Material: Mid-Semester Grade Report
    a. Compare "anticipated" and "actual" grades for all courses
    b. Discuss possible reasons for unexpected passing and failing grades
   2. Analyze Probable Causes of Scholastic Difficulty
   Material: Scholastic Difficulty Analysis Form (Appendix D-2)
    a. Check appropriate reasons for each course

    b. Discuss appropriate corrective actions for each reason checked

3. Analyze Consequences of College Failure

    a. Discuss effect on future employment

    b. Discuss effect on present self-respect

APPENDIX J

Scholastic Difficulty Analysis Form

Factors which, in the judgment of the student, are contributing to scholastic difficulty in specific subjects. Please indicate subject (history, biology, etc.) and check appropriate items.

	Subject	Subject	Subject
Do not study.......................	☐	☐	☐
Have reading problem	☐	☐	☐
Do not hand work in on time	☐	☐	☐
Am excessively absent	☐	☐	☐
Am frequently late to class	☐	☐	☐
Do not spend enough time on lessons	☐	☐	☐
Have health or other personal problem ...	☐	☐	☐
Do not seek help from teacher	☐	☐	☐
Have poor background for subject	☐	☐	☐
Am not interested in subject	☐	☐	☐
Am working too much outside school	☐	☐	☐
Have too many outside activities	☐	☐	☐
Other	☐	☐	☐
Other	☐	☐	☐
Cause Unknown	☐	☐	☐

In conference, the student and I effected the following actions relating to the above:

....

Student   Date   Advisor

APPENDIX K

Activity Sequence Outline: Note Taking Instruction

A. Check Counselee's Experiences and Expectations
  1. Review Counselee's Biographical Data
  Material: Student Information Form (Appendix C-2)
    a. Discuss past and present participation in nonacademic activities
      * Part-time and summer work experiences
      * Nature and extent of dating activity
      * Extracurricular awards and honors
    b. Discuss past and present acceptance of academic activities
      * Least liked and most liked high school subjects
      * Academic rank in high school graduation class
      * Reaction to current college courses
  2. Question Counselee's Needs and Wants
    a. Probe counselee's perceptions of problem
      * Specific nature of problem
      * Possible causes of difficulty
    b. Probe counselee's attitudes toward counseling
      * Response to previous counseling suggestions
      * Expectations from current counseling session
B. Discuss Common Note Taking Problems
  1. Examine Tendency to Take Notes Verbatim
    a. Unable to keep up with instructor
    b. Too busy to evaluate what is said
    c. Organization and relationship of material is lost
    d. Meaningfulness of material is reduced
  2. Examine Difficulty in Maintaining Concentration Level
    a. Continued lecturing is new experience
    b. Uninterrupted lecturing does become boring
    c. Daydreaming and distraction are normal result
    d. Effective note taking helps maintain concentration
  3. Examine Tendency to Take Notes "Paragraph" Style
    a. Easy because little thinking is required
    b. Lends itself to taking notes verbatim
    c. Lacks organization into major and minor points
    d. Difficult to study because hard to read

NOTE: Appendix numbers cited in this outline are for the appendices in the *Student Counselor's Handbook*.

C. Review Note Taking Process
   Material: Effective Study Guide (pp. 24–25), *Student's Guides to Effective Study*, no. 3: *Guide to Taking Lecture Notes*, and Sample Lecture Notes on Taking Lecture Notes (Appendix A-7)
   1. Discuss Listening Process
      a. Explain Rule #1: Be Prepared
         * Read textbook assignments beforehand
         * Review previous lecture notes beforehand
      b. Explain Rule #2: Learn Your Professor
         * Organization of lectures
         * Cues to major points
      c. Explain Rule #3: Listen-Think-Write
         * Be attentive to what is said
         * Critically evaluate what is said
         * Restate what is said in your own words
      d. Explain Rule #4: Use Proven Procedures
         * Separate notes from different courses
         * Date notes and number pages
         * Use ball-point pen or fountain pen
         * Use standard abbreviations only
         * Write legibly and on one side of paper
         * Use underlining and other emphasis marks
   2. Discuss Reviewing Process
      a. Explain Rule #1: Review Lecture Notes Immediately after Class
         * Do clarify and expand your notes
         * Don't waste time recopying your notes
      b. Explain Rule #2: Correlate Lecture Notes with Reading Assignments
         * Check for differences in interpretation
         * Check for differences in emphasis
      c. Explain Rule #3: Recite Major Points Presented in Lecture
         * To reinforce learning of material
         * To identify poorly understood material

D. Analyze Student's Lecture Notes
   1. Check for Use of Standard Outline Form
      a. Roman numerals, capital letters
      b. Indention to different depths
   2. Check for Use of "Listen-Think-Write" Rule
      a. Brief but comprehensible sentences
      b. Notes in student's own words
      c. Separation of major and minor points

3. Check Use of Recommended Reviewing Techniques
   a. Notes expanded and clarified
   b. Notes correlated with reading assignments
4. Check Use of Proven Procedures
   a. Notes dated and pages numbered
   b. Notes written on only one side of paper
   c. Notes written legibly
   d. Notes taken in ink
   e. Notes contain standard abbreviations only
   f. Notes underlined and marked for emphasis
E. Determine Appropriate Corrective Steps
   1. Review Deficiencies Discovered during Session
   2. Have Counselee Suggest Effective Corrective Actions
F. Decide on Follow-Up Counseling
   1. Determine if Follow-Up Session Is Desirable
   2. Confirm Time and Place of Next Meeting

APPENDIX L
Personal Data Form

NOTE: This is a confidential form for use in vocational counseling.

Name.................................. Sex...... Age......

Date................. Address...............................

High School................................ Size..........

Type Course.................... Scholastic Quarter: 1 2 3 4

Most Liked Subjects	Least Liked Subjects
1)	1) ....
2)	2) ....
3)	3) ....

Awards and Honors

1)	4) ....
2)	5) ....
3)	6) ....

Memberships

1)	4) ....
2)	5) ....
3)	6) ....

Hobbies

1)	4) ....
2)	5) ....
3)	6) ....

Sports

1)	4) ....
2)	5) ....
3)	6) ....

Social Activities

1)	4) ....
2)	5) ....
3)	6) ....

Health Data

1)	3) ....
2)	4) ....

Employment Data

Job Description	Duration	Attitude
1)................................	....	SL L ? D SD
2)................................	....	SL L ? D SD
3)................................	....	SL L ? D SD

4).................................   ....   SL   L   ?   D   SD
5).................................   ....   SL   L   ?   D   SD
6).................................   ....   SL   L   ?   D   SD

Family Data

Father's Occupation ....
Father's Education: 1 2 3 4 5 6 7 8 9 10 11 12   1 2 3 4 5 6 7........
Mother's Occupation ....
Mother's Education: 1 2 3 4 5 6 7 8 9 10 11 12   1 2 3 4 5 6 7........

Vocational Plans

1st Choice: ....
2nd Choice: ....
3rd Choice: ....

Educational Plans

Major		Minor
....	1st Choice	....
....	2nd Choice	....

Directions for Preparing Personal Data Form

NAME: Record last name, first name, middle name or initial.

SEX: Record M or F.

AGE: Record current age.

DATE: Record current date as 10/25/60.

ADDRESS: Give college dorm and room number or home address and telephone if living off campus.

HIGH SCHOOL: Record name and location of high school.

SIZE: Give classification of high school (B, A, 2A, 3A, 4A).

TYPE COURSE: Record type of high school program completed (college preparatory, commercial, technical, etc.).

SCHOLASTIC QUARTER: Indicate rank in high school graduation class by circling 1st, 2nd, 3rd, or 4th quarter.

MOST AND LEAST LIKED SUBJECTS: List 3 most liked and 3 least liked subjects actually taken in high school.

AWARDS AND HONORS: List significant awards and honors received while in high school (valedictorian, class or club president, cheerleader, ROTC officer or sponsor, editor of annual or paper, most popular boy or girl, leading role in senior play, scholarship, debating trophy, etc.).

MEMBERSHIPS: List significant clubs or organizations joined while in high school (FFA, FTA, Science Club, Dramatics Club, Debating Society, Band, etc.).

HOBBIES: List significant hobbies during the last five years (stamp collecting, photography, gardening, raising pigeons, painting, building model airplanes, hot-rod racing, etc.).

SPORTS: List major sports participated in and write "L" for letters won (track, tennis, basketball, baseball, golf, bowling, swimming, hunting, fishing, etc.).

SOCIAL ACTIVITIES: List social activities commonly engaged in for recreational purposes (going dancing, playing bridge or poker, attending concerts or exhibits, working on church or club projects, participating in "bull sessions," going to the movies, etc.).

HEALTH DATA: List health problems or physical disabilities which might have occupational significance (asthma, diabetes, high blood pressure, rupture, color blindness, impaired vision or hearing, etc.).

EMPLOYMENT DATA: Beginning with current or most recent employment, give the following information for each job held: (1) description of work performed; (2) duration of employment; and (3) attitude toward job duties (SL=Strongly Liked; L=Liked; ?=Undecided; D=Disliked; SD=Strongly Disliked).

FAMILY DATA: Indicate each parent's occupation and education by writing current job title (insurance salesman, carpenter, history teacher, grocery store owner, secretary, housewife, etc.) and circling highest grade completed (1–12=school; 1–7=college; in blank list highest degree held).

VOCATIONAL PLANS: List three occupations that should be considered in vocational planning.

EDUCATIONAL PLANS: List two possible major fields of study and two possible minor fields of study that should be considered in educational planning.

APPENDIX M

Occupational Analysis Form

Occupational Title ....

I. *Job Characteristics*
   A. Job Description (describe the nature of work performed):
      ....
      ....
      ....
      ....
      ....
      ....
      ....
   B. Employment Trends (describe occupational outlook in terms of future supply and demand):
      ....
      ....

II. *Qualifications and Training*
   A. Personal Qualifications (describe desirable personality and intellectual traits):
      ....
      ....
      ....
      ....
   B. Formal Education (fill in appropriate blanks):
      1. Undergraduate Work
         Academic Major? ....
         Academic Minors? ....
         Other Subjects? ....
      2. Graduate Work
         Location? ....
         Academic Major? ....
   C. Training (fill in appropriate blanks):
      Internship? .... Length?........
      License or Certification? ...... Type? ....
      Other ....
   D. Related Experience (describe desirable work, hobby, or other background experience):
      ....
      ....
      ....
      ....

III. *Remuneration and Advancement*
  A. Earnings (fill in appropriate blanks):
    1. Beginning earnings? ....
    2. Average earnings? ....
    3. Maximum earnings? ....
    4. How long does it usually take to reach maximum? ....
  B. Advancement (answer each question fully):
    1. Where and how does one enter this occupation? ....
       ....
       ....
    2. What are the opportunities for promotion? ....
       ....
    3. What is the usual method of promotion?
       Merit System?....... Seniority?....... Other?.......
       If other, what is usual procedure? ....
       ....

APPENDIX N
Problem Summary

Name.................. Counselor............. Date.......

Problem Summary:

Additional Information:

Topics Discussed:

Action Initiated:

Action Recommended:

Counselor's Evaluation:

Test Results Report Form [front]

Name .... Age......... Sex....... Date......... Major.........

Score	Centile
....	....

American College Test Results

.... Your *English Usage* score indicates your mastery of the basic elements of correct and effective writing: punctuation, capitalization, diction, phraseology, and organization of ideas. About ...... out of 100 college freshmen are *lower*; about ...... out of 100 college freshmen are *higher*.

.... Your *Mathematics Usage* score indicates your mastery of the mathematical principles used in the solution of quantitative problems and in the interpretation of graphs and charts. About ...... out of 100 college freshmen are *lower*; about ...... out of 100 college freshmen are *higher*.

.... Your *Social Studies Reading* score indicates your ability to read, evaluate, and draw significant conclusions from social studies reading materials as well as your general understanding of basic social concepts and terminology. About ...... out of 100 college freshmen are *lower*; about ...... out of 100 college freshmen are *higher*.

.... Your *Natural Science Reading* score indicates your ability to read, evaluate, and draw significant conclusions from natural science reading materials as well as your general understanding of basic scientific principles and terminology. About ...... out of 100 college freshmen are *lower*; about ...... out of 100 college freshmen are *higher*.

.... Your *Composite Achievement* score is the average of your scores on these educational development tests and provides *one* basis for an overall estimate of your general ability to succeed in college. About ...... out of 100 college freshmen are *lower*; about ...... out of 100 college freshmen are *higher*.

Davis Reading Test Results

Score	Centile
....	....

.... Your *Reading Speed* score indicates the rapidity and accuracy with which you read the kinds of material that college students are ordinarily required to read. About ...... out of 100 college freshmen are *lower*; about ...... out of 100 college freshmen are *higher*.

.... Your *Reading Level* score indicates the depth of understanding that you achieve while reading the kinds of material that college students are ordinarily required to read. About ...... out of 100 college freshmen are *lower*; about ...... out of 100 college freshmen are *higher*.

Test Results Report Form [back]

Name .... Age........ Sex...... Date........ Major.........

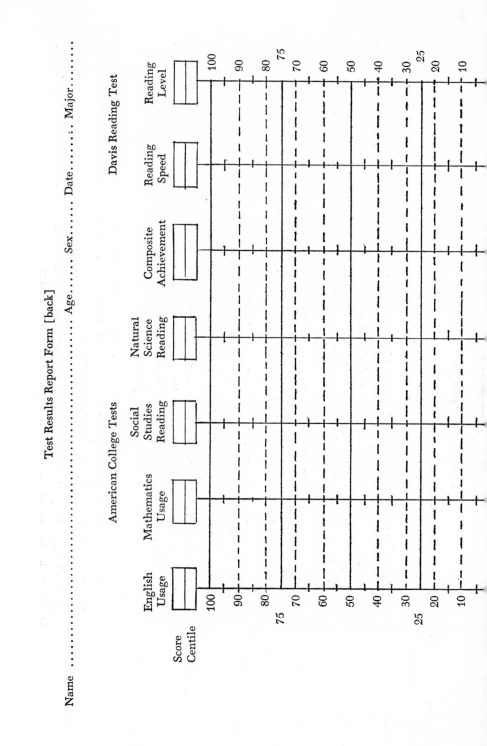

American College Tests

Davis Reading Test

APPENDIX P

Educational Analysis Form

1. My occupational choice is: ....
2. Educational requirements for my occupational choice include:
....
3. Type of college degree desired: BA.... BS.... Other...........
4. I plan to major in: ....
5. I plan to minor in: ....

Academic Requirements

A. General Requirements (all students):

Course	Hours	Course	Hours
English:		Science:	

English:
....
....
....

Mathematics:
....

Humanities:
....
....
....

Speech:
....

Foreign Language:
....
....

Science:
....
....
....

Social Science:
....
....
....

Physical Education:
....

Other:
....

B. Major Requirements: ....

(Name of Major)

Course	Hours	Course	Hours
....	....	....	....
....	....	....	....
....	....	....	....
....	....	....	....
....	....	....	....
....	....	....	....
....	....	....	....
....	....	....	....

C. Minor Requirements: ....
                                          (Name of Minor)
      Course   *Hours*   *Course*   *Hours*
....
....
....
....

D. Other Requirements:
      Course   *Hours*   *Course*   *Hours*
Military: Education:
....
....
....
....
....
....
....
....

E. Electives:
      Course   *Hours*   *Course*   *Hours*
....
....
....
....

Extracurricular Activities
I am interested in participating in the following extracurricular activities:
(a) Sports: (d) Religious groups:
....
....
(b) Departmental clubs: (e) Others:
....
....
(c) Social organizations: ....
....
....
....

APPENDIX Q

Counseling Evaluation Questionnaire

Directions

The statements in this questionnaire are designed to sample your attitudes toward the Test Interpretation Program. Your answers will be made anonymously so please answer all questions frankly.

You will mark your answers on a separate answer sheet. Make no marks on this booklet. There are 60 statements in this questionnaire. You are to indicate the extent to which you agree with each statement. Read each statement and decide how *you* feel about it. Then mark your answer on the space provided on your answer sheet.

	SA	A	?	D	SD
If you *strongly agree*, blacken the space under *SA*	▥	//	//	//	//
If you *agree*, blacken the space under *A*	SA //	A ▥	? //	D //	SD //
If you are *undecided* or *uncertain*, blacken the space under *?*	SA //	A //	? ▥	D //	SD //
If you *disagree*, blacken the space under *D*	SA //	A //	? //	D ▥	SD //
If you *strongly disagree*, blacken the space under *SD*	SA //	A //	? //	D //	SD ▥

There are no "right" or "wrong" answers to these statements. If you will honestly and thoughtfully mark all the statements, however, your attitudes can help us to improve the Test Interpretation Program. Work as rapidly as you can without being careless, and do not spend too much time on any one statement. PLEASE RESPOND TO EVERY ITEM.

1. All entering freshmen should have their test scores interpreted to them by a counselor.
2. Discussing my test scores helped me to understand better my academic adjustment problems.
3. I enjoyed discussing the test results with the other students.
4. The "facts" revealed by the test scores are not accurate in my case.
5. I benefited from hearing the views of other students on the problems that were discussed.
6. Discussing desirable study habits has made me more conscious of the time I waste each day.

7. The discussion of attitudes toward school and teachers was time well spent.

8. Discussing my academic attitudes has made me more tolerant of teacher deficiencies.

9. My counseling group was unable to agree on how to improve one's study methods.

10. I did not have an adequate opportunity to present my views on the problems that were discussed.

11. Discussing my academic attitudes has increased my ambition for academic accomplishment.

12. Discussing my test scores has enabled me to better plan my educational and vocational future.

13. The students at my table were unable to agree on how to improve one's academic motivation.

14. The counselor allowed one or two members of our group to monopolize the discussion too much.

15. The counselor did not give sufficient explanation of the various forms used during counseling.

16. I gained very little from hearing the questions and comments of the other counselees at my table.

17. A lot of time was wasted in discussing things that were irrelevant or unimportant.

18. We failed to discuss the academic adjustment problems that trouble students most.

19. My problems were not the same as those of the other students seated at my table.

20. The Test Interpretation Program gave me a lot of useful information about myself.

21. Too much time was spent in telling us how to study.

22. The Test Interpretation Program was too idealistic in content, and the activities and materials should be made more practical.

23. My time was largely wasted because my problems are different from those that were discussed.

24. The pace of the Test Interpretation Program was too fast to permit effective discussion.

25. I didn't have an adequate chance to ask questions or discuss problems that were bothering me.

26. I would prefer to discuss my test scores with the counselor individually instead of in a student group.

27. I didn't feel relaxed or comfortable during much of the counseling session.
28. I had difficulty tying together all the information that I received from the tests.
29. The discussion would have been improved if students of both sexes had been seated at the same table.
30. Our counseling group was too large to permit each student to state his views.
31. The differences in our test scores made the members of my group uncomfortable.
32. Our group was too large for the counselor to work efficiently.
33. The counselor presented his materials too rapidly to permit effective discussion.
34. I had difficulty understanding what the counselor was talking about.
35. The counselor appeared to lack understanding of the needs and interests of students.
36. The counselor tended to be overbearing and conceited at times.
37. The counselor seemed to be unsure of himself.
38. The counselor did not allow enough discussion of the ideas that were presented.
39. The counselor tried to distribute his time and attention equally among all those seated at my table.
40. The counselor was well prepared to discuss the problems a student encounters in adjusting to college.
41. I had difficulty tying together all the information that I received from the counselor.
42. The counselor hindered free discussion of problems created by dormitory life.
43. The counselor appeared to doubt the value of some of the materials being used.
44. Discussing my scores on the Effective Study Test started me thinking about how to improve my study skills.
45. Reading the *Effective Study Guide* helped me to better understand some of the reasons for my academic difficulties.
46. The Daily Activity Schedule that I made out should help me to use my time more wisely.
47. Discussing the organization of my study area was a waste of time and effort.

48. I found the counseling session to be tiresome and boring.
49. The group at my table did not appear to be very interested in this counseling program.
50. It is unlikely that the members of my group will change their study habits as a result of this counseling.
51. Planning a Daily Activity Schedule is a waste of time and effort.
52. I didn't get enough useful information from the counseling to make any real decisions.
53. Some straight advice would help me more than this program of discussing test results.
54. All entering freshmen should be given an opportunity to discuss their academic adjustment problems with a counselor.
55. I expect my grades to improve as a result of this academic adjustment counseling.
56. The counseling session lasted longer than was really necessary.
57. I enjoyed taking the tests and learning about my test scores.
58. My test scores gave me a realistic picture of my academic strengths and weaknesses.
59. I plan to follow up the Test Interpretation Program by correcting the weaknesses revealed by my test scores.
60. I would like to discuss other adjustment problems with a counselor when I have the time.

APPENDIX R
Distribution of Item Responses for Counseling Evaluation
(Questionnaires Completed Anonymously by 265 Freshmen Counseled
during October, 1959)

Item	Wording	SA	A	U	D	SD	Item	Wording	SA	A	U	D	SD
1	Positive	175	78	9	2	1	31	Negative	4	11	33	148	69
2	Positive	109	118	30	7	1	32	Negative	1	5	7	152	100
3	Positive	96	122	32	12	3	33	Negative	0	3	11	153	98
4	Negative	12	41	80	103	29	34	Negative	1	5	8	152	99
5	Positive	73	141	34	12	5	35	Negative	2	1	16	134	112
6	Positive	116	109	19	15	6	36	Negative	2	3	12	108	140
7	Positive	70	123	36	25	11	37	Negative	0	7	11	127	120
8	Positive	24	119	69	42	11	38	Negative	3	5	13	146	98
9	Negative	5	14	18	130	98	39	Positive	154	91	6	9	5
10	Negative	1	4	13	110	137	40	Positive	118	115	21	7	4
11	Positive	72	123	49	16	5	41	Negative	3	11	21	167	63
12	Positive	52	105	66	29	9	42	Negative	3	26	35	126	75
13	Negative	1	7	40	142	75	43	Negative	5	13	32	136	79
14	Negative	5	3	15	92	150	44	Positive	98	134	23	6	4
15	Negative	4	5	17	135	104	45	Positive	76	145	29	8	7
16	Negative	8	14	25	141	77	46	Positive	88	122	30	12	13
17	Negative	3	15	22	140	85	47	Negative	7	7	36	141	74
18	Negative	5	20	31	145	64	48	Negative	9	19	38	126	73
19	Negative	11	50	43	130	31	49	Negative	10	18	44	134	59
20	Positive	80	122	34	24	5	50	Negative	17	34	113	80	21
21	Negative	7	18	36	152	52	51	Negative	8	17	44	122	74
22	Negative	5	30	90	116	25	52	Negative	10	16	47	146	46
23	Negative	3	15	23	163	61	53	Negative	12	42	72	103	36
24	Negative	3	9	29	153	71	54	Positive	134	97	21	6	7
25	Negative	1	6	13	151	94	55	Positive	32	95	108	21	9
26	Negative	13	10	41	127	74	56	Negative	4	9	27	125	100
27	Negative	1	14	13	131	106	57	Positive	53	136	43	23	10
28	Negative	1	19	40	137	48	58	Positive	84	139	30	8	4
29	Negative	23	45	77	67	53	59	Positive	51	153	51	7	3
30	Negative	5	4	11	118	127	60	Positive	44	100	76	29	16

NOTE: The abbreviations *SA*, *A*, *U*, *D*, and *SD*, respectively, designate response categories Strongly Agree, Agree, Undecided or Uncertain, Disagree, and Strongly Disagree.

APPENDIX S

Counseling Comprehension Test

Directions

Each of the following statements is either true or false. You are to evaluate the truth or falsity of each statement and mark your answer in the appropriate column provided on the separate answer sheet. Thus, for example, you will mark the space under T on your answer sheet if you believe a statement to be true. If you believe a statement to be false, you will mark the space under F on your answer sheet. If you are undecided or uncertain about the truth or falsity of a statement, mark the space under the ? on your answer sheet. Read each statement carefully before marking your answer. Please answer all questions.

1. Only a few four-year colleges now have a selective admissions program.

2. In order to stay off scholastic probation a freshman must earn at least fifteen quality points each semester.

3. To obtain a bachelor's degree you must complete a minimum of 140 semester hours with a "C" average.

4. Approximately seven out of ten entering freshmen fail to continue beyond the first year of college.

5. Dormitory and classroom construction have kept pace with anticipated enrollment increases of most four-year colleges.

6. Freshmen earning less than nine quality points will be "campused" during school nights for the next semester.

7. Fifty-four semester hours are required for a major in most departments.

8. A daily activity schedule cannot be deviated from if it is to be effective.

9. The average college freshman is expected to study about fifty hours per week outside class.

10. The rule for reviewing is to review just before lecture courses and just after participation courses.

11. Studying for less than two hours on any one course at one time is considered to be inefficient.

12. Foreign languages are usually considered to be lecture courses.

13. Off hours between classes should be used for recreation and relaxation.

14. Saturday afternoon is the best time to schedule a "catch-up" study period.

15. It is best to concentrate your classes on M-W-F or T-T-S so as to leave the other days free for studying.

16. You should place your desk facing a window so that you will have adequate light to study by.

17. You should surround your study area with many interesting objects so that you do not become bored.

18. Freshmen should avoid joining any organizations if they hope to earn good grades.

19. Loaning money and clothing is a recommended procedure for making friends in college.

20. You must obtain your faculty advisor's approval to drop a course after the grace period has expired.

21. Your academic attitude is one of the four basic factors that directly influence your scholastic success and satisfaction.

22. Knowing the number of questions answered correctly is less important than knowing your centiles on a standardized test.

23. The centiles used in reporting your test results indicate how you compare with the other freshmen at this college.

24. Your test results will be influenced by such external factors as your emotional state and physical condition at time of testing.

25. High verbal ability indicates that you have the potential to do well in foreign language courses.

26. Scoring at the 45th centile means that 45 percent of your freshman class made a score lower than yours.

27. There are no "right" or "wrong" answers to the questions in the Survey of Study Habits and Attitudes.

28. Faculty advisors are responsible for helping freshmen decide what courses to take and when to take them.

29. Your opinion of teachers and their classroom behavior will influence your study motivation.

30. Faculty advisors are responsible for explaining departmental policies and programs to freshmen.

31. Scoring at the 50th centile means that you are below average.

32. High Scores on the American College Test guarantee academic success in college.

33. Procrastination is a quality every freshman should strive to develop.

34. Scoring at the 80th centile means that you answered 80 percent of the test questions correctly.

35. Bob Benchley's essay demonstrated that he possessed the maturity and self-discipline necessary for scholastic success in college.

36. The difference between the average lifetime earnings of high school and college graduates is about a half million dollars.

37. The Occupational Information Library is located in the Student Employment Office.

38. Students who are undecided about their major field of study are required to sign up for vocational guidance.

39. The Reading Laboratory charges 50¢ per hour for use of the reading accelerators.

40. A $2.50 service fee is charged for the tests administered to students during the course of vocational guidance.

41. The SQ3R Method is a procedure for taking lecture notes.

42. Stopping frequently to recite the major points in a reading assignment is too time-consuming to be practical.

43. You should recopy your lecture notes as soon as possible after class.

44. The standard outline form of note taking is best for following the unorganized lecturer.

45. The paragraph form for taking notes clearly differentiates major and minor points for later study.

46. Outlining an in-class theme before starting to write it is too time-consuming to be practical.

47. When writing an in-class theme you should first prepare a rough draft.

48. You should skip the survey through a textbook reading assignment if study time is limited.

49. When preparing for an objective test you should completely reread your textbook assignment.

50. You should wait until dead week to start your intensive studying for final exams.

51. The average freshman should spend two hours on outside preparation for each hour spent in class.

52. You should take a ten-minute break after each hour of concentrated studying.

53. The SQ3R Method produces an 80 percent improvement in remembering for the same amount of study time.

54. Underlining key words and phrases in the textbook is a good way to practice the active reading principle.

55. The "3R's" of the SQ3R Method are read, recite, and review.

56. Efficient textbook reading emphasizes comprehension rather than speed.
57. The standard outline form of note taking makes maximum use of the listen-think-write rule.
58. You should read true-false questions at least twice before answering.
59. Periodic reviewing is more effective than last-minute cramming when preparing for an essay test.
60. You should distribute your time according to the point value of each question when taking an essay test.

APPENDIX T

Sentence Completion Survey

Age . . . . . . Sex . . . . . . High School . . . . Date . . . . . .

Please complete each of the following sentences by writing whatever ending you think most appropriate to express your feelings. Do not be concerned about using correct grammar or punctuation and do not spend too much time on any one sentence.

The course . . . .
. . . .
I most liked . . . .
. . . .
I least liked . . . .
. . . .
The information presented . . . .
. . . .
The classroom atmosphere . . . .
. . . .
The handout materials . . . .
. . . .
The student counselors . . . .
. . . .
The professional counselors . . . .
. . . .
Add . . . .
. . . .
Eliminate . . . .
. . . .
My study habits . . . .
. . . .
My study attitudes . . . .
. . . .
The course helped me most . . . .
. . . .
My grades . . . .
. . . .
I believe that . . . .
. . . .

Additional Comments

....

....

....

....

....

....

....

....

....

....

....

....

....

APPENDIX U

Rating Scale for Evaluating Student Reaction to the College
Adjustment Seminar Study Habits Content

Rating	Statement
9 Strongly positive	My study habits will be greatly improved because I am going to start using all the study procedures that we were taught.
8 **	....
7 Positive	The suggested study methods look pretty good, and I plan to use most of them.
6 **	....
5 Ambivalent or none	The various study methods could be helpful if the student decides to use them.
4 **	....
3 Negative	I believe that many of my present study methods are as good as or better than those suggested during the course.
2 **	....
1 Strongly negative	The suggested study methods are either too hard to follow or waste too much study time.

NOTE: Although a nine-point rating scale was desired, only five points on the scale were defined. The points marked by asterisks and dots should be considered as about midway between two defined points.

APPENDIX V
Rating Scale for Evaluating Student Reaction to the College
Adjustment Seminar Study Motivation Content

Rating	Statement
9 Strongly positive	The seminar really opened my eyes as to what college is all about and why I must improve my study skills.
8 **	. . . .
7 Positive	Now I have a better understanding of what college will expect from me and how and why it will benefit me.
6 **	. . . .
5 Ambivalent or none	The seminar repeated the same stuff that our teachers have been telling us.
4 **	. . . .
3 Negative	To improve the seminar you should stick to study habits instead of preaching about our study attitudes.
2 **	. . . .
1 Strongly negative	All this stuff about the importance of good study attitudes was a lot of nonsense and a waste of time.

NOTE: Although a nine-point rating scale was desired, only five points on the scale were defined. The points marked by asterisks and dots should be considered as about midway between two defined points.

BIBLIOGRAPHY

1. Berg, Paul C., and Rentel, Victor M. "Improving Study Skills." *Journal of Reading* 9 (1966): 343–346.
2. Blake, Walter S. "Study-Skills Programs." *Journal of Higher Education* 26 (1955): 97–99.
3. Brown, Cathy W. "Upward Bound." *The Texas Outlook* 51, no. 4 (1967): 30–32.
4. Brown, William F. "A Study-Attitudes Questionnaire for Predicting Academic Success." M.A. thesis, University of Texas, 1952.
5. ———. "Motivational Orientations and Scholastic Achievement." Ed.D. dissertation, University of Texas, 1955.
6. ———. "Relationship between Peer-Group Affiliation and Initial Academic and Social Achievement in College." *American Psychologist* 12 (1957): 395.
7. ———. "A Priori Subscales for the Survey of Study Habits and Attitudes." Paper read at Southwestern Psychological Association, Austin, Texas, December, 1958.
8. ———. "Sex Differences in Scholastic Behavior." Paper read at Southwestern Psychological Association, Austin, Texas, December, 1958.
9. ———. "Factors Influencing the Scholastic and Social Achievement of College Freshmen." *American Psychologist* 14 (1959): 380.
10. ———. "Academic Adjustment Counseling through Peer-Group Interaction." In *Personality Factors on the College Campus*, ed. Robert L. Sutherland and associates, pp. 131–135. Austin: Hogg Foundation for Mental Health, University of Texas, 1962.
11. ———. "College Students as Academic Adjustment Counselors." Paper read at Southern College Personnel Association, Washington, D.C., November, 1962.
12. ———. "Reducing College Dropouts through Student-to-Student Counseling." Paper read at National Academy of Science, Austin, Texas, November, 1962.
13. ———. Effective Study Test: College Level and High School Level. San Marcos, Texas: Effective Study Materials, 1964.
14. ———. *College Adjustment Course Instructor's Manual.* San Marcos, Texas: Effective Study Materials, 1964.

15. ———. *Effective Study Course Instructor's Manual.* San Marcos, Texas: Effective Study Materials, 1964.

16. ———. *Study Skills Surveys.* San Marcos, Texas: Effective Study Materials, 1965.

17. ———. "Student-to-Student Counseling for Academic Adjustment." *Personnel and Guidance Journal* 18 (1965): 821–830.

18. ———. "Student-to-Student Counseling as a Systematic Guidance Procedure." *Naya Shikshak* 9 (1966): 78–87.

19. ———. *Student's Guides to Effective Study.* San Marcos, Texas: Effective Study Materials, 1966.

20. ———. "Systematic Utilization of Peer Counseling on the College Campus." Paper read at American Personnel and Guidance Association, Dallas, Texas, March, 1967.

21. ———. *Student Counselor's Handbook.* San Marcos, Texas: Effective Study Materials, 1967.

22. ———. *Faculty Advisor's Guide.* San Marcos, Texas: Effective Study Materials, 1967.

23. ———. "Consejos que de un estudiante a otro para ayudárlo a orientárse en los métodos y técnicas de estudiar eficazmente." *La contribucion de las ciencias psicologicas y del comportamiento al desarrollo social y económico de los pueblos,* I, 91, 1–8. Mexico City: Sociedad Interamericana de Psicología, Universidad Nacional Autónoma de México, 1967.

24. ———. "Student-to-Student Counseling in Perspective." Paper read at American Personnel and Guidance Association, Las Vegas, Nevada, April, 1969.

25. ———. "Student-to-Student Counseling: A Survey of the Pluses and Minuses." Paper read at Personnel and Guidance Association, Las Vegas, Nevada, 1969.

26. ———. *Encuesta sobre las hibilidades de estudio.* San Marcos, Texas: Materiales para el Estudio Efectivo, 1970.

27. ———. *Prueba sobre el estudio efectivo.* San Marcos, Texas: Materiales para el Estudio Efectivo, 1970.

28. ———, and others. "The Division of Student Personnel." In *Emphasis upon Excellence,* pp. 74–96. San Marcos, Texas: Southwest Texas State College Press, 1964.

29. ———, and others. *Student-to-Student Tips.* San Marcos, Texas: Effective Study Materials, 1964.

30. ———, and Abeles, Norman. "Façade Orientation and Academic Achievement." *Personnel and Guidance Journal* 39 (1960): 283–286.

31. ———; Abeles, Norman; and Iscoe, Ira. "Motivational Differ-

ences between High and Low Scholarship Students." *Journal of Educational Psychology* 45 (1954): 215–223.

32. ———, and Galvan, Robert A. *Aconsejamiento académico de estudiante a estudiante.* Sound filmstrip: 80 frames, color, 22 minutes, tape. San Marcos, Texas: Materiales para el Estudio Efectivo, 1968.

33. ———; García, Eduardo H.; and García, Fernando C. *Orientación de estudiante a estudiante.* Sound filmstrip: 80 frames, color, 24 minutes, tape. San Marcos, Texas: Materiales para el Estudio Efectivo, 1969.

34. ———, and Gunn, Mary E. *Student-to-Student Counseling to Aid Academic Adjustment.* Sound filmstrip: 80 frames, color, 22 minutes, tape. San Marcos, Texas: Effective Study Materials, 1967.

35. ———, and Gunn, Mary E. *College Adjustment Seminars to Motivate Effective Study.* Sound filmstrip: 80 frames, color, 22 minutes, tape. San Marcos, Texas: Effective Study Materials, 1969.

36. ———, and Haslam, Warren L. *Study Skills Instruction to Motivate Academic Achievement.* Sound filmstrip: 80 frames, color, 24 minutes, tape. San Marcos, Texas: Effective Study Materials, 1968.

37. ———, and Holtzman, Wayne H. *Survey of Study Habits and Attitudes.* New York: Psychological Corporation, 1953 and 1956.

38. ———, and Holtzman, Wayne H. "Study Habits and Attitudes in the Prediction of Academic Success." *American Psychologist* 8 (1953): 369.

39. ———, and Holtzman, Wayne H. "The Importance of Study Habits and Attitudes in the Scholastic Achievement of High School and College Students." *American Psychologist* 9 (1954): 341–342.

40. ———, and Holtzman, Wayne H. "A Study-Attitudes Questionnaire for Predicting Academic Success." *Journal of Educational Psychology* 46 (1955): 76–84.

41. ———, and Holtzman, Wayne H. "Use of the Survey of Study Habits and Attitudes for Counseling Students." *Personnel and Guidance Journal* 35 (1956): 214–218.

42. ———, and Holtzman, Wayne H. *Effective Study Guide: High School Edition and College Edition.* San Marcos, Texas: Effective Study Materials, 1964.

43. ———, and Holtzman, Wayne H. Survey of Study Habits and Attitudes: Form C and Form H. New York: Psychological Corporation, 1964, 1966, and 1967.

44. ———, and Holtzman, Wayne H. *Encuesta de hábitos y actitudes hacia el estudio.* New York: Psychological Corporation, 1971.

45. ———; McGuire, Carson; and Holtzman, Wayne H. "Motivation-

al Orientations and Scholastic Achievement: A Factorial Investigation." *American Psychologist* 10 (1955): 353.

46. ————, and McGuire, Carson. "Peer Acceptance Data as a Predictor of College Achievement." Paper read at Southwestern Psychological Association, Little Rock, Arkansas, April, 1957.

47. ————, and Seals, Jim. "Sex-Related Differences in Study Habits, Study Attitudes, and Study Knowledge." Paper read at Southwestern Psychological Association, Oklahoma City, Oklahoma, April, 1965.

48. ————; Wehe, Nathan O.; and Haslam, Warren L. "Effectiveness of Student-to-Student Counseling on the Academic Achievement of Potential College Dropouts." *Journal of Educational Psychology* 62 (1971): 285–289.

49. ————, and Zunker, Vernon G. "Student Counselor Utilization at Four-Year Institutions of Higher Learning." *Journal of College Student Personnel* 7 (1966): 41–46.

50. Campbell, Glenn. "Student Evaluation of a College Preparation Seminar before and after College Attendance." M.A. thesis, Southwest Texas State College, 1964.

51. Chase, Clinton I. "The Non-persisting University Freshman." *Journal of College Student Personnel* 9 (1968): 165–170.

52. Chestnut, W. J. "The Effects of Structured and Unstructured Group Counseling on Male College Students' Underachievement." *Journal of Counseling Psychology* 12 (1965): 388–394.

53. Cole, Charles W., and Ivey, Allen E. "Differences between Students Attending and Not Attending a Pre-College Orientation." *Journal of College Student Personnel* 8 (1967): 16–21.

54. Colvin, B. L. "Adapting Academic Adjustment Counseling through Peer-Group Interaction to a Required College Orientation Course." Paper read at Southwestern Psychological Association, San Antonio, Texas, April, 1964.

55. Cope, Robert G. "Limitations of Attrition Rates and Causes Given for Dropping Out of College." *Journal of College Student Personnel* 9 (1968): 386–392.

56. Cordes, Carolyn L. "A Normative, Validity, and Subscale Intercorrelation Analysis of the Revised Brown-Holtzman Survey of Study Habits and Attitudes for Grades 7–12." M.A. thesis, Southwest Texas State College, 1964.

57. Davis, P. H. "Trustees Take Heed of Attrition." *Liberal Education* 47 (1962): 479–486.

58. Demos, George D. "Analysis of College Dropouts—Some Manifest and Covert Reasons." *Personnel and Guidance Journal* 46 (1968): 681–684.

59. De Weese, H. L. "The Extent to Which Group Counseling Influences the Academic Achievement, Academic Potential, and Personal Adjustment of Predicted Low-Achieving First-Semester College Freshmen." Ed.D. dissertation, University of Illinois, 1959.

60. Dickenson, Walter A., and Truax, Charles B. "Group Counseling with College Underachievers." *Personnel and Guidance Journal* 45 (1966): 243–247.

61. Duncan, D. R. "Effects of Required Group Counseling with College Students in Academic Difficulty." Ed.D. dissertation, University of Florida, 1962.

62. Eddy, Edward D. *The College Influence on Student Character.* Washington, D.C.: American Council on Education, 1959.

63. Entwisle, Doris R. "Evaluation of Study-Skills Courses: A Review." *Journal of Educational Research* 53 (1960): 243–251.

64. Farquhar, Winfred G. "Further Refinement and Validation of Brown's Survey of Study Habits and Attitudes." M.A. thesis, University of Texas, 1953.

65. Foxley, Cecelia H. "Orientation or Disorientation?" *Personnel and Guidance Journal* 48 (1969): 218–221.

66. García, Eduardo H.; García, Fernando C.; and Brown, William F. "Orientación de estudiante a estudiante." Paper read at Congreso Mundial de Orientación, Mexico City, August, 1969.

67. García, Fernando C.; García, Eduardo H.; and Brown, William F. "Orientación académico de estudiante a estudiante." *Revista Interamericana de Psicología* 4 (1970): 203–204.

68. Gelso, Charles T. "How Much Do Students Study?" *Journal of College Student Personnel* 8 (1967): 373–375.

69. Gilbreath, Stuart H. "Group Counseling with Male Underachieving College Volunteers." *Personnel and Guidance Journal* 45 (1967): 469–475.

70. Goodstein, Leonard D. "Five-Year Follow-up of Counseling Effectiveness with Probationary College Students." *Journal of Counseling Psychology* 14 (1967): 436–439.

71. ———, and Crites, J. O. "Brief Counseling with Poor College Risks." *Journal of Counseling Psychology* 8 (1961): 318–321.

72. Griffin, Mary H., and Donnan, Hugh. "Effect of a Summer Pre-College Counseling Program." *Journal of College Student Personnel* 11 (1970): 71–72.

73. Hannah, William. "Withdrawal from College." *Journal of College Student Personnel* 10 (1969): 397–402.

74. Hardee, Melvene D. "General Education and General-educational Counseling." *School and Society*, July 7, 1951.

75. Harren, Vincent A., and Jenkins, Thomas V. "Student-to-Student

Academic Adjustment Counseling of Fraternity Pledges." *Journal of College Student Personnel* (in press).

76. Hart, David. "A Study of the Effects of Two Types of Group Experiences on the Academic Achievement of College Underachievers." Ph.D. dissertation, Michigan State University, 1963.

77. Haslam, Warren L. "Student-to-Student Counseling on the High School Campus." Paper read at American Personnel and Guidance Association, Las Vegas, Nevada, 1969.

78. ———, and Brown, William F. "Effectiveness of Study Skills Instruction for High School Sophomores." *Journal of Educational Psychology* 59 (1968): 223–226.

79. ———, and Brown, William F. "Study Skills Counseling for Disadvantaged High School Students." Research report submitted to the Upward Bound Program, U.S. Office of Economic Opportunity, Washington, D.C., August, 1968.

80. ———; Brown, William F.; and Dibrell, Bill. "A Student-to-Student Guidance Program for High School Freshmen." Paper read at American Personnel and Guidance Association, Dallas, Texas, March, 1967.

81. Hendrix, Oscar R. "The Effect of Special Advising on Achievement of Freshmen with Low Predicted Grades." *Personnel and Guidance Journal* 44 (1965): 185–188.

82. Hill, A. H., and Grieneeks, L. "An Evaluation of Academic Counseling of Under- and Over-Achievers." *Journal of Counseling Psychology* 13 (1966): 325–328.

83. Holtzman, Wayne H., and Brown, William F. "Attitudes of Students toward School, Teachers, and Classmates as a Factor in Scholastic Success." Paper read at Southwestern Psychological Association, Oklahoma City, Oklahoma, December, 1954.

84. ———, and Brown, William F. "Evaluating the Study Habits and Attitudes of High School Students." *Journal of Educational Psychology* 59 (1968): 404–409.

85. ———; Brown, William F.; and Farquhar, Winfred G. "The Survey of Study Habits and Attitudes: A New Instrument for the Prediction of Academic Success." *Educational and Psychological Measurement* 14 (1954): 726–732.

86. Iffert, R. E. "Retention and Withdrawal of College Students." *Bulletin*, 1958, No. 1, U.S. Office of Education. Washington, D.C.: Government Printing Office, 1958.

87. Ivey, A. E. "A Three-Year Evaluation of a College Freshman Week Program." *Journal of College Student Personnel* 5 (1963): 113–118.

88. Jessep, Joe R. "Pre-College Orientation Conferences and Subse-

quent Behavior of Freshmen." *Journal of College Student Personnel* 7 (1966): 289–294.

89. Karraker, W. J. "Student-to-Student Counseling for Academic Achievement of Students on Probation." Paper read at American Personnel and Guidance Association, Dallas, Texas, March, 1967.

90. Klingelhofer, E. L. "The Relationship of Academic Advisement to the Scholastic Performance of Failing College Freshmen." *Journal of Counseling Psychology* 1 (1954): 125–131.

91. Kronovet, Esther. "Current Practices in Freshman Orientation throughout the United States." Paper read at American Personnel and Guidance Association, Washington, D.C., April, 1966.

92. Lum, Mable K. M. "A Comparison of Under- and Over-Achieving Female College Students." *Journal of Educational Psychology* 51 (1960): 109–114.

93. Maroney, K. A. "Effectiveness of Short-Term Group Guidance with a Group of Transfer Students Admitted on Academic Probation." Ed.D. dissertation, North Texas State University, 1962.

94. Marsh, Lee M. "College Dropouts—A Review." *Personnel and Guidance Journal* 44 (1966): 475–481.

95. Murry, John P. "The Comparative Effectiveness of Student-to-Student and Faculty Advising Programs." *Research Report No. 18*, Office of Educational Research. Manhattan: Kansas State University, 1971.

96. Northman, Fred H. "The Effectiveness of Three Methods of Group Counseling with College Students on Probation." *American Psychologist* 19 (1964): 455.

97. Pappas, John G. "Effects of Three Approaches to College Orientation on Academic Achievement." *Journal of College Student Personnel* 8 (1967): 195–196.

98. Pickett, Dorothy C. "Student-to-Student Study Skills Instruction at Phillis Wheatley High School." Research report submitted to the Hogg Foundation for Mental Health, University of Texas, Austin, Texas, August, 1968.

99. Popham, W. J. "The Validity of the SSHA with Scholastic Overachievers and Underachievers." *Educational Research Bulletin* 39 (1960): 214–215.

100. ———, and Moore, M. R. "A Validity Check on the Brown-Holtzman Survey of Study Habits and Attitudes and the Borow College Inventory of Academic Adjustment." *Personnel and Guidance Journal* 39 (1960): 552–554.

101. Posey, Jewell. "Personality Characteristics Predictive of Social Achievement." M.A. thesis, Southwest Texas State College, 1960.

102. Powell, Orrin B. "The Student Who Assumes Counseling Respon-

sibilities." In *The Faculty in College Counseling*, by Melvene D. Hardee. New York: McGraw-Hill Book Co., 1959.

103. Roth, R. M.; Mauksch, H. O.; and Peiser, Kenneth. "The Non-Achievement Syndrome, Group Therapy, and Achievement Change." *Personnel and Guidance Journal* 46 (1967): 393–398.

104. ———, and Meyersburg, H. A. "The Non-achievement Syndrome." *Personnel and Guidance Journal* 41 (1963): 535–546.

105. Rothman, Leslie K., and Leonard, Donald G. "Effectiveness of Freshman Orientation." *Journal of College Student Personnel* 8 (1967): 300–304.

106. Schroeder, Wayne L., and Sledge, George W. "Factors Related to Collegiate Academic Success." *Journal of College Student Personnel* 7 (1966): 97–104.

107. Seals, James M. "Sex Differences in Scholastic Behavior." M.A. thesis, Southwest Texas State College, 1964.

108. Shafer, Elizabeth G. "Student Tutorial-Counseling Program at Madison College." Ph.D. dissertation, Florida State University, 1969.

109. Sheldon, W. D., and Landsman, T. "An Investigation of Non-Directive Group Therapy with Students in Academic Difficulty." *Journal of Consulting Psychology* 14 (1950): 210–215.

110. Speegle, P. T. "The Effectiveness of Two Techniques of Counseling with Students on Academic Probation." Ed.D. dissertation, North Texas State University, 1962.

111. Spielberger, C. D.; Weitz, H.; and Denny, J. P. "Group Counseling and the Academic Performance of Anxious College Freshmen." *Journal of Counseling Psychology* 9 (1962): 195–204.

112. Staff. "Students Counsel Students at SMHS in an Effort to Prevent Dropouts," *San Marcos Record*, December 13, 1962, p. 6.

113. Staff. *Upward Bound Guidelines 1966–1967*. Washington, D.C.: Office of Economic Opportunity, 1965.

114. Staff. *Occupational Briefs No. 1-274*. Chicago: Science Research Associates, 1962.

115. Staff. "Counseling by Students." *Innovator* [School of Education, University of Michigan] 1, no. 1 (1969): 1.

116. Staff. "Explosive Growth in College Enrollments," *U.S. News and World Report*, October 20, 1969, pp. 38–39.

117. Staff. *Freshman/Sophomore Attrition Rates, 1964–65 to 1968–69*. Austin, Texas: Coordinating Board, Texas College and University System, 1970.

118. Summerskill, John, and Darling, C. Douglas. "Sex Differences in Adjustment to College." *Journal of Educational Psychology* 46 (1955): 355–361.

119. Thelen, Mark H., and Harris, Charles S. "Personality of College Under-Achievers Who Improve with Group Psychotherapy." *Personnel and Guidance Journal* 46 (1968): 561–566.
120. Tiebout, H. M. "The Misnamed Lazy Student." *Educational Record* 24 (1943): 113–129.
121. Upcraft, M. Lee. "Undergraduate Students as Academic Advisors." *Personnel and Guidance Journal* 49 (1971): 827–831.
122. Van Cleve, Morris. "Male, Female, and Higher Learning." *Journal of Higher Education* 30 (1959): 67–72.
123. Vaughan, Richard P. "College Dropouts: Dismissal Vs. Withdrawal." *Personnel and Guidance Journal* 46 (1968): 685–689.
124. Waits, Marilyn. "Ivy in the Ghetto." *American Education* 5, no. 10 (1969): 27–29.
125. Wehe, Nathan O. "Effectiveness of Student-to-Student Counseling upon Subsequent Scholastic Adjustment of Potential College Dropouts." M.A. thesis, Southwest Texas State College, 1968.
126. Wharton, William; McKean, John; and Knights, Ruth. "Student Assistants for Faculty Advisors." *Journal of College Student Personnel* 7 (1966): 37–40.
127. Williams, Henrietta V., and McQuary, John P. "The High-School Performance of College Freshmen." *Education Administration Supervision* 39 (1953): 303–308.
128. Winborn, B., and Schmidt, L. G. "The Effectiveness of Short-Term Group Counseling upon the Academic Achievement of Potentially Superior but Underachieving College Freshmen." *Journal of Educational Research* 55 (1962): 169–173.
129. Wolff, Thomas. "Undergraduates as Campus Mental Health Workers." *Personnel and Guidance Journal* 48 (1969): 294–304.
130. Zunker, Vernon G. "A Comparison of the Effectiveness of Student and Certified Counselors in a Selected Program of Academic Adjustment Guidance." Ph.D. dissertation, University of Houston, 1964.
131. ———, and Brown, William F. "Comparative Effectiveness of Student and Professional Counselors." *Personnel and Guidance Journal* 44 (1966): 738–743.

INDEX

Abeles, Norman: findings of, on high- and low-scholarship students, 22–23

academic ability: in men and women, 32; independence of, from other factors, 34; as success factor, 36, 37; and scholastic success, 45, 46

academic achievement: related to SSHA, 28; related to EST, 30; in men, 32; and positive attitudes, 33; and peer acceptance, 33–34; and academic ability, 34; and life-style orientation, 34; and scholastic success, 45, 46; comparison of, in testing, 101, 102; as affected by academic adjustment counseling, 106–107; improved by student counselors, 127, 128; as affected by College Adjustment Seminar, 140–141; as affected by required orientation, 146; available literature on, 190–191

academic adjustment: increasing emphasis on, 4; and the SSHA, 26–27; and scholastic success, 45, 47; in counseling activity sequence, 52–53; counseling procedures for, 75–80; tested, 101

academic attitude: in men and women, 32; and sex differences, 33, 39, 40; as success factor, 36, 37; and scholastic success, 45, 47, 48

academic improvement: in counseling activity sequence, 53; counseling procedures for, 80–86

academic success. SEE scholastic success

achievement tests: as predictive instruments, 20–21; measure student's potential, 23

ACT. SEE American College Test

Allegheny College: uses student counselors, 202

American College Test (ACT): used in counselor selection, 61, 62; used in Test Interpretation, 79; used in educational advising, 91; used in ranking students, 111, 140, 144; used to pinpoint low-ability students, 123–124

aptitude tests: as predictive instruments, 20–21; measure student's potential, 23; and SSHA, 25–26; and EST, 30

Arlington State College: conducts scholastic probation clinic, 145–150

Association of Women Students' Handbook: used in freshman orientation, 70

attrition rate. SEE freshman students

Auburn University: orientation program at, 189

Brown, William F.: survey made by, 7, 9–17, 192–193; findings of, on high- and low-scholastic students, 22–23; and peer-group affiliation, 37; develops high school how-to-study course, 162; how-to-study course by, used in Project Upward Bound, 167

Bucknell University: counseling program at, 189

buddy system: in counselor training, 64

CEEB Scholastic Aptitude Test: used in ranking students, 151, 154; used to predict grade-point average, 200

chi-squares: results obtained from, 42, 43

chi-square significance test: 38–39, 40

College Adjustment Seminar: initiated, 130–131; nature of, 131, 133–134; course outline for, 132–133; evaluation rating scales for, 134, 290–291; first systematic evaluation of, 134–139; student comments on, 138–139; second systematic evaluation of, 139–143

college preparation project: purpose of, 156–157; participants selected for, 157–158; activity outline for, 158; results of, 159–160

colleges: population explosion in, 3

Colorado State University: orientation program at, 188

Date Due